THE YOUTH LEADER'S SOURCEBOOK

THE YOUTH LEADER'S SOURCEBOOK

Gary Dausey

Zondervan Books
Zondervan Publishing House
Grand Rapids, Michigan

The Youth Leader's Sourcebook
Copyright © 1983 by The Zondervan Corporation
Grand Rapids, Michigan

Zondervan Books are published by Zondervan
Publishing House, 1415 Lake Drive, S.E.,
Grand Rapids, Michigan 49506

Zondervan Publishing House, 1415 Lake Drive, S.E.,
Grand Rapids, Michigan 49506

Library of Congress Cataloging in Publication Data

Main entry under title:
The Youth leader's sourcebook.

1. Church work with youth—Addresses, essays, lectures.
I. Dausey, Gary.

BV4447.Y58 1983 259'.23 82-25618
ISBN 0-310-29310-3

Designed by Louise Bauer
Edited by Edward Viening

Printed in the United States of America

86 87 88 89 / 9 8 7 6

Contents

IV SHARPENING THE TOOLS OF YOUTH WORK

V RESOURCES FOR THE YOUTH LEADER

Contributors

Yohann Anderson President, Songs and Creations, P.O. Box 559, San Anselmo, California 95960

Dan Baumann Senior Pastor, College Avenue Baptist Church, 4747 College Ave., San Diego, California 92115

Robert Bland Executive Director, Teen Missions International, P.O. Box 1056, Merritt Island, Florida 32952

David Carlson Professor of Counseling, Trinity Evangelical Divinity School, 20065 Half Day Road, Deerfield, Illinois 60015

Craig Clapper Minister of Junior High, The Chapel in University Park, 135 Fir Hill, Akron, Ohio 44304

Wayne Cordeiro Counselor, Faith Center, 1410 W. 13th, Eugene, Oregon 97402

Gary Dausey Executive Vice President, Youth for Christ/USA, P.O. Box 419, Wheaton, Illinois 60187

Bob Davenport Founder/Director, Wandering Wheels, Taylor University, Upland, Indiana 46989

Richard Hagstrom President, Hagstrom Consulting, Inc., 83 Barrie Road, East Long Meadow, Massachusetts 01028

Jay Kesler President, Youth for Christ/USA, P.O. Box 419, Wheaton, Illinois 60187

David Mann Missionary Youth Fellowship International, 3901 S. Wayne Avenue, Fort Wayne, Indiana 46807

Bill Muir National Campus Life Director, Youth for Christ/USA, P.O. Box 419, Wheaton, Illinois 60187

John Musselman Minister of Youth, Coral Ridge Presbyterian Church, 5555 N. Federal Highway, Fort Lauderdale, Florida 33308

Edward Oulund International Representative, Christian Camping International, 434 Union Street, Heritage Village, Vero Beach, Florida 32960

John Pearson Executive Director, Christian Camping International, U.S. Division, Box 646, Wheaton, Illinois 60187

Gary Richardson Associate Editor, GROUP Magazine, P.O. Box 481, Loveland, Colorado 80537

Rusty Rogers Regional Field Director, Youth for Christ/USA, 1830 N.E. 35th Avenue, Topeka, Kansas 66617

Mark H. Senter III Assistant Professor of Christian Education, Trinity Evangelical Divinity School, 20065 Half Day Road, Deerfield, Illinois 60015

Marshall Shelley Adjunct Professor, Denver Theological Seminary, P.O. Box 10,000, Denver, Colorado 80210

Paul Simmers Director of Christian Education, Second Presbyterian Church, 4055 Poplar Avenue, Memphis, Tennessee 38111

E.G. von Trutzschler Minister of Youth, Clairemont Emmanuel Baptist Church, 2610 Galveston Street, San Diego, California 92110

Mike West Executive Director, Rockfordland Youth for Christ, P.O. Box 4221, Rockford, Illinois 61110

Bud Williams Athletic Department, Wheaton College, Wheaton, Illinois 60187

Rory Wineka Minister of Senior High, The Chapel in University Park, 135 Fir Hill, Akron, Ohio 44304

David Zehring Senior Pastor, Covenant Baptist Church, 1769 West Kiowa, Mesa, Arizona 95203

Foreword

I am excited about church youth work today.

I became a full-time youth worker 26 years ago, and at that time I remember that church youth work was like a tacked-on function at the edge of the church's activity. Some churches hired CE Directors and asked them to double in youth ministry or music. Most Sunday schools were separate from the youth program and there was little integration of their functions.

Most people didn't take church youth work seriously. When they would ask me what I did and I would tell them I was a youth worker, they would often say, "What do you plan to do when you grow older?" or "Have you ever thought of going into the ministry?"

Over the years I began to counter with, "I am in youth work just like the president of the state university is in youth work, or the principal of the high school, or the superintendent of schools, or the math teacher." The reason these people are respected is because they take their work seriously.

I take Christian youth work seriously as well. As you look at the list of contributors to this book, you will discover that the book has been written by people who take youth work seriously and have indeed distinguished themselves by their successes in the various fields represented by each chapter.

Gary Dausey directed the Youth for Christ training program for a number of years and has carried a burden for equipping youth workers. This is a book that excites me because it takes the best of the contributions of some of the finest youth workers in the country. I am happy to introduce this book to you and encourage you to make it part of your library and resource shelf. It should be on the four-foot shelf of every youth worker.

Jay Kesler, President
Youth for Christ/USA

Introduction

Have you ever wished that you could gather together a group of seasoned youth leaders so that you could learn from their successes and failures? Have you ever thought to yourself, "Surely somebody has been in this situation before; I wonder what others have done"?

Through this book we are seeking to bring to you the resources and insights of a highly selective group of Christian youth leaders, so that you may, in fact, learn the lessons they have learned.

Some time ago I wrote to our staff in Youth for Christ and asked them to identify the most effective youth leaders they knew of serving churches in their cities. I wasn't necessarily looking for a list of those who were best known; I simply wanted to know who was doing the job.

From a rather sizeable list, I've chosen several of those people, identified an area of ministry that I felt was particularly strong, and have asked them to tell you about it in this book. I have supplemented their information with some additional helpful content from others who are serving in interchurch or parachurch ministries.

The content of this book therefore is not the theory of youth ministry, but the collective insights from those who are doing it well. Our combined prayer is that through the sharing of this information, your ministry with high school students may be strengthened.

Gary Dausey
Wheaton, Illinois

I BUILDING THE FOUNDATION FOR A SUCCESSFUL YOUTH MINISTRY

1

Exploring the World of the High-school Student

Put on your best hiking shoes, load your knapsack with plenty of provisions, and join me through the hills and valleys, the plateaus and plains, the ecstasy and the agony of a place known as *Teen-Age Country*. The only route open to those who are sojourners is the one requiring passage through the bordering state to the south known as *Childhood*. At the edge of this country they check your "passport," and if you are twelve or under, or twenty and above, you must be accompanied by a teen-ager. As singular as the entrance into this *Teen-Age Country* is, there are many exits. (I don't want to alarm you, but some travelers never leave this place, but wander aimlessly through it for years.) The most desirable exit, however, is through the border state to the north known as *Adulthood*.

As we begin this exciting journey, it is important for us to spend a few minutes scouting out the territory. To the east and west are the bordering states of *Depression, Poor Self-Image, Outrage, Disgust, Hate, Poor Family Relations*, and *Peer Pressure*. The traveler must be constantly aware that the main hiking trails can subtly, without warning, lead into one of these border states without the hiker being aware of the

---

Paul Simmers is the Director of Christian Education and Recreation at Second Presbyterian Church, Memphis, Tennessee.

change in direction. Let's look together at what the teen-ager encounters in his journey from childhood to adulthood.

PHYSIOLOGICAL AND PSYCHOLOGICAL CHANGES

Soon after the journey begins, due to a unique interaction of forces within, the teen-ager becomes aware of a difference—it is a beginning of looking and sounding different; an awakening to the feeling of a very strange but wonderful thing happening inside the body that has never been experienced before—an awareness of development that is progressing at a faster rate than ever before. In both physical and emotional growth variations, there is the realization that these teen-age residents are immature, maturing, and mature.

At the outset, the girls will generally be more physically and socially advanced than the boys. The emotional, social, and mental changes that set these individuals distinctly apart are concomitant with this physical change. Socially, homogeneous interests give way to heterogeneous interests. The brain will be continuously bombarded with questions about what to do with all of these feelings that are so new and so demanding: "How can I relate to the opposite sex?" "What do I have to do in order to get a date?" "What is my role in the society in which I am living?" During this time the peer group exerts a strange, almost mystical power on the sojourner, and how its clarion call is accepted or rejected influences the pattern of the individual's behavior.

Emotionally, an unrest develops during this period that causes inconsistency in behavior. More than ever, this lethargic/energetic, pliable/moody, interested/apathetic, positive/negative being seeks the security of acceptance and guidance needed to stabilize his or her self-concept. Gradually an awareness of being freed from the external constraints that once were imposed formulates. As the freedom from these former constraints develops, the knowledge that the capacity to think, the ability to make decisions about how things are doing, comes more clearly into focus. As the teen-ager progresses along the trail from childhood to adulthood, more old constraints and psychological shackles should drop off. The ultimate constraint is imposed by "apron strings." With this nagging need to sever this constraint comes the question, "How in the world can the teen-ager untie these strings without feeling bad about doing it?"

With this persistent question comes the dawning of the knowledge that each individual must answer according to his or her uniqueness. As this question vies for answers, there is one thought that looms highest on the horizon: "Who am I?" At least a partial answer to this must be obtained before posing any other questions concerning "Where am I going?" and "How will I get there?" The question, "Who am I?" is intimately tied to the questions, "Is there really a God?" "Does He really have a plan for my life?" "Are these detours merely the ones that my parents and friends have identified clearly that I should avoid?" "How can I venture outside the safety of the path on which I am now hiking; my own little 'safe' path that I have been on all the way through my childhood?" "How am I to handle this new self that is developing?"

As the journey progresses, the sojourner becomes more conscious of the feelings of loneliness, self-criticism, and worthlessness, which are all tied to the guilty feelings engendered by the natural process related to this new body.[1]

THE ROLE OF THE FAMILY

One of the major contributions to either the success or failure of the teen-ager's journey from childhood to adulthood is the role of the family. Presently, nearly half of all mothers with children under 18 are working, more than double the number 30 years ago. This means that only 7% of the American families can be thought of as being "traditional," meaning the father is working and the mother is keeping house and exercising direct influence over the children at home. In addition, we find that there are more than 8 million homes in which the mother is the only parent present and 1.6 million homes where the father is the only parent present.[2] Projections from these statistics indicate that more than half of all the children born today will live in a single parent family.

A further look into this reveals a startling change. The home, once a relative place of safety and security, is gradually losing that image. Matthew 12:43–45 states that when one "thing" is cast out or stopped, it will definitely be replaced. Often that replacement is much less desirable. A supporting principle from the world of thermodynamics states that "things left to themselves will deteriorate."[3] Let's consider the homes represented by our teen-agers and see how this principle is operating. What is replacing this safe and secure haven of home? Although a home environment with an emphasis on raising children with strict discipline and respect for authority still exists, a shift in the opposite direction is replacing these beliefs.[4]

This antithesis is best represented by a category called the "New Breed" which, among other beliefs, considers religion a very unimportant value for themselves, and therefore of very little value for their children. Patriotism, success, and saving money are also falling prey to the lack of value placed on these areas. However, there is a conflict in the teachings of this "New Breed" in that they do want their children to embrace somewhat traditional values. The problem arises when parents live a lifestyle that does not model any of the traditional values that are verbalized to their children. The hallmark of this new belief system is a preoccupation with self-fulfillment. This god of self-fulfillment produces a conflict that is increasingly shaping the nature of the American family. The seeds of this conflict are planted as values shift from the traditional beliefs in marriage as a primary institution, parents' sacrifices to get their children through college, and unhappy parents staying together for the sake of their children. The fruit of this belief is seen in the fact that these parents are sacrificing less and less for their children.[5]

This belief brings with it an implied contract that exists between parents and children. More than 67% of parents interviewed in a recent study believe that children have no obligation to their parents regardless of what their parents have done for them. What does this mean? A laissez-faire attitude of parents to children is becoming the norm for child-rearing practices. Accompanying this preoccupation with self-fulfillment is the delusion of freedom—"I want to be myself, so why shouldn't my children be free also?" The logical extension of this belief would mean that children would be allowed complete control to eat what they want, sleep when they want, do what they want, and all as often as they want.[6] Has this freedom brought about the desired results? Let's look carefully at some of the indicators of the success of this new trend.

Every year, 6.5 million children are harmed by a parent or other family member. Eight million children, or 18 out of every 100 children, are currently assaulting their parents.[7] Violence within the home is increasingly alarming. For example, the National Institute of Education estimates that each month, 5,200 junior and senior high school teachers are attacked (more than 62,000 per year) and 6,000 are robbed by force (72,000 per year).[8] More than 282,000 teen-agers are assaulted and more than 112,000 of them are robbed. Teen-agers have also pulled off 270,000 school burglaries and destroyed school property worth $200,000,000. The National Association of Secondary School Principals indicates that absenteeism tops the scale as the worst problem facing teachers, even above poor motivation, lack of discipline, vandalism, tardiness, and drug abuse.[9] After more than a decade of vaunted "innovation" in education, not only is violence continuing to climb, but today's students are more poorly equipped in basic skills than were their predecessors. One measure of this downward trend in academics is seen in the scores on college entrance exams: after holding steady for decades, the average scores on the Scholastic Aptitude Test have slowly but steadily fallen.

Directly related to this problem with the family is another horrendous one: young people are running away from home in unprecedented numbers. In 1975 a federal study indicated that 260,000 teen-agers—age 17 or younger—ran away from home for more than a week—triple the numbers from 1964. In order to find more data to support the unhealthy fruits of this new freedom found in the New Breed families, the Department of Health, Education and Welfare searched further into this problem and estimated that more than 733,000 youngsters leave their homes and stay away overnight without permission each year. The main reason why teen-agers ran away from home was basically "trouble" with their parents. This "trouble" ranged from minor fights to drunken brawls, which often included not only physical, but also sexual abuse.[10] As the teen-ager's world of today becomes more complex, crowded, and self-centered, and as authority diminishes in churches as well as in schools, we find parents taking out their frustrations on their children. As a consequence, more children are finding family life so intolerable that they feel they must run away for survival. This has resulted in the changing of attitudes on the part of the entire surrounding society toward the runaway. No longer are runaways charged with committing a crime; they are now given counseling rather than jail, or they are placed in detention homes.

SOCIETAL INFLUENCES

Further challenges the teen-ager must face along his journey from childhood to adulthood include the societal changes involving drugs and sex. As we look down this path, we find more and more teen-age girls having sexual intercourse earlier and with more partners. The prevalence of sexual activity among unwed teen-age girls has increased dramatically so that by age 19, more than 55% have had sexual relations. These sexual relations are occurring boldly within the home setting rather than being "stolen" in secluded places—a direct result of the laissez-faire attitude on the part of the parents. A Johns Hopkins scientist, when asked why teen-agers were more sexually active today, replied, "Why shouldn't they be? Sex is a relatively pleasant experience and the teen-agers today have access to contraceptives, a place to have sex in comfort, and everything in our society keeps saying, 'You ought to.' Is it really surprising that they agree?"[11] An interesting addendum to "freedom" directions, often supported by court decisions, is that teen-age girls can have abortions on demand, yet need a parent's permission to have their ears pierced!

As we look further into the results of earlier and more frequent sexual relations among teen-agers, we find that pregnancies are reaching epidemic proportions with one out of every ten teen-age girls getting pregnant each year, which means more than a million pregnancies a year. Thirty thousand of these girls are under 15 at the time of conception. Although most of the girls come from low-income families, we are now finding this trend enveloping the middle-class non-minority home as well. It is particularly interesting that this rise in teen-age pregnancies has occurred during a time of increased emphasis on sex education in the schools. This is happening at a time when there is a greater availability of professional sex counselors than ever before, a time when there is more openness and discussion of sex problems, and a time when there is a greater availability of contraceptive pills and devices. Planned Parenthood, which has been investigating this trend, blames this on three basic postures of our society: 1) loose morals that result in early sexual activity; 2) ignorance of sex facts; and 3) inaccessibility of contraceptive services. In addition to this, pro-life advocates attribute the increase in pregnancies not to inaccessible contraceptives, but to abortion on demand. Neither refer to family degeneration very much in promoting their causes. The stigma that was once attached to having a child out of wedlock has disappeared, and for many girls the baby becomes living proof that she made it sexually, which has been confused with a belief that she has made it as a human being.

Why is this happening? Again we must look back to the family unit. What becomes readily apparent is that the current concept of "family" is different. One major part of this difference is amplified by the noticeable absence of the close, loving relationship that had been a hallmark of the family for years.[12] Parents move about in their world of work and activity leaving several unsupervised, unattended, free hours existing between the time a teen-ager comes home and the time that parents arrive on the scene (in many cases there is only a single parent to perform both parent roles). When this free time is accompanied by a lack of parental love, care, and supervision, some girls are led to believe that giving birth will enable them to "get" someone who will love them. In addition, this trend toward a sexually-open society has surrounded the teen-ager with constant sexual performance pressure. Parents, without the standard given by Jesus Christ, can easily be led into believing that their offspring are mature enough to handle sex at an early age. Here we are exposed to a paradox, for it is the permissive society in which we find ourselves that is also blaming the teen-ager for the increased number of pregnancies. To cope with this problem, the general solution has been to come up with a technical sex-education program and a vague "values clarification" program.

The confluence of all of these pressures often results in the ultimate cry for help that culminates in both the attempted suicide as well as the "successful" suicide. In 1978, 5,000 teen-agers and young adults committed suicide. Psychologists believe that for every teen-ager who succeeds, more than fifty try. Over all, a quarter of a million young adults tried to take their lives in 1978.[13]

Television has played a major role in shaping the mind of the teen-ager. We find that during twelve years of school, an average teen-ager will have spent 15,000 hours watching television compared to 12,000 hours in the classroom.[14] The addictive results of television are at once apparent when entering any room with a TV set on. This stimulus will take precedence over conversation or other interaction that may be taking place, and cause all eyes to respond by commanding total attention. A careful study of the content of this monster finds programs portrayed on television replacing violence with sex. Actual or implied sexual intercourse will take place approximately 2.7 times every hour, with 88% of all sex represented taking place outside of marriage. If we were to add up all the instances of sexual intercourse, sexual comments, and suggestive sexual scenes appearing on the networks in 1978, the total would be 20,000.[15] In addition, those computing this alarming detail have indicated that visualized drinking is on the rise. Someone drinks 3.5 times per hour, 4 times per hour during prime time. For every time coffee is consumed, alcohol is consumed 10 times; for every time milk is consumed, alcohol is consumed 44 times. Water is consumed once for every 48 times someone drinks alcohol.

What happens to the students who are bombarded with this imagery? Their exposure to the insidious brainwashing techniques employed by television has resulted in more than 3,000,000 youths experiencing problems at home, schools, and on the highways as a result of drinking.[16] More than 1,000,000 girls between the ages of 15 and 19 have become pregnant each year; 270,000 of these pregnancies end in abortion; 235,000 result in illegitimate births, and 100,000 try to legitimize their situation by a marriage that is often doomed to failure. One out of every 5 new mothers today is a teen-ager, with more than 30,000 of them being 15 years of age or younger.[17]

There are changes in our religious values that affect the teen-ager as well. It is easy to see why young people are turning to cults and experiential religious groups when many traditional church institutions have lost their ability to provide concrete answers to meet the needs of an amorphous society. The "lack of identity" is found to be strongest in the upper middle-class and upper income groups. The basic question that confronts the teen-ager is "Who am I?" This question indicates the beginning of a search for this identity. There is in every human being a profound desire for a clear answer to this question. This often means that anyone who comes around with a seemingly authoritative firm answer is almost guaranteed a following. Therefore, the dearth of institutions including family, school, and church speaking firmly to this "identity need" makes youth vulnerable to authoritarian movements or cults. Teen-agers respond to those who tell them who they are and respond to their quest for personal identity. With the urgency of this need being expressed in a variety of ways, it is often a matter of which groups get to them first with an answer.

What does all of this mean? It means that as a youth leader you must be aware of all the insidious side paths waiting to attract and trap the young people to whom you seek to minister. It means that everyone needs to examine the moral fiber of society and the directions taken by the media. It means that working families need support for the supervised, active care of teen-agers to eliminate the frustrations that bring violence and abuse. It means awareness, attention, and commitment from all to make the journey better.

FOOTNOTES

[1]Richard DeHaan, *The Wonderful Difficult Years* (Wheaton: Victor Books, 1973).

[2]"Working Mothers and Their Children," *Youth Letter,* July, 1977.

[3]Lane Adams, *Come Fly With Me* (Ventura, CA: Regal Books, 1973).

[4]Merton P. Strommen, *Five Cries of Youth* (New York: Harper & Row, 1974).

[5]Tim Stafford, *The Trouble With Parents* (Grand Rapids: Zondervan, 1978).

[6]Yankelovick, Skelly and White, Inc., *Raising Children in a Changing Society* (New York: Harper, 1964).

[7]*Family Circle,* June 26, 1979.

[8]Ibid.

[9]"Youth," *Time,* November 14, 1977.

[10]Department of Health, Education and Welfare. *The Youth Route,* 1975.

[11]"Family Planning Perspectives," *A Journal of Parenthood,* April, 1977.

[12]Gene A. Getz, *The Measure of a Family* (Ventura, CA: Regal Books, 1977).

[13]*Good Housekeeping,* May, 1979.

[14]"TV Comedy: What It's Teaching the Kids," *Newsweek,* May 7, 1979, p. 67.

[15]National Federation for Decency, Fall 1978.

[16]"New Alcohol Program to Focus on Women, Teenagers," *Los Angeles Times,* May 2, 1979.

[17]*Family Circle,* June 26, 1979.

2

Determining Your Theology of Youth Ministry

Someone has said, "What you believe is the most important thing about you." In fact, the apostle James has reminded us that our conduct eventually will verify or deny what we say we believe. For this reason, the theology of the youth worker is ultimately more important than his or her strategy or methodology. Of course, the study of theology does not eliminate the need for the study of methods, but methods must flow from a sound theology. Clever and industrious people who have no knowledge of God can achieve the saturation of a market. My concern is, "What are we delivering to that market?" Or, to put it another way, "What are young people hearing from us by life and word about God and the Christian life?"

Your personal theology will have an effect on everything you do in youth work. It will influence the type of message you bring, the response you expect, the progress of the youth among whom you minister, your method of counseling, your attitude toward others, and how you measure results. In short, all we do relates to what we actually believe.

OUR VIEW OF AUTHORITY

We must be biblical Christians; that is, we accept the Bible as authoritative for faith and practice. We are

Jay Kesler is President of Youth for Christ/USA.

among those Christians who believe the Bible to be inspired, infallible, and communicated by the Holy Spirit through the personalities of men.

In today's youth culture we are up against a dangerous reaction to the relativism of the past few years. Many Christian young people who are experiencing the general conservative swing in society and the insecurity brought about by the failure of humanistic promises are opting for a new literalism that is either unaware of or ignores the basic rules of hermeneutics.

Some of them quote 1 Corinthians 1 and 2 in an arrogant and cocksure manner far beyond what Paul intended. Paul was not attempting to rule out all of our learning and progress and establish the Bible as a textbook for *all* learning. He was pointing out that with all of our wisdom we cannot get to God without the revelation of Scripture and the person of Jesus Christ. Paul certainly was not suggesting that we can know nothing about anything without being Christian.

Such a stance on the part of today's youth is understandable to a degree. Utopian ideals were encouraged in the early and middle '60s. The failures of political and social activism and the massive commitment to the war on poverty resulted in disillusionment. Idealistic youth found an unresponsive establishment and problems that remain stubbornly unsolved even after massive commitment. As a result, many young people simply dropped out and concluded that things couldn't be changed.

The theological result has been an escapist attitude on the part of many, with emphasis on the Second Coming, new legalism, passivism, and apathy. The resulting situation is characterized by an anti-intellectualism that insists that Christians know everything because they are possessed by the Holy Spirit.

It is very important that we communicate to youth a firm belief that the Scriptures properly interpreted, properly understood, and properly applied give the Christian fantastic insights that seem to elude those who use only the "wisdom of men." It is interesting, for instance, that Karl Menninger has only recently asked modern psychology, "Whatever happened to sin?" Christians have known about sin by revelation.

It is also important, however, that in our enthusiasm over biblical authority we do not create a compartmentalized mind-set. Many try to live that way. One compartment is for God's truth. It includes concepts such as "How long is a Sabbath day's journey?" "How many smooth stones?" "What is grace?" "How old was Jesus when He confounded the elders in the temple?" The other compartment deals with information such as "How do you keep from getting hit by cars?" "How do you build a skyscraper?" "What is Newton's law?" Some of our brethren are frightened that if the barrier is broken down, secular truth will devour God's truth.

We must teach our youth that truth is truth. God and truth are not exclusive of one another. They are consistent with one another. If there seems to be conflict, either God is misunderstood or truth is misunderstood. This is not to infer that truth is easy to ascertain. It is not. It takes care, honesty, hard work, time, experience, and humility, just for starters. However, a rabbit dissected at a Christian college looks just like a rabbit dissected at a secular college. A statement is not any more anti-Christian just because it comes from a nonbeliever than certain clothing is Christian because it is worn by a Christian. Truth is outside of oneself. Truth is truth. But it is not inconsistent with the rest of truth that God has allowed us to discover.

My plea to youth workers is that we advocate a faith based solidly on Scripture with a stance that is unthreatened and confident, not frightened and reactionary. It should be a faith that assures us that when we meet God He will not have perspiration on His palms, afraid that any minute we are going to do Him in. Of all people, Christians should be curious to learn new truth. The more we learn about our world, the more we know about Him who is the Creator. "Through him all things were made; without him nothing was made that has been made" (John 1:3).

This frightened form of evangelical existentialism needs to be rooted and grounded not merely in Bible verses, but in faith in God who is all authority and who made heaven and earth.

OUR VIEW OF GOD

Pollsters tell us that today more people in public and private life are claiming belief in God than ever before. At the same time, people are facing identity crises, struggling with tremendous insecurity about the future, and reading horoscopes. If our view of God includes His omnipotence, omnipresence, omniscience, holiness, sovereignty, mercy, righteousness, and a personal interest, then it would seem to follow that He "will keep [him] in perfect peace . . . whose mind is steadfast, because he trusts in" Him (Isa. 26:3).

Not so, however, in our culture. It would seem that the God of many Christians is less able than even the government. Christians struggle with personal identity and question whether or not God knows or cares that they exist in the midst of an exploding world. The same people seem confident that Uncle Sam can find everyone on April 15 to pay income taxes. It would appear that Uncle Sam has been keeping up but God has not. Uncle Sam has computers! Now think of the absurdity of that.

Take a statement like, "In the beginning God created the heavens and the earth" (Gen. 1:1). What a thing to say you believe! Here we are on a planet lighted by a sun that is a mediocre star, in a universe that is just a bright spot in the tail of the Milky Way, part of a galaxy that is one of more than 100 million galaxies, and we wonder if God is able.

People often betray this inadequate view of God by asking questions like, "Do you think God will let man go to Mars?" They asked the same thing about man going to the moon a few years ago. This is just a quantitative rather than a theological problem. It's like asking, "Do you think God will let me jump on my desk?" Although grossly oversimplified, going to the moon or Mars is only a quantitative extension of the problem of getting on my desk.

What does a frightened attitude about space exploration say to young people who have always assumed that man can go to Mars and much farther? They have been from DNA to the moon. We must allow our belief in God to accommodate the expanding universe. We must emphasize not only the imminence of God, but His transcendence as well. God is bigger than our limited experience.

"Don't bother me, I can't cope," dare not be the view telegraphed to young people about the nature of God. We evangelicals have often created an unnecessary antithesis between faith and science by our defensive stance. We must teach our children that "can" and "God" cannot be together in a question. By definition the words are incompatible in a question. "Can God make a fish big enough to swallow a man?" The question is not "can God?" The question is, "Is there a God?" If there is, then by definition, He can.

The God of the Scriptures is not an extension of man who is learning to cope with His world a step at a time. God, the same yesterday, today, and forever, is not playing "catch up" ball. We reveal much about what we believe concerning the nature of God by that which makes us defensive. In today's youth culture our God must not be threatened by the universe even though it is so overwhelming to us at the present time.

OUR VIEW OF MAN

There is a theology that makes God big by making man small. This view has insisted on underlining verses like "All our righteous acts are like filthy rags" (Isa. 64:6), and ignoring, "I praise you because I am fearfully and wonderfully made" (Ps. 139:14). We have been afraid that we would err as do the humanists by ignoring the basic sinfulness of man. As a result many of us have been guilty of an evangelical overkill that maims man to the degree that even the blood of Christ doesn't seem to cleanse from all sin.

Christian psychologists are inundated with these casualties of evangelistic zeal. We must guard against the wishful thinking that would tempt us to ignore man's sinful state and his absolute lostness outside of redemption in Christ. But we must also help restore the value of the individual that has been so sorely eroded by the many dehumanizing influences of the twentieth century.

We must emphasize the fact that all have sinned, but we must not forget the good news that assures today's youth that God personally cares for them. He even cares for the ordinary kids who do not meet the standards of the models in our advertising. The movies and the novelists have recognized this need in the creation of the anti-hero. It is not incidental that Dustin Hoffman has become a symbol of ordinary young people.

We must clarify to youth that when Paul says, "I

have been crucified with Christ" (Gal. 2:20), he is not advocating "personality kamikaze," but is speaking to the basic egotism and selfishness of man. Jesus encourages us, "Love your neighbor as yourself" (Lev. 19:18). If we are filled with self-hate, contempt, and worthlessness, our neighbors are in real trouble. In fact, this may say more of the present social situation than we suspect.

A youth worker whose theology does not have this scriptural balance between the need for repentance and the availability of redemptive love may find that by default he is driving youth to the arms of some Eastern cult with its eclectic humanism.

Our principles must include an acceptance of young people as persons, an unwillingness to violate personal integrity, an unconditional love, and the consistent directing of young people past ourselves to the person of Christ. Manipulation, exploitation, and panaceas encourage a view of man that is unworthy of the New Testament. In our zeal to win youth to Christ, we must refuse to do anything to another person that God Himself would not do.

OUR VIEW OF THE WORLD

The Edict of Milan in A.D. 313 opened the way for Christians to embrace a majority strategy to convert the world by purely political and armed means. Constantine's desire to see a "christianized" world fell far short of the ideal even to our own time. The equation of Christianity with various forms of nationalism contributed to the cry of the youth of the '60s, "Christ, yes; Christianity, no."

This world is "no friend of grace." The New Testament is a minority manual. It teaches believers how to live and grow in a hostile climate. Satan is the "prince of this world" (John 12:31). The Christian must learn to listen to the voice of the Holy Spirit through the Word of God. He marches to a different drum. The attempt to equate the message of Christ with any of man's institutions or structures will lead to disillusionment and failure. The gospel message is not equal to any other message—it stands alone. Others are measured against it; it is the standard.

We must help young people to see God at work in history. They must see the larger picture of His redemptive plan spread out from the beginning of time with His church crossing all national, racial, economic, and ethnic barriers. We must help them to *see* God's broken heart for the family of man. He does not countenance greed, lust, bigotry, racism, and war any more than He does murder, stealing, or adultery.

Our God has a social conscience larger than that of liberal politicians. He is not a deaf God whom we are trying to make hear, an insensitive God we are trying to sensitize, a forgetful God we are trying to cause to remember, or an inactive God we are trying to move to action. "Surely the arm of the LORD is not too short to save, nor his ear too dull to hear. But your iniquities have separated you from your God; your sins have hidden his face from you, so that he will not hear" (Isa. 59:1–2).

We must help young people to see ourselves as active in the world with responsibility for our actions. It is not that God made us and the world with inherent flaws or that our environment is a detrimental influence. We have sinned and have corrupted the world. We are not only responsible for our sin and in need of personal redemption, but when we become redeemed people we are participants in the kingdom of God to confront and heal this present world.

We can conclude from listening to the testimonies of many young people that in much preaching, psychology may have replaced the Word of God, and that experience is more important than truth. We applaud together the helpful insights of the study of man in the speculative areas of psychology and sociology and surely want to gain all we can from them, but left alone they will not bring people to God, or fill their lives, or save their souls. Relationships and relational theology are certainly important and valid, but they must bring young people to an encounter with the living Christ, not merely to an encounter with "significant others" or with community.

When all is said, we as Christian youth workers must follow Christ's example who "did not . . . cling to his rights as God, but laid aside his mighty power and glory . . . becoming like men" (Phil. 2:6–7 LB). We must relate vulnerably and lovingly to youth.

We must interpret youth to adults and adults to youth. We must point youth to the church and to responsible churchmanship. We must encourage healthy, growing social relationships. We must be friends to the family and build respect for the authority of the home. And while doing so we must present the God of the Bible and a Christian view of man and his world. All of this must be done in language, both verbal and relational, that is understandable to the adolescent. This is a large, even impossible task in its entirety.

Young people are open today as never before to the supernatural. The Christian youth worker can be the influence to assist the home, the church, and the school to convey truth—God's truth—to today's youth.

3

Analyzing and Planning the Youth Program

You've just accepted a position in a church as the director of youth ministries. You and your family have moved and, while you are in the process of unpacking boxes, you suddenly realize that the pressure is on you. You are expected to take a weak, almost nonexistent youth ministry and turn it into something exciting. Or perhaps worse, you are following a former youth director who has had a very successful ministry. In either case, it's clear that all eyes are on you, and the expectations of the kids, the parents, and the board are all high. Where do you begin? How do you start? How do you plan for success?

A youth ministry is unique and, although there are some principles of planning that can be taken from big business, there are many that can not. A youth group is a voluntary organization and hence its program is designed for people who may want to participate in it for a variety of reasons. Their motivation for participation is "I want to," and that's much different from "I have to."

Planning and evaluating in a youth program setting are more complex and less objective than for a business. For example, how do you evaluate the fact that after several weeks of absence, Tom is beginning

---

Richard Hagstrom is the President of Hagstrom Consulting Inc., East Long Meadow, Massachusetts.

to participate again? How do you evaluate a "good" meeting? Or, even if the group is growing numerically, how do you assess the fact that the kids are becoming more rowdy, the adult advisors are becoming disgruntled, and cliques are forming?

Most would recognize that in any successful youth ministry good planning must take place. Yet we must also be cautious, so that our planning doesn't become so sophisticated, so professional, so specific that we "put God in a box" and leave no breathing room for His Holy Spirit.

Planning for any ministry must be open-ended enough so that those who participate in it may function in an atmosphere and climate enabling them to "catch the wind of His Spirit" (see John 3:8). If planning itself prepares minds and hearts to "hear His still small voice," then planning is okay.

Writing in a totally different context, E. Kirby Warren states:

> The biggest single failure in most . . . companies has been the failure to recognize that . . . it is the process, the mechanism for planning and not the plan itself that is of greatest importance. It can not be overemphasized that with few exceptions, the purpose of long-range planning is not nearly so much having a plan as developing processes, attitudes and perspectives which make planning possible. Developing formal, comprehensive, long-range plans is merely a means to an end. The plan itself is likely to be obsolete a week after it is developed. The process which created the plan, if carefully conceived, nurtured, and controlled is not. It is instead the basis for sensing needs and making adjustments continuously.[1]

And that's what planning should be: a mechanism for sensing needs and making adjustments continuously. Planning must be an immensely spiritual experience, just like other things we do for God.

Our attitudes must demonstrate personal caring, two-way sharing, bearing one another's burdens, and encouraging one another. This is foundational to the "whats" and "hows" of planning which, in its simplest form, asks the questions, "How well are we doing?" "What should we be doing?" and "Who's going to do it?"

HOW WELL
ARE WE DOING?

Asking, "How well are we doing?" means taking a close look at the present situation, based on past experience. It involves evaluating Key Result Areas (KRAs). A Key Result Area is defined as an activity essential to achieving the group's purposes and goals. The first step is to identify the Key Result Areas for your group. One youth group identified their KRAs as:

- Sunday school or prechurch
- Sunday evening meeting
- Wednesday Bible study
- Winter retreat
- Summer camp

You'll note that these are all events and can be measured with a fair amount of objectivity. Other Key Result Areas that could apply to a youth group, but which are more difficult to analyze are:

- Outreach and service
- People relationships
- Communications
- Personal spiritual growth

The next step is evaluating from one to three of your Key Result Areas. This evaluation should be done by those who are participating in the program. The planners and doers should generally be the same. In a large group, this isn't always possible. But whenever practical, those who carry out plans should be involved in the planning process.

In one church, the youth leader uses a brief, one-page questionnaire periodically. It works for two reasons: it's specific and deals with just one area of concern. Secondly, the leader always follows with a report of the findings to the group. Whether you gain your information for evaluation from a questionnaire or through a small group process is relatively unimportant. What is important is the level of participation. Young people don't expect to make all the decisions, but they usually want to feel that their opinions are valued and acted upon in one way or another. Involving others in evaluations and decisions usually facilitates cooperation. Remember, if you have to sell a solution or program, you've got the wrong solution.

Once you've determined how you are going to

secure your evaluative information, you must decide what you need to know to answer the question, "How well are we doing?"

I have found the following questions to be useful in evaluating most Key Result Areas:

1. What is going well? Why? (strengths)
2. What is not going well? Why? (weaknesses/problems)
3. What are two *priority* problems? Why?
4. What are the opportunities?
   a. Something we aren't doing enough.
   b. Something we aren't doing at all but should.
   c. Something we've tried before, perhaps briefly, then stopped.
   d. Things we've never done before, or any other new ideas.

When appropriate, ask:

5. What are the trends, if any?
6. What changes ought to be anticipated?

Once we have determined the strengths, weaknesses, and opportunities within our present program, it's time to decide what it is we want to do in the future.

WHAT SHOULD WE BE DOING?

This is the heart of the planning process. Before you can develop goals, you must decide what your mission or purpose will be. A mission statement should be written that is specific enough to give direction yet broad enough to allow flexibility. It dare not be something that is committed to paper and then forgotten. The participants in the group must feel a sense of ownership and commitment to it.

One of the parachurch groups with which I work is Youth for Christ. Several years ago they developed a mission statement that provides the focus for their ministry. As a part of their ongoing planning process, they rediscuss and recommit themselves to this mission. On visits to their national service center in Wheaton, Illinois, and to their local offices in other parts of the country, I see their mission statement prominently displayed as a reminder to their staff of their purpose for existing.

Their mission is:

> To participate in the body of Christ in responsible evangelism of youth, presenting them with the person, work and teachings of Christ and discipling them into the Church.

In addition to their overall mission, each of their ministry departments has a mission that relates to its specific functions within the organizational mission.

A church youth group should have a mission statement that describes its reason for existence. In addition, there can be secondary mission statements related to specific parts of the program such as the Bible study, a retreat, or the Sunday school period.

The form that the mission or purpose statement takes is far less important than the fact that you do have one.

"The Student Body," the high-school group of the Wheaton Bible Church, under the leadership of Ridge Burns, expresses its mission in these terms:

> First, we are looking for changed lives, for students who are willing to change their lifestyles, their attitudes or their rhetoric in order for them to live in obedience to Jesus Christ.
>
> Second, we are looking for integrated lives. Our goal is not to have some sort of monastery where people live out their lives in a vacuum apart from the real world. We want students to take their faith into the everyday world, into their schools and jobs to change their world for Christ.
>
> Third, we want committed lives. We are looking for students who are willing to commit themselves to Jesus Christ and to accomplishing God's purpose for "The Student Body."

Once you know what it is you want to accomplish in your group and can state it clearly, you must then translate your mission into goals.

The goal-setting phase of planning involves much subjective judgment. Hard facts are usually difficult to come by. Attendance-related goals are one of the few exceptions. However, when setting goals that relate to growth, commitment, and discipleship, you'll find that they are very difficult to measure and you can become easily discouraged if you have no solid way of knowing if you are making progress.

The type of goals that can be measured are called "action goals." That is, things done or things people do to reach a goal. Your action goals should reflect a specific task to be done in a specified amount of time.

Examples of action goals are:

1. Create a parents' breakfast by September 15.
2. Create a college tour for high-school seniors by October 1.
3. Plan and secure the basics, date, location, speaker for a winter retreat by August 1.

You should plan for both long- and short-term goals with the short-term ones being most specific. Remember once again that the goals will change with the dynamics of your group. It is the process through which you set the goals that is more important than a goal for which no one feels ownership but you. The group must not only feel a sense of ownership of the goals but the priorities placed on the goals as well. "What is most important?" "What must be done now?" "What is an investment in the future of the group?" The answers to these questions will help you decide on the scheduling of the tasks to be performed and, in fact, which become short-term and which long-term goals.

WHO IS GOING TO DO IT?

Any plan is only as good as the person who carries it out. You may have decided that in order to have a quality youth program, you have to do it all yourself. Many good youth leaders feel this way. They have seen good plans become mediocre programs because the kids didn't follow through with their responsibilities. If you've been in youth work for any length of time you also know that some years you will have a group with many good leaders and other years you'll feel that there isn't a person in the group you would trust with anything important.

It is not my task in this chapter to address the issue of student leadership versus leadership from the paid staff; that's addressed elsewhere in this book There have been, however, numerous studies done for the business world that I believe can be helpful to you in your work with young people. These studies have invariably shown a very high correlation between job satisfaction and productivity with the individual's abilities and skills.

Those whom I have found to be successful in youth work put great emphasis on getting to know the gifts and abilities of the students and using the students in their areas of strengths whenever possible. This not only affects their satisfaction with the program, but develops them as well.

Regardless of who you decide to use, what is important is that for each goal you set, there be not only an appropriate time frame, but also a specific assignment to some individual or group.

IN SUMMARY

Many books have been written on the subject of planning. There are charts and diagrams one can use to express the various forms planning may take. In this chapter, I have attempted to be nontechnical and relate only to the most basic detail essential for good planning for your youth ministry. I have attempted throughout this chapter to express something I feel very deeply: Planning is just words put on paper. Relationships are fundamental; without a relationship, a person has no right or authority to hold another person accountable. When relationships are positive, then whatever method you use, you and others will be more apt to be prepared to be sensitive to the Spirit of God. Then you will be depending on Him, willing to trust Him with the results—"the final outcome is in God's hands."

FOOTNOTES

[1]E. Kirby Warren, *Long-Range Planning* (Englewood Cliffs: Prentice-Hall, 1966).

4

Youth Ministry Is More Than a Meeting

In the '50s and '60s youth work consisted primarily of meetings. All you would have to do was show up once or twice a week and put on a meeting. Often those meetings came right out of a book, and we had many of them. It was very easy—you simply duplicated a church service with some different names and a slightly different approach.

But as I look back on my thirty years in youth work, I find that my most successful ministry with kids was not related to meetings, but rather to my one-on-one times with individuals. It could be said, I'm sure, that Christ's most meaningful times with His disciples were not in the mass meetings by the seaside, but rather in the more intimate moments as they walked together and prayed together and learned to know and love one another. How does one structure a ministry to provide for these types of one-on-one opportunities and what are the cautions related to such a ministry?

MINISTERING ONE-ON-ONE

The most effective way to meet kids one-on-one is to go places they go, and do things with them. Many youth pastors are just hirelings—they produce a program. A youth pastor with a shepherding mentality,

---

E. G. von Trutzschler is Minister of Youth, Clairemont Emmanuel Baptist Church in San Diego, California.

rather than that of the hireling, will produce a ministry. He wants to accomplish several things. First, he wants to give his young people a taste of what he has—a personal faith in Christ. Secondly, he wants to help them mature and begin grooming them for the future—training and developing them so that they, too, can minister.

The first step in this process is to discover the surroundings. What facilities are available at the church, in the schools, in the area? The next is to find out about the kids. Where do they hang out? What do they like to do? Who are they? It's essential to search them out, to go where they are, to meet them on their own level, talk with them . . . observe them . . . listen to them. When I'm driving kids around in my car, I listen to their dialogue: What are they interested in? What is current? To know who and what my kids are, I need to study them. This involves a sacrifice of my time and desires . . . to be with them, go where they want to go, and do things they want to do.

One important, often overlooked aspect of meeting kids one-on-one is to do so when they're available, and when they're ready. I remember watching a youth group on the beach some years ago. The director had quite a large group, yet he was playing volleyball with just a few of the older boys. It looked like good, specialized contact, until I noticed the rest of the group . . . bored, idle, just sitting around. It is essential that the youth worker see that all of his group are occupied, are enjoying themselves, and are getting involved. When most of the group is involved in the activity, it becomes possible to talk to the individuals who haven't gotten into the activity for one reason or another, and to get to know them personally. I look for this opportunity at camps and retreats, trying to find individuals who are available for communication. This develops a style of leadership that emphasizes respect and love, rather than one that is strictly positional. I have control and authority. Both are essential for communication with the group. The youth worker must watch for opportunities to meet kids on an individual basis.

Getting Kids Involved

Some families are simply church attenders. The parents set an example of going to a meeting without getting involved, and their kids learn to do the same.

Other families drive across town to another neighborhood. The young people either don't have a close attachment to the youth group, or it is just one of two worlds in which they live. They never develop a sense of loyalty, and thus never really become involved. Perhaps their parents do not really encourage involvement. How can the youth director involve this kind of kid?

First, we need to sell the parents on the program. In many cases, the youth director *is* the program, and if the parents are sold on the youth director, they will begin to see a need to get their children involved. As a result, they'll be more likely to encourage their children to participate.

Friendships are also an important part of involvement. Special activities like camping or overnight trips allow a cohesive bond to grow within a group of kids. Loyalties develop, and kids are more likely to become involved in the program itself because they feel comfortable. They feel that they are part of the group. Participation becomes more than going along and being a spectator. Friendship and love draw them into the group, as well as their love and respect for the leader, who encourages them to be part of the group. The program is not as attractive to the kids as is the friendship of the group and their love for their leaders.

Using Your Time Wisely

No matter who is in your youth group, someone will constantly claim more of your time than you can give. A kid comes to you with a new problem every week, or keeps bringing back the same problem time after time. Kids today are very insecure, and often their basic need is attention. Whether this need is a result of their home life or because they are just selfish individuals, it's important to hear them out. Growing up today is difficult.

Try to correct the problem by exposing it and helping the individual learn to deal with it and work it out himself. Rather than solve the problem for him, I would much rather salvage the problem kid. Perhaps there is some area of ministry in which this young person can begin to achieve and gain recognition on his own, in a positive way.

Many parents, pastors, and youth workers are too lenient here, and in the name of love have crippled many kids. The adults get bogged down with solving the problems and struggles for the kids, when actually the kids must experience these things themselves before they can become individuals God can use.

Dealing With Kids' Admiration

Every kid has heroes and, depending on his age and maturity level, he may make the youth director his hero. This is a normal phase in a young person's development, although this adulation is generally short-term. Often, as the young person gets to know the youth leader more personally, the fantasy he's attached to him begins to give way to reality and the youth leader becomes more of a real person to him. It's hard to tell an immature, young kid to look to Christ when his whole being is crying out for a flesh-and-blood model. I believe God has intended that young people should learn through this modeling and, because of this, the youth director is to be the model, or one of his models. Young people must see Christ in their leaders if they are to learn to be Christlike.

Occasionally, a girl from the youth group develops a crush on the youth director. It's a part of growing up that can happen without any apparent reason or encouragement. This is a temporary thing that needs sensitive handling. Spend some time in a counseling session, dealing with the problem in a delicate way. It's a difficult experience for a young girl, but such sessions have often given me an opportunity to share some important values with them.

Many young people from broken homes will look up to the youth director as a father figure. This can be a healthy thing. These young people then have someone they can look up to with respect, and someone they can seek out for counsel. The time the youth leader has with his young people is often a transitory one, a time when he becomes part of the young person's life, to influence what he can, when he can.

Keeping Confidences

Once trust and respect are established between the youth leader and the young people, kids may begin to feel that confidential information can be shared with the director. It is essential that such information be held in strict confidence; the breaching of that confidence could cost the youth leader the respect of not just the individual involved, but of the entire youth group. A youth leader cannot afford to break a kid's trust and, as a result, impair his ministry by breaking the trust of the group.

Even if the parent would request confidential information, I could not give it out. Most parents understood. This confidence allowed me to work with the kids on a level of respect and friendship that took time to develop.

Maintaining this confidence can become a very lonely position for the youth director. There are many such moments in youth work . . . lonely moments when the majority of the kids don't understand, the deacons don't understand, the pastor doesn't understand, and the parents don't understand. The youth director can find himself on an island of loneliness, waiting for everything to work out.

BALANCING WORK AND HOME

It's not easy to strike a balance between the demands of individual kids for your time, and a sane home life for yourself and your family. Every pastor faces this and tries to get over a nagging feeling of inadequacy. "Am I doing enough?" "Could I have done this better?" Sometimes this causes guilt feelings, but after some time in the ministry a youth pastor, or any pastor, realizes that he's only one person, and can only do so much. Anyone who becomes so involved in what he's doing that he overextends himself past his physical, emotional, and spiritual limits, does himself no good. Knowing how to budget time and establish priorities is important.

The youth leader's family is very important. This is difficult for someone just starting out to adjust to, but it is a matter of establishing priorities and meeting needs. You must have a happy, healthy relationship at home. I once asked the teen-age children of a pastor ministering at a large west coast church at what age they rebelled. (I assumed that all pastors' kids rebelled.) They said they never had, and it shocked me. When I asked them why, one of the boys responded, "Our father was the same at home as he was in the pulpit." That says a lot for the man. His children respected him completely. When I talked to the pastor later, he explained that he gave each of his boys some special time each week. He felt that it wasn't the amount of time that was important, but the quality of the time spent together. So he took a half day each week for each of his kids. They certainly turned out well.

MINISTERING TO INDIVIDUALS IN A GROUP CONTEXT

Warming Up to Kids

One of the most awkward moments for any youth leader is when he stands before a group for the first time and wants to feel accepted and be in control.

One way to overcome this problem is to start working with younger children and work your way up until you feel comfortable with the high-school group. This will allow you to develop confidence in your role. When you are yourself, relaxed and at ease, you are attractive to the group and there shouldn't be much of a problem communicating.

Getting to know the kids as individuals is important too. It's hard to break into a group mentality. It's better to see the group as a collection of individuals who love and respect him. He will be able to develop good rapport much more easily than if he tried to break into a group mentality.

It is possible for an introvert to become an extrovert. The introvert must learn to lose his obsession with himself and how he appears to others. As soon as he does this, he takes a few steps in the right direction, becoming free to be the person he wants to be.

Involving Kids Who Don't Participate

It's unfortunate, but we have trained our kids to be spectators. We bring in singing groups, or a media presentation, and the kids become an audience. They sit at a distance and watch. The criteria set by the media is in their subconscious thinking. They judge the youth worker in everything he does and says, but there is no way the youth worker can compete with media professionalism, the fast-moving, exciting program, whether it bears a Christian label or not. Instead of trying to compete with the media's image, I think being an honest, loving individual is a much more viable alternative. Young people need a chance to see the youth leader on a one-on-one basis, where they love him as a person, and can see that he's not putting on a show.

What kind of involvement do we want? Worship? Singing? Whatever the case, kids are always conscious of what's going on around them. For instance, in singing, often kids will just sit and listen; very few will actually sing. Maybe it's because the songs of the church aren't too appealing to them. But many have a low self-image, and if they can't sing, they're not about to prove it to the entire group. Maybe we're trying to get them to sing and be joyful, but they don't have much joy to sing about. Perhaps they're more honest than their leaders. There are other factors to consider: the individual who is sick, the one who was pushed into coming to the meeting, the individual who feels that the whole of Christianity is just a group of hypocrites sitting together.

The most important factor in increasing involvement is to first find out why your young people aren't becoming involved. There's no real involvement in a meeting where a group of spectators sit and listen to someone speak. Activities should be planned so that they are not a threat to individuals. If an activity emphasizes athletic ability, it will attract jocks, but nonathletic kids won't become involved for fear of making fools of themselves. Once you find out why kids are not becoming involved, get in with them, and encourage them. Perhaps you can plan programs and activities where involvement is not going to be a threat or make them feel unnatural. Normally, kids will become as involved as the leader is, so it's best to change a whole program into one of involvement; start working with your kids and let them see you become involved yourself.

Dealing With Cliques and Disruptive Groups

Every group leader has to deal with cliques at one time or another in most cases. These groups are not intentionally malicious; they just enjoy each other's company and aren't aware of anyone else. There's a difference between a clique, or self-interest group, and a special interest group. Special interest groups share a special interest, like surfing or biking. They all speak the same language and are into the same things.

I have found cliques tend to form more frequently in groups that have a number of couples. We try to put a damper on romance, making it a very low-key thing. We stress friendship and we try to get everyone involved as a family. Teaching that emphasizes love, the group as a body, and the individuals' need for each other promotes interest in the whole of the body. This attracts a group that is not oriented toward coupling or steadies. If cliques still stick together, I get the clique together and speak candidly to them about the destructive effect of their action. The best way to deal with this counterproductive element is to head into the clique as it forms, and keep it from becoming the kind of group where a newcomer feels like he needs an ice pick to get in.

You can often tell the feeling of members of the group by observing where they sit in relation to you. Those who are just about out, but not quite, will be sitting in the back, having their own little meeting. They just don't want to be involved. There could be many reasons as to why those four guys sit back there on the periphery of the group. They may think it's smart, or they may think the whole youth group thing is a rather immature waste of time. They may be fighting God. This group is counterproductive, maybe even subversive, and may try to undermine and destroy what you're trying to build. I've had groups like this in my youth programs. One even came to me after every meeting to tell me what he and his group were doing to destroy the youth group, how many kids were following them, and how many were following me. It was very interesting working with him. It drove me to my knees and gave me a challenge. One by one, you can win the respect of individuals to yourself and your Lord. If you make a special effort in this area, they'll listen to you. They'll see how counterproductive these activities are to the group; they'll see that cliques and disruptions destroy all that you and they are reaching for.

I try to approach these disruptive groups on a one-on-one basis, not together. If you can wean the leader back to the rest of the group, the others are likely to follow. Often this is a spiritual thing. If they're right with God, they're going to be right in the middle of things.

Developing Student Leadership

In the '50s and early '60s youth work placed a strong emphasis on student leadership. Individuals were elected to positions, and we had traditional Sunday night meetings: Step right up and preach . . . lead the songs . . . do this and that. This kind of meeting, and those who lead them, seem to foster a "platform" mentality that can become an ego thing, and many times the kids aren't really ready for it.

In the last few years, I've changed my philosophy about this. I used to work hard with my junior highs, giving them leadership responsibilities in meetings and platform exposure. There were kids in the group who could handle programs and speak. I could walk out of the room, leaving no adults present, and come back an hour later to a controlled meeting, going on exactly as planned in our elections. We had a board of leading youth directors and pastors who checked out those who wanted to run for office, gave special awards for outgoing officers, and recognition for those who stood out. All this was on the junior-high level. But I lost many of those individuals when they became 11th and 12th graders, and I was disappointed because I had put so much time into them. They were doing so well when suddenly they would peel off and go into the world. I encountered some of them later, and these were their comments: "We had enough of this Mickey Mouse church stuff. We wanted to go into the world where it's real. We wanted to have some fun. We wanted to live." That hit me hard. In growing more mature many of my best potential leaders threw off their junior high lifestyle, and along with it went their intense involvement in the youth program. So I changed my philosophy. Many of us have been pushing too soon and too fast, trying to develop what we see as leadership. Kids are good mimics (in the platform sense), but they often lack the maturity, judgment, and wisdom it takes to make a real leader.

Our junior-high program is light, full of fun and games. If kids can be kids when they're young, they won't be acting like kids when they're men and women. Too many adults are still acting like children because they've never had the chance to do nutty things as kids. We have a light program that takes kids as fast as they want to go. The curriculum includes knowing that the Word of God is truth, knowing that there is a will of God for them, and that they need to submit to the Lord. They learn about lordship, and they memorize verses, going about as fast as they can and as far as they can. But they are not pushed beyond their maturity level. When they reach the senior-high group, we involve them in ministry and serving, and work on from that level. I would rather develop leadership and responsibility in activities, and reserve "platform" leadership for those who are more mature and have proven themselves.

Leadership should be developed in those who have the desire and the ability. I don't believe you can create leaders as such. But you can develop them to their maximum potential, using them in limited responsibilities for activities, and groom them step by step, until they prove themselves in basic responsibilities. Remember, most adolescents have an up and down history. If one of your teen leaders falls he will take others with him.

Turning Spectators Into Participants

Our church culture has groomed spectators. We have too many activities where you "put in your quarter and watch what happens." We've got to recognize that this is a particular problem among young people and must find ways to develop participants. Getting life and enthusiasm into the group will help change spectators into participants.

If you yourself are a participant, preaching involvement, participation, and ministries, and don't just sit around in endless circles of Bible studies and churchianity, if you're going somewhere and doing something, you'll attract participants. It is the simple concept of modeling in action. There are enough drones in the beehive of God, so it's not necessary to attract more. I want to attract winners, but they're hard to attract because they're already involved. You have to use an entirely different strategy to get winners than you do to get losers. Losers are always around if there is a good program, just like the multitudes who followed Christ. He gave lunches and had a good show, but the multitudes were never the disciples.

I came to a point where I wasn't interested in having a big, spectacular group. We had more than 700 attending every week, and it was a fat group. We just weren't doing anything. What do you do with someone who's obese? Just like the group that's obese, you change their diet and put them to work. We changed the "diet," and attendance certainly dropped off a lot. Many went and sat in another church. We put our group to work, and attendance dropped off more. But we ended up with a better caliber of individuals, and I could start giving them some responsibility.

Most youth leaders want to have participants in their group, but the activities they provide are designed for spectators. If the activities are planned for participation, you'll have participators. Our church has all kinds of programs, and this attracts those who get involved in ministry. Most kids want to get involved in the reality of living and demonstrating their faith. It's a shame that so many youth leaders don't provide these young people with a meaningful area for demonstration of their faith and a ministry in which they can function.

As I look at it, I guess we've sort of been programed to think the meeting is so important and I certainly feel that proclamation or preaching is critical. It just seems so simple to turn on the meeting, do your job, and then walk away, and yet we don't seem to question what kind of an individual this produces. Kids today want to be known for themselves. They want to be ministered to as individuals; they want to be taken as individuals. They're tired of being spectators and being simply a statistical number. In California, the graduation ceremony in many of our schools is simply a farce: on occasion the graduates get up and, as a whole group, walk right out, leaving the parents there. One kid told me how, in their graduation ceremony, they blew bubbles . . . it was a big joke. Young people are tired of being clumped together as a big group. The big-group mentality left as the Jesus Movement tapered off, and kids have come to me now more than any other time in my ministry asking "Do you know my name?" "Do you know who I am?" What does this say? They want to be taken as individuals and they will respond as individuals. But the problem is that this is very costly, and we would rather wrap it up in very neat, tidy program packages, and call it a meeting. I think this is where we often fail. Christianity was meant to be a person-to-person thing—a dynamic living experience, not necessarily canned and pushed through as a meeting or program. So we have to face the fact that our kids demand to be ministered to as individuals. This means that I'm going to have to multiply myself so that I minister to individuals and teach them by modeling, to minister to each other. This is the only way that hurt, that thirst, that vacancy is going to be filled.

There is no other way to get around it, but the individual who is going to be a successful youth worker is going to have to pay for his success. And it's going to have to be met in the area of individual work. Many times it will be one-on-one, many times a small group ministry, taking kids to and from, talking with them, calling them by name, being sure that the youth worker is an example and a model that they can see under many conditions. High-profile discipleship, high-profile leadership is indeed expensive.

5

The Youth Leader As a Model

Jeff was a junior in high school when I met him. He was a popular guy with a sharp sense of humor. He was a guard on the varsity football team and his athletic build looked like an endorsement for Universal Gym Equipment. What was special about Jeff was his faithful attendance at the Bible studies I led during his last two years of high school. He always seemed hungry to know more. He was diligent in studying Scripture and very involved in church activities. He became a leader in his church youth group, and near the end of his senior year he decided to go into the ministry.

We kept in touch during the years that followed. We had lunch together during his senior year in college and he really startled me.

Jeff said, "Bill, I can't remember much of what you taught us. . . ." I found myself wanting to slip under the table. I could feel my face flush with embarrassment. In that second, my mind flashed back to all those hours I spent in the office preparing those great lessons of truth, creativity, and everyday applications. If Jeff had not had a B+ average in high school and college, I might have blamed his lack of retention on a poor intellect, instead of my teaching.

Bill Muir is the National Director of Campus Life, the high-school campus ministry of Youth for Christ.

Then Jeff finished his statement. ". . . But I remember everything about *you*—the way you went out of your way to pick up people, the fact that you never put people down, your enjoyment of life, and your desire to be like Jesus Christ."

What a lift! I had feared that Jeff had missed it all and was about to announce his abandonment of the faith. Instead, he revealed a principle of youth ministry that I've never forgotten: my availability and relationships with youth are as important as teaching them in the classroom. One of the most commonly overlooked areas of youth ministry is the quality of relationships between the young people and the youth leader. And yet the amount of time spent with them and the quality of those relationships are fundamental to an effective youth ministry. A ministry that produces change in young people will not be lacking in meaningful relationships.

BENEFITS OF RELATIONSHIPS

Good relationships with the youth in our charge have several advantages to us leaders. One benefit is the improved quality of our teaching. Larry Richards, in his book *A Theology of Christian Education,* says, "By spending time with the student individually or collectively we begin to complement our teaching. Relationships provide opportunities to allow our youth to see the Word lived out in real life." And from the students' perspective Richards notes,

> For God's Word to catch at our hearts and be most effectively applied for transformation, we also need an intimate relationship with the teacher. We need to see ourselves (and desire ourselves to be) like the teacher. We need to know the teacher well, to have access to his feelings and his values and his attitudes, and his way of responding in life. We need to be with the teacher outside the formal learning setting, in life. And the teacher needs to be a person who *lives* his faith, and who in his own personality reflects the meaning of truths Scripture communicates in words.[1]

In other words, relationships with youth provide opportunities to engage in some valuable role modeling.

Modeling the Christian life is somewhat like modeling clothes, except that we don't shed the Christian life like an article of clothing. When models are on display in a clothing store, they show the viewer what that particular item looks like on a real person. It's one thing to look at a dress on a rack and another to see it on a person. The models are simply answering the unspoken question of the audience—"What might these clothes look like on me?" When we model the Christian lifestyle we are *showing* youth the real-life application and the meaning of words like "love," "servanthood," and "obedience." It has been said that we retain:

10% of what we read,
20% of what we hear,
30% of what we see,
50% of what we see and hear,
70% of what we speak, and
90% of what we speak and do.

The old axiom appears to hold true: actions *do* speak louder than words.

Adolescents are notorious followers. They respond to the adult who shows interest in them like plants respond to sunlight. Teen-agers, like adults, as social beings, need and want relationships. As children enter their teen years, they become very aware of their interactions with other people. They plug into models that help them know how adults act. Adolescents copy people they like and admire, since they are in the process of developing independence from their parents and are attempting to find their own identity. The person they like who moves alongside of them will become a powerful influence in helping them determine who they will be. Teen-agers are open to and looking for an adult relationship.

The Scriptures confirm the importance of relationships in ministry. Letters to believers as recorded in 1 Thessalonians 2:1–10 and 1 Timothy 1:16 say—

> You know, brothers, that our visit to you was not a failure. We had previously suffered and been insulted in Philippi, as you know, but with the help of our God we dared to tell you his gospel in spite of strong opposition. For the appeal we make does not spring from error or impure motives, nor are we trying to trick you. On the contrary, we speak as men approved by God to be entrusted with the gospel. We are not trying to

> please men but God, who tests our hearts. You know we never used flattery, nor did we put on a mask to cover up greed—God is our witness. We were not looking for praise from men, not from you or anyone else.
>
> As apostles of Christ we could have been a burden to you, but we were gentle among you, like a mother caring for her little children. We loved you so much that we were delighted to share with you not only the gospel of God but our lives as well, because you had become so dear to us. Surely you remember, brothers, our toil and hardship; we worked night and day in order not to be a burden to anyone while we preached the gospel of God to you.
>
> You are witnesses, and so is God, of how holy, righteous and blameless we were among you who believed (1 Thess. 2:1–10).

> But for that very reason I was shown mercy so that in me, the worst of sinners, Christ Jesus might display his unlimited patience as an example for those who would believe on him and receive eternal life (1 Tim. 1:16).

Paul acknowledged modeling as a teaching method. He encouraged people around him to watch how the Christian life was being lived. His emphasis on righteous living was undoubtedly not only to obey God, but also that the believers' words and deeds might be consistent with one another to the end that the gospel would be clearly proclaimed.

Jesus placed tremendous importance on His relationships with people. In Mark 3:13–14 we discover that He chose twelve to be *with* Him. He took the time to be with people. We find Jesus attending parties of large groups of all sorts of people. He also sat down with individuals to talk about spiritual questions. We tend to focus on His explicit teaching and lose sight of the hours and days He spent with His twelve disciples walking from one location to another. But words alone were not sufficient for our Lord. He chose to communicate the gospel over a period of three years and through hundreds of relationships and conversations.

Carl Rogers summarizes the importance of the relationship between the teacher and student. He describes it as one that rests not on the teacher's skills, knowledge, planning, or resources, but the attitudinal qualities of the personal relationship between the teacher and the learner.

Relationships serve another important function. They enhance our ability to counsel. Psychologist Rollo May has written, "If you don't listen to the little things, the big things won't come." People confide in those in whom they trust. Teen-agers will open up to those they believe know them and are concerned about them. Spending time laughing, playing, traveling, and talking with kids allows them to get to know us, and makes it easier for them to talk with us.

Teen-agers with whom I've worked who are now living out the Christian life in college or at work, are those with whom I spent time and shared deep experiences. The odds of a young person developing a virile, active faith seem from the experiences of many youth workers to be directly correlated with the individual time the leaders spent with them in the formative stages of their faith.

THE RESULTS OF RELATIONSHIPS IN TEEN-AGERS' LIVES

Simply *being with* someone isn't sufficient to communicate the gospel in its fullness. Modeling through relationships isn't meant to be a substitute for communication of content. Rather, it is an enabling methodology as well as an obvious application of scriptural examples in our lives. Meaningful relationships benefit the adolescent in several ways.

One basic result of the role-model relationship is that it shows the teen-ager that the Christian life has practical, daily applications. When young people notice someone going out of his or her way to run an errand for another, they realize that it is possible (and positive) for them to do the same. Many truths easily written on a chalkboard often seem impossible to live. But when those truths are demonstrated in someone's life, others see that they *can* be practiced. A teen-ager who watches a respected person can be reassured that the Christian life *can* be lived. A youth leader can run out of gas telling a teen-ager that God can give a person peace of mind, but when that teen-ager watches the leader exhibiting that peace of mind under stress, the teen-ager learns firsthand someone's experiencing of God's peace.

Relationships can help teen-agers remember biblical truth. When a person watches you go out of your way to help a stranded motorist get to a gas station, that picture will not easily be forgotten. When you are seen returning to the cashier the money he or she overpaid you, honesty is contextualized.

Our relationships with teen-agers impress on them our personal concern for them. You can back up a phrase like "I love you and so does God" by showing them you care enough to give up a free evening to have them over for ice cream. Teen-agers have learned that youth leaders are *expected* to be at youth meetings. But taking extra time out of your busy schedule for a young person may just *prove* that you care. By spending time with someone, you are communicating to them their worth. Furthermore, the kids we spend time with will become genuine acquaintances. We can celebrate their happy moments with them and invite them to share ours. Through repeated exposure to individuals by means of errands, talks, and activities, they begin to know what makes us tick. They begin to understand our ministries and why and how Jesus Christ is important to us.

One evening after midweek Bible study, I asked Mark if he would be interested in getting together that weekend to play racquetball. Mark's response was, "Sure! You mean you want to play racquetball with me? You're so busy. What time should I walk to your house?"

"Mark, I'll pick you up at your house in my car," was my response. Most effective youth leaders have found that through a simple gesture like this and hundreds more, you can show your concern for a teen-ager in a way that words alone could never match.

Another benefit of relationships to your ministry is that they help open up teen-agers to you and to God's Word. As you spend time with youth, they will share problems like guilt, home difficulties, thought life, and dating, subjects they formerly would have avoided discussing because of pride or fear of rejection.

One afternoon I invited Pete to my apartment so he could go swimming in our pool. Like any youth leader, I attempted to be fun-loving, exciting, and creative. I had a list of pool games that would keep us busy. After a few minutes of pool games and other attempts to be "funny, exciting, and creative," I decided just to be myself. I was tired that afternoon, so I decided just to climb out of the pool and relax in the sun. But as I did, I became extremely uncomfortable because I was afraid that Pete would get bored with me and leave. Out of the corner of my eye I watched to see how he was doing. He would swim, get out and lay in the sun, get back in and float around. Eventually, Pete came over and sat next to me.

"Bill, my girl friend says it's okay with her if we go all the way. What do you think?" That provided a great opportunity to talk about important issues. I strongly believe that if I had kept trying to be *what I thought* he wanted me to be rather than *what I was,* he would never have asked me that question. By being the person God made me and spending authentic time with Pete, I freed him to be himself and to talk about things that were important to him.

Relationships can motivate and convict. A good model encourages people to act in the same way. When I hear someone read the Bible with conviction, I find myself wanting to read it with renewed interest. When I am praying with someone whose prayers reflect deep communication with God, I find myself wanting to take advantage of the privilege and opportunity of communing with my Lord. Good models remind people of what they should do as well as point us toward what we could do. It's easy to put off doing the things we ought until we see someone else doing that particular "ought." We often become convicted to ask ourselves why we are not acting in the same way.

THE BENEFITS OF RELATIONSHIPS FOR YOUTH LEADERS

It is evident that providing meaningful relationships with teen-agers benefits us as well as them. When we spend time with people in order to demonstrate truth and love, it remolds us as well. Knowing kids are watching everything about us and, through that observation are determining how the Christian life should be lived, will affect our actions. Paul states in 2 Corinthians 3:2–3 that we are living letters

> . . . written on our hearts, known and read by everybody. You show that you are a letter from Christ, the result of our ministry, written not with ink but with the Spirit of the living God, not on tablets of stone but on tablets of human hearts.

Actions in which we are tempted to compromise our principles will be much harder to engage in if we are being watched! Realizing that our strengths and weaknesses are being observed and even mimicked by young Christians will help us to correct and not rationalize those besetting sins. This is the concept found in a statement by the Lausanne Committee for World Evangelization, "We believe that the key principle to persuasive Christian communication is to be found in the communicators themselves in what kind of people they are."[2]

In short, when we realize we are models, we become motivated to live out the basics. If we want our kids in the Word daily, we must also be studying daily. If we want them to witness to their friends, we must witness to ours. If we want them to pray, we must live a life of prayer.

Time with teen-agers allows us to get feedback. It is important in youth work to know whether we are teaching the right concepts in the right ways. In a casual setting, teen-agers can tell us what they and their friends think about the effectiveness of our ministry. That feedback enables us to make the appropriate changes to tailor our ministry more effectively to their needs.

Fostering credibility is another benefit gained through developing relationships. Teen-agers listen to people they love and people who love them. When they watch our lives during the week and find us to be real and honest, they will also listen to our words during a meeting or a conversation. They will tend to be more open to believe our teaching and our answers because they have seen that teaching illustrated in our lives.

Credibility with teen-agers can be gained or lost all too easily by what we neglect. Recently Youth for Christ and Michigan State University did a joint research project to determine what teen-agers consider to be the desirable and undesirable behaviors of adults. The results included the following information:

> Implications of this finding are if a leader wishes to be effective, he or she should emphasize behaviors that involve relating to followers as people. For example, listening, communicating and seeking help when needed are more important than preoccupation with program details, arrang-

ing chairs, soliciting volunteers, planning next week's refreshments or setting up the projector and screen. The research suggests that young people are less interested in the program an adult leader has planned for a given occasion than with how he treats them when they come together.[3]

CHARACTERISTICS OF GOOD AND BAD RELATIONSHIPS

Teen-agers indicate that the most desirable quality in an adult leader is the ability to simply listen. Many times we as youth leaders have thought being funny, outgoing, talkative, and creative would make students respond to us. But what they really want is someone who will listen to them. Youth leaders need to spend more time enabling the youth to talk, rather than monopolizing every encounter.

The second most desirable quality in a youth leader is an understanding of teen-age concerns. It is important for adult leaders to be aware of the youth culture in general and the specific concerns of the youth to whom we relate.

It is easy for adults to minimize the problems teen-agers face. Dating, grades, friends, and pimples don't seem quite as significant as negative bank balances, gas bills, broken arms, mortgage payments, and conflicts with neighbors and co-workers. Youth respond to the adult who empathizes with their concerns, values, interests, and desires. Remember your high school years; concerns you had then shaped your approach and response to much of what followed later in life. Adult leaders have an advantage: we've been there.

A third desirable quality of leaders, according to the survey, is the ability to communicate. Teen-agers respond to adults who feel free to talk with them *as adults* and not as if they were small children. When we communicate with them as adults, it is more likely that they will respond as mature youth. It is important for teen-agers to get to know us and see us as *people,* and not simply as *roles.* Teen-agers don't like unexpected surprises that embarrass them. They have fragile egos. If things are going wrong in a meeting or activity, we should tell them in a way that preserves their dignity.

There are also undesirable qualities that should be avoided by youth leaders.

The most undesirable quality in leaders, according to these teen-agers, is the habit of saying one thing but doing another. And this hypocrisy isn't only expressed in big issues such as theology or morality. Does this sound familiar? "I'll call you this week and we'll do something." But have we always kept such promises? It is easy for a leader to make promises on the spur of the moment that he or she easily forgets. But teen-agers don't forget as easily. Teen-agers may not remind us of broken promises, but they *do* remember them. I can *still* remember my youth leader telling me that the leaders of the youth group were going on a retreat that never materialized. That hurt. Hypocrisy is ranked as the most serious undesirable behavior exhibited by both peer and adult leaders. "The high ranking of hypocrisy as a negative behavior seems to imply that to be effective with young people, the leader's words and deeds should match. 'Practice what you preach' is good advice for effective leadership."[4]

Other undesirable qualities are:

1. doesn't relate to me,
2. doesn't show concern for me,
3. doesn't trust me,
4. doesn't follow through—is irresponsible, and
5. looks down on me.

An acronym to keep in mind when seeking to develop meaningful relationships with teen-agers is LEAN—Love, Example, Acceptance, Nearness. Each of these words should characterize our relationships with our youth.

Without a doubt the greatest relationship builder is our Lord Jesus Christ. He displayed all the characteristics of LEAN and continues to do so to this day.

L. As a *Lover,* we see Him serving. He did not place Himself above those with whom He came in contact. He served them (John 13:12–14). He did not brag or boast of who He was or what He did. He simply demonstrated love to others. To love someone is to make sacrifices in serving them. "For even the Son of Man did not come to be served, but to serve, and to give his life as a ransom for many" (Mark 10:45).

E. We must provide a living *Example* of what the Christian life is all about. If our disciples are to grow we must "flesh out" for them the life Christ demands that we live. Someone like Jesus needs to be seen at a ballgame. You may not mention His name every time you're with kids, but you should be living as Jesus would if He were there in the flesh. Our aim should be that our God-pleasing lifestyle would become contagious and that we could say with Paul, "Imitate me as I imitate Christ." We must show that in obedience to Christ we express care and kindness in all our relationships.

A. Jesus demonstrated *Acceptance* in His relationship with the Samaritan woman, the woman caught in adultery, the great religious leader Nicodemus, the greed-stricken Zacchaeus. He reached out to befriend people so openly and unconditionally that He was accused of being a glutton and drunkard because of His association with the despised tax collectors and sinners. He accepted the unacceptable. Being a friend means that we dare not hold on to any preconceived mindsets that result in our discriminating against those who don't measure up in looks, performance, popularity, and influence. We must accept students where they are in their own pilgrimage. We must look below the surface to identify and appreciate their unique characteristics and qualities. But we must not confuse acceptance of the person with acceptance of his or her harmful or objectionable activities. Jesus was not afraid to confront any one of His disciples if they got out of line.

N. We must practice *Nearness*. Jesus knew it was impossible to care for someone from a distance. A loving relationship and lifestyle cannot exist without close contact. We cannot help or teach when we allow a chasm of distance to develop as a result of a lack of time or commitment, insecurity, laziness, apathy, or fear of rejection or failure. Spending time with teenagers allows them to get to know us as real people. It provides us with the opportunity to live out our teaching. We are communicating to them that they are more than an occasional number at a meeting. It costs us time, but it allows us to demonstrate truth, right values, right qualities, and right priorities.

By God's grace and the empowering of His Holy Spirit, we must exhibit an attitude that is accepting and a lifestyle that is contagious. We must be a *Lover* (a sacrificing servant), an *Example* (exhibiting God's intended lifestyle), an *Acceptor* (accepting others as

Christ has accepted us), and *Nearby* (one who spends time with young people and seeks to befriend them).

Those with whom you choose to spend time will tell you something about yourself. You might have preferences as to who you would like to be with, but to have an effective ministry it is *essential* that you spend time with teen-agers from various backgrounds and of many interests, ages, at various levels of performance and social graces. God does not display favoritism. Neither can we.

Larry Richards summarizes what needs to take place in a modeling relationship:

> 1. There needs to be frequent, long-term contact with the model(s) (youth leaders).
> 2. There needs to be a warm, loving relationship with the model(s).
> 3. There needs to be exposure to the inner states of the model(s).
> 4. The model(s) need to be observed in a variety of life settings and situations.
> 5. The model(s) need to exhibit consistency and clarity in behaviors, values, etc.
> 6. There needs to be a correspondence between the behavior of the model(s) and the beliefs (ideal standards) of the community.
> 7. There needs to be an explanation of lifestyle of the model(s) conceptually, with instruction accompanying shared experiences.
>
> These factors help us see that instruction and modeling are not contradictory or mutually exclusive. Instead, they point us to a situation in which Truth concepts are taught, explained, and expressed in words. But they also point us to other dimensions of the teaching/learning situation which make it more likely that the concepts will be perceived as realities to be experienced rather than simply as ideas to be believed.[5]

QUANTITY AND QUALITY OF RELATIONSHIPS

Perhaps the most essential ingredients in relationship building are the quality and quantity of time. Using time effectively demands decisions about how, when, and where we use it. The following is a list of common activities through which leaders can spend time with teen-agers:

- sandlot football, soccer, baseball
- shopping
- picnic
- volunteer tutoring
- TV watching at home
- skin diving
- skiing/tobogganing
- polar games
- trips to "away" games, tournaments
- charm school
- eating after games
- stuffing envelopes
- practicing a skit
- camping
- surfing/beach trips
- bike riding
- hiking
- slumber parties
- "rap" sessions
- working on your car
- swimming
- chess
- ping pong
- canoeing
- riding along (running errands, calling, etc.)
- working out with school team
- throwing a Frisbee
- going out for a Coke
- water skiing
- weekend trips

Investing a quantity of time with teen-agers is important because relationships can't grow unless people spend time with one another. But the quality of that time together is equally important. A youth leader can ensure that there is quality in the quantity of time spent by always looking for teachable moments. There will be times when the teen-ager will get angry, criticize someone, or gossip. And the youth leader must be ready to use such times to talk to the teen-ager about improper conduct. This *does not* mean preaching. A simple comment like "Boy, Sue, you really got mad back there; would you like to talk about it?" is usually an effective way to begin dialogue.

Essential to "redeeming" or building quality into time together is the leader's sensitivity to the teen-ager. Late one afternoon I picked Pete up at school for a Coke break. He climbed into the front seat. He seemed defeated. His eyes were red, his head was bent down, and his shoulders were slumped over. My simple opener of "Can I help in any way?" allowed him to open up about his being turned down by a girl for a date. The rest of our time together turned into a sharing about rejection and dating.

Sometimes it is not as obvious that there is a problem. A teen-ager will drop a sentence into a conversation that shows a need in a subtle way. He or she will appear to be happy, but while shopping might say, "I don't need any new clothes, I never date." Such a statement may indicate a feeling of rejection. And a helpful response could be, "Does it bother you that you are not dating right now?"

POTENTIAL PROBLEMS IN RELATIONSHIPS

Of course, when we invest large amounts of time with teen-agers, we will discover new issues and problems in our own lives, some of them very personal.

A top priority is that you protect your family and your time with them. As you develop meaningful relationships with kids, it will be easy for them to begin to drop in at your home, sometimes with no warning. You may have to say things such as, "Frank, I enjoy spending time with you, but I also need to spend time with my family." I tell some teen-agers to call before they come over. The main thing to keep in mind is that it is okay to tell your youth that you can't spend all your time with them. If they call, don't be afraid to say no. If you are developing good relationships with them they will understand. Part of being a good model for them is showing that a good Christian is also a good husband/wife, mother/father. If your family agrees, you could occasionally have kids over for dinner, painting, TV, yard work, and other activities. It's important not to take your family for granted. They need you too.

Since there is no substitute for time, adult leaders must plan carefully so that time spent on relationships does not devour time that must be spent in preparation for other responsibilities. For example, in the midst of a people-oriented ministry, some leaders must work on three-year goals, this month's curriculum plan, details for an upcoming activity, and the publicity for the camp. It is too easy to neglect the behind-the-scenes preparation in order to be out in the sun or off to a show with the kids. But when you have regularly scheduled meetings on Sunday mornings and midweek, you must be prepared. Purposeful meetings take time to plan if you care about the individuals attending the meeting.

One way to use time effectively is to be with youth in groups. Gather a group together to go to a baseball game. Play basketball with five rather than one. Instead of doing your grocery shopping alone, do it with someone. But take care not to spend all your time with the same group. A youth leader can over-concentrate on one group and neglect others. Youth who feel left out will drop out of your group's activities. A notebook with the names of your teen-agers and how much time you spend with each of them will help protect you from this problem. And while you're keeping records, include a page for yourself.

It's easy to lose your private self to people. A youth leader needs time alone to study, pray, meditate, plan, and review. Don't neglect your own needs because of busyness with others. This will ultimately hurt your ministry. On occasion we all just need to be alone. When we are alone, it is essential that we protect that space by telling people in advance that we are unavailable at a certain time.

Finally, avoid the danger of group loyalty rallying to you rather than to the church. Your goal in relationships is the growth and maturity of teen-agers, not your own ego gratification. One way to avoid this pitfall is to develop tentative goals for each individual's growth. Then make sure that the relationship you have with him is moving the teen-ager toward those goals. Ultimately, you must point teen-agers away from you and toward their own niche in the Christian life.

Relationships are work. We cannot afford to reduce Christianity to the confines of a classroom or pages shown on an overhead. Jesus taught from everyday circumstances, real problems, and the normal events of life. On the other hand, relationships must not be seen as substitutes for teaching. Rather, they can be supportive of teaching and help produce maturity.

Jeff was wrong when he said he hadn't remembered anything that he had been taught. He had. He simply couldn't remember the specifics. Without knowing it, he had begun to assimilate those truths into his life. The relationship we had has borne fruit. That's a good feeling.

FOOTNOTES

[1]Lawrence O. Richards, *A Theology of Christian Education* (Grand Rapids, MI: Zondervan, 1975), p. 85.

[2]Lausanne Committee for World Evangelization, *Lausanne Occasional Papers, #2: The Willowbank Report—Gospel and Culture* (Minneapolis: World Wide Publications, 1978), p. 15.

[3]Edward D. Seely, "Leadership Skills of Adult Leaders and Youth-Peer Leaders," (Summary of Doctoral Dissertation, Michigan State University, 1980), p. 3.

[4]Ibid., p. 4.

[5]Richards, *Theology of Christian Education,* pp. 84–85.

6

Developing a Volunteer Team

For both quantitative reasons (the number of kids being ministered to) and qualitative reasons (the significance of that ministry), it is imperative to build a ministry team that includes volunteers. There are too many tasks that need to be done for even the best "Lone Ranger" to do alone. In every church there are individuals who volunteer their time and abilities to do the variety of tasks required to run a church youth program. Proper training and supervision provide the structure and encouragement they need to do their ministry effectively. The skills necessary to work with volunteers can be developed in people who have the desire, discipline, and persistence to help other people use their gifts and abilities. It is important for the leader to see himself or herself as a facilitator, an enabler, a manager of other Christians. A Christian leader may compare his responsibilities to those of a coach. A coach brings individuals together, helps them to develop their personal skills, and molds them into a corporate oneness where their solo efforts are amplified by the strengths of the whole.

In working with volunteers there are certain basic assumptions that need to be understood.

■ *Every volunteer is motivated for his or her own reasons.* To work with volunteers effectively you must dis-

---

Mike West is the Executive Director of Rockfordland Youth for Christ (Illinois), and coordinates associate (volunteer) staff training for Youth for Christ/USA.

cover their motivations and seek to meet them in appropriate ways. While from a human perspective some motivations could be more noble than others, they all touch the core of our emotional makeup. To deny these motivations is to deny our humanness. Some are motivated by the challenge of starting something new, others by the feedback of teaching a class, still others by the desire to organize that which has been unorganized. Like full-time staff, volunteers are motivated by the mission of our work. The task of working with kids must always be kept in front of them as something that is noble.

■ *Like full-time staff, volunteers "get paid" for their work.* Only the currency is different. Successful youth leaders think of their volunteer staff with the same sensitivity and awareness they give to the "salaried professional." These leaders believe that volunteers need to be involved in decisions that affect them. Volunteers need to feel appreciated, know what is expected of them, and be given regular feedback. They need to be told and shown that they are important.

■ *In most cases, volunteers are more effective when they feel they are part of a team.* This means you must systematically strive to show your volunteers how their individual efforts are supporting the group. As they see how these efforts fit into the larger scheme of things, a positive group atmosphere will be developed that will encourage their spirit and sustain their efforts. Such a group can be a vivid demonstration of Christ's love and the impact Christians can have when they work in an atmosphere of corporate commitment.

■ *To improve volunteer results you must train and supervise them to maximize the satisfaction they are receiving from their tasks.* This means developing certain skills such as planning, interviewing, running meetings, confronting the volunteer's performance, and problem-solving. As individuals who have been given the responsibility of working with others, we cannot assume that the right things will just happen. We must be faithful to our volunteers by ministering to them through training and supervision, and in so doing we are also faithful to God.

EIGHT STEPS TO A COMPLETE TRAINING PROGRAM

1. Identify the task to be accomplished.

At the beginning of your work with volunteers, it is crucial that you have a clear idea of what your ministry needs are. It can be overwhelming when you think of all that needs to be done. By listing the specific task, you will establish an objective foundation for determining the needs your training program will address.

2. Identify skills and knowledge needed to accomplish each task.

Paralleling each task that needs to be done are the individual ingredients that will bring that task to reality. For example, if one of the tasks listed is to have a winter retreat, the skills required for that task would be to organize, schedule, coordinate, recruit, motivate, and run meetings. The type of knowledge needed would be familiarity with needs of the group, possible locations, potential resources, budget restrictions, and awareness of what has happened in the past with the winter retreat.

3. Prioritize tasks according to overall impact.

There are certain tasks that are necessary for the spiritual health of your group. Such things as the development of student leadership, small group Bible studies, personal appointments, and well-run retreats are almost indispensable items to a healthy youth group.

There are other tasks that establish a "tone" for your ministry. They could include the quality of group singing, the enthusiasm of the opening sessions in Sunday school, and the general appearance of your meeting area. Whatever you see as important must be given a high priority.

4. Match people with tasks.

This is a crucial step. In the process of selecting your volunteer staff, you will have obtained a clear idea of what their gifts are. Your training program should place people in positions that allow them to exercise those gifts, and at the same time accomplish the task that you have identified as important to your group. By placing people where they belong, you will also be cutting down on turnover. When people are using their strengths and contributing to the success of your program, their motivation for staying will be increased greatly, their commitment to the group sealed, and the quality of ministry increased.

5. Determine training needs of volunteers based on the task they will be performing.

After you have associated a task with a person you will be in a position to ask the question, "What can training do to help this person do that task?" If a person has the task of leading the singing and is an expert in that field, training is not important for the performance of that task. In such a case, training could help in integrating that person and function into the larger scheme of things so that he or she feels like part of a team. Training should direct itself at solving problems, answering questions, and meeting needs of your volunteers. You will do these at a variety of levels.

6. Develop a training curriculum that imparts the right kind of knowledge, teaches the needed skills, and builds a positive attitude.

Such a curriculum can be divided into three different categories. First, volunteers need input that teaches them the "how to's" of ministry. Such skills as leading small groups, building personal relationships, leading students to Christ, discipling Christians, giving a "talk-to" or "wrap-up," and leading discussions are some of the skills your volunteers will be using. As you help your staff develop these skills, they will not only increase their efficiency, but also their sense of satisfaction on mastering a ministry skill that they will be able to use in other situations.

A second level of instruction should deal with the reasons behind the "how to's." Because volunteers are usually involved in tasks that represent a piece of the "ministry pie," it is easy for volunteers to lose their perspective and get bogged down in just what they are doing. As volunteers are exposed to ideas that deal with understanding the youth culture, being an adult in a teen-age world, the spiritual decision process and other materials that touch on the "reasons" behind their activities, their individual contributions will be interpreted with the value they actually have. For example, if someone is doing a Bible study for a group of typical high school sophomores, it could be discouraging if they interpret "sophomore indifference" as a true reflection of what is happening. If they understand what normal adolescent behavior is like and have a grasp of discipleship as a process, the volunteer will be able to persist in the light of what can happen as the kids mature emotionally, physically, and spiritually.

A third area that your training program should deal with is the personal needs of your staff. As you do things for your volunteers that speak directly and indirectly to their world, they will benefit as people. From time management to encouragement about their spiritual, family, and personal relationships, you can help them feel better about who they are as people.

In each of these areas you may feel it appropriate to use outside resources. You do not have to be the expert—only the facilitator, the coach.

7. *Initiate concentrated training sessions.*
The purpose of such sessions is to create a positive group identity and communicate the basics of what would be common to everyone's ministry (concepts of discipleship, personal ministry, communication, understanding adolescents). Consequently, these sessions need to be well thought out. They should be an example of a good group meeting.

There is no "one best way" of organizing these sessions. Principles of learning such as motivation, reinforcement, transfer of learning, and retention should be utilized. The timing of such meetings needs to be something that is appropriate for your group. For some churches it means meeting quarterly for an all day teach-in, for others it's a yearly weekend retreat followed by two or three day-long sessions held during the year. Still others meet twice a month for two- or three-hour sessions. Again, do what is best for your volunteers.

8. *Monitor and adjust your training objectives.*
As your ministry year develops, you will become better aware of the changing needs of your volunteers. Don't be locked into any system, but be sensitive to the needs of the people God has given you to work with.

SUPERVISION

Because ministry does not take place in the classroom, a responsible training program follows through to the supervision of volunteers as they do their tasks. Supervision is a structured way of relating to people. It is a consistent extension of a philosophy of training that cares for both people and programs. Proper supervision tells the volunteers they are important and that what they are doing is important.

As a supervisor you will encourage people in their tasks, be a mirror of what is happening, monitor the process of their ministry, serve as a catalyst for their abilities, and be stimulus for new learning.

Supervision requires consistent contact with a specific purpose. That purpose is the personal edification of the volunteer and the enhancement of the kingdom of God.

Supervision is a cooperative effort where the relationship between the people involved is the most important part of the learning experience. The word "supervision" should not be interpreted as a relationship that is forced by an organizational chart. Supervision is discipleship. It is a relationship where there is trust, a common spirit of commitment, a desire to learn on the part of each person involved, a willingness to pursue truth, and a belief that God will bless the faithfulness of that relationship.

STRUCTURE AND CONSIDERATION

In this relationship there are two key ingredients: structure and consideration. Structure provides the parameters or the guidelines of the relationship. Consideration provides the affirmation needed in the relationship.

Structure consists of:

- written task descriptions for volunteers
- specified review times
- an agreed-upon time commitment
- an agreed-upon longevity commitment
- clearly defined expectations of the volunteer's performance
- a standardized screening process

Consideration consists of:

- including volunteers in decision making when it affects them
- including volunteers on appropriate mailing lists
- doing personal favors
- having a comfortable space for volunteers to relax
- sending special occasion cards

- writing the volunteers' spouse a note of appreciation
- seeing (visiting) volunteers in "their world"
- public recognition
- providing fun, social events

The assessment form on the following page can act as a sounding board for the level of structure and consideration you are giving. If possible, duplicate the form so you can fill it out on yourself and then have the volunteers fill it out on you. To use the Volunteer Manager Assessment Form:

1. Write number scores in each box: 5 equals "always" through 1 equals "never" except where there is a "–" sign after the statement, and then reverse the order of numbering (1 equals "always" and 5 equals "never").
2. Draw a line under "Sees to it that all volunteers are working up to capacity."
3. Add up all the numbers above the line to get a total.
4. Add up all the numbers below the line to get a second total.
5. "Acceptable" scores for those above line (reflects structure) are 42–47.
6. "Acceptable" scores for those below line (reflects consideration) are 47–51.

The Volunteer Manager Assessment Form will let you know if you are providing the "structure" and "consideration" your volunteers need. Use it as a learning experience to increase your sensitivity to your volunteer needs.

SKILLS NECESSARY IN PROVIDING SUPERVISION

There are six basic skills a supervisor needs to develop:

1. Establishing and maintaining the "right relationship," the "right distance."
2. Setting of goals.
3. Encouraging strategies to reach goals.
4. Facilitating a field experience.
5. Listening and asking the right questions.
6. Interviewing and evaluating.

Volunteer Manager Assessment Form

The Volunteer Manager:

always	often	sometimes	seldom	never	
					Makes his/her attitudes clear to the volunteers.
					Tries out his/her new ideas with the volunteers.
					Rules with an iron hand. (–)
					Criticizes poor work.
					Speaks in a manner not to be questioned.
					Assigns volunteers to particular tasks.
					Works without a plan. (–)
					Maintains definite standards of performance.
					Emphasizes the meeting of deadlines.
					Encourages the use of uniform procedures.
					Makes sure his/her role in the program is understood by all volunteers.
					Asks that volunteers follow standard rules and regulations.
					Lets all volunteers know what is expected of them.
					Sees to it that all volunteers are working up to capacity.
					Does personal favors for volunteers.
					Does little things to make it pleasant to be a volunteer.
					Is easy to understand.
					Finds time to listen to volunteers.
					Keeps to himself/herself. (–)
					Looks out for the personal welfare of individual volunteers.
					Refuses to explain his/her actions. (–)
					Acts without consulting the volunteers. (–)
					Is slow to accept new ideas. (–)
					Treats all volunteers as his/her equal.
					Is willing to make changes.
					Is friendly and approachable.
					Makes volunteers feel at ease when talking with them.
					Puts suggestions made by volunteers into operation.
					Gets volunteer approval on matters affecting them before going ahead.

1. Establishing and maintaining the "right relationship," the "right distance."

In normal working relationships there are four stages that evolve: 1) a tentative stage, 2) an infatuation stage, 3) a realistic stage, and 4) a love 'em/leave 'em stage. Such relationships are always changing, never perfect, and usually fragile. For your sake and your volunteer's sake, you need to establish a relationship that is both personal and professional.

Professionalism defined: 1) attention is given to skill development, 2) "tough" decisions are not avoided, 3) objectivity is sought, 4) being/becoming thick-skinned, and 5) confronting and supporting.

Personalism defined: 1) there is a personal investment, 2) sensitivity is maintained, 3) people are drawn into each other's experiences, and 4) sympathy and empathy are exercised.

The goal is to create a balance between professionalism and personalism. The way to create this balance is to pace the relationship by moving from professionalism to personalism. Professionalism could be equated with discipline and personalism with spontaneity. You should move from a disciplined relationship to a spontaneous relationship. This is done by saying no when it is appropriate, resisting the tendency to be constantly informal, not compromising in assuming responsibility, and by having an impersonal criteria for measuring performance.

2. Setting of goals.

As a supervisor, have each volunteer start the year off with individual goal setting. Each goal should be as specific as possible. For a goal to be useful it must be measurable, realistic, and involve a time factor. Goals should be achievable within the designated time span. As the year develops it may be necessary to rewrite the goals. An example of a goal statement would be: to bring one new student to Bible study every Wednesday from September through January. Such goals will not only give direction to your volunteers, but will also serve as a basis for future dialogue between volunteer and supervisor.

3. Encouraging strategies for reaching goals.

After the volunteer has established his or her goals, you must take the process to its logical next step by

Goals Worksheet

(to be filled out by volunteers at the start of each semester)

Goal	*Measurement*
What is it you want to accomplish?	How will you know it happened?

1. My goals for ministry are: (prioritize)

2. My goals for my personal growth are: (prioritize)

3. What I would like others doing as a result of my efforts:

encouraging the volunteers to think through a plan to realize those goals. The following questions can be used to develop that strategy:

1. What specific activities do you need to do to make these anticipated accomplishments a reality?
2. What problems will you face?
3. How will you go about solving these problems?
4. What "helps" will you need?
5. What will you do to get the process started?

4. Facilitating a field experience.
The volunteers you work with will have varying degrees of experience. However, a general rule to follow is that everyone will benefit by having a healthy model of the right way of doing things. One of your more experienced volunteers may be that model. As with everything else in training, you do not have to see yourself as the only person able to help others. When possible, use volunteers to train and supervise other volunteers. After seeing how the task is performed, the next step is for the volunteer to do the task with an experienced person. This guided field experience gives the volunteer an opportunity to "practice" in a somewhat protected situation. Finally, the volunteer will do it on his or her own with the supervisor observing. In this whole process there is constant dialogue that takes the following direction: What has worked and why? What hasn't worked and why? What are the problems? What are the changes that need to be made?

5. Listening and asking the right questions.
A necessary skill to develop in working with volunteers is that of listening. You should talk only 20-30 percent of the time and allow the volunteer to verbalize his or her feelings, attitudes, and impressions. In so doing you will be able to objectively understand the dynamics of the ministry situation. Here are some principles of listening to help that process:

- Most people listen, but few hear.
- Inability or unwillingness to listen is the major cause of poor communication.
- A major index of emotional maturity is the ability to listen.

- Observe the good listener: even his or her physical posture shows concentration.
- If it's worth saying, it's worth listening to.
- Speak with enthusiasm, but listen with calmness.
- A top professional at anything is a master listener.
- If you must speak, ask questions.
- Poor listeners: shuffle papers, look away, change the subject.
- Good listeners: stop the phone, look you in the eye, give you all the time you need.
- To listen with art, practice a listening attitude, a listening posture, and concentration.
- There is no such thing as an unpopular listener.
- To succeed, one must understand. To understand, one must hear. To hear, one must listen!

To complement the art of listening it is also necessary to ask the kind of questions that precipitate a good conversation. Ask these questions or make these statements and you'll have much to listen to:

- How do you feel about . . . ?
- What would you like . . . ?
- Looks like you're . . . .
- I sense that . . . .
- It sounds like . . . .
- How do you see . . . ?
- Say a little more about that . . . .
- What I hear you saying is . . . .
- It feels as though . . . .
- How do you see the problem . . . ?

6. Interview and evaluation.
One skill that you must develop is a guided conversation that reflects on the direction and progress of the volunteer's ministry. This interview should take place on a regular basis. The purpose of the interview is to: 1) review task description, 2) go over goals, and 3) preview future plans. These simple questions are enough to accomplish what needs to be done:

a. What is going well?
b. What needs to be improved?
c. How can I help?

In addition to these regularly scheduled interviews, there will be other opportunities for proper feedback. Here are examples of how that dialogue should and should not be made.

Situation 1—Negative

Volunteer: Well, how did I do?
Supervisor: Good, real good.
Volunteer: Come on, level with me—what do you really think—what did I do wrong?
Supervisor: Well, to tell you the truth, there are some things I would have done differently.
Volunteer: Yeah? (somewhat apprehensively)
Supervisor: You know when you . . . , now let me tell you what I would have done. . . . Now the other thing was . . . ; you shouldn't have done it. You should have. . . . I remember the time I did that, and it really worked well. Kids loved it.

Situation 2—Positive

Volunteer: Well, how did I do? Lay it on me.
Supervisor: Well, I'd be happy to share my thoughts with you, but first I'd like to ask you how you felt you did. What did you feel you did well?
Volunteer: . . .
Supervisor: Why do you feel it went well?
Volunteer: . . .

In summary, training and supervision are necessary ingredients of every church's ministry. God's main resource in building His kingdom is His people. Those people need the opportunity to exercise their gifts. These gifts will be maximized through a program of training and supervision.

ADDITIONAL READING

Institute for Fund Raising, *Managing Volunteers for Results,* 1978.
Marlene Wilson, *The Effective Management of Volunteer Programs,* Volunteer Management Associates, 279 S. Cedar Brook Rd., Boulder, CO 80302, 1976.
Eva Schindler-Rainman and Ronald Lippitt, *The Volunteer Community: Creative Use of Human Resources.* NTL Learning Resources Corporation, 1975.

Research and Development Division, *Training Volunteer Leaders,* National Council of Young Men's Christian Associations, New York, NY 10007, 1974.

J.A. Reyes Associates, Inc., *A Training Guide for Volunteer Programs,* ACTION, 1976.

Training Division, *Associate Staff Development: People and Program,* Youth for Christ International, Wheaton, IL 61087, 1976.

7

Developing Student Leadership

The outstanding trademark of almost every successful ministry is found in the reproduction and transition of consistent leadership. As important and primary as developing leadership is, it is one of the most delicate aspects of ministry. Leadership transferred too prematurely can seriously inhibit and even destroy potential qualities in a student, and leadership never developed stunts a youth worker's ministry to remedial stages.

Before we can adequately talk about the timing, strengths, and weaknesses of an adult vs. student-centered leadership, we must determine if there are the tools necessary to get the job done. Are there students in your youth group who have the scriptural qualities and requirements necessary for leadership? And if not, are they potentially available for you to develop? These questions must preface this chapter. Let's begin our search from the foundation upward.

In 2 Timothy 2:2, we find a four-generation process in discipling to leadership. "And the things you have heard me say in the presence of many witnesses entrust to reliable men who will also be qualified to teach others." This four-generation proc-

---

Wayne Cordeiro is the high school pastor with Faith Center in Oregon and is the Pacific Northwest Youth Director with the denomination he is affiliated with.

ess is usually lumped into one or two, but as we look closely at this discipleship mandate from Paul, we find four distinct stages. The four are: 1) Paul, 2) Timothy, 3) reliable men, and 4) others who were reached by the "reliable" ones Timothy discipled. It begins with Timothy's receptivity of Paul's message and ends with those whom Timothy discipled into leadership. This encompasses the total discipleship role of Timothy, and the process ending prematurely will only limit a youth leader's approach to developing leadership.

Student leadership, in lieu of Paul's instructions to Timothy, is the goal of discipleship, and this should be the goal of each youth leader as well. To disclose huge amounts of information alone would be inadequate, but to simultaneously build leadership so the knowledge can be implemented would be a noble challenge.

Where can we look to find some practical and functional direction in this all-important balance? The best place to look is in the life of Jesus from the Gospels. Here we find four levels of involvement that are imperative in reproducing and transferring leadership.

THE MODEL

To conquer
adverse circumstances
conquer yourself.
To accomplish much, be much.
In all cases
the doing must be
the mere unconscious expression
of the being.[1]

No one can build successfully without laying the groundwork. This is true in building spiritual people as well as in building physical things!

What do I mean by groundwork? Your primary responsibility as a youth leader is not to build a huge youth program. Your first responsibility is you! It is your relationship with the Lord Jesus, the Head. If you're not growing and learning, don't expect your ministry to. The curriculum of your discipleship is written by what you are currently learning and how you are presently growing.

Jesus was the disciples' ever-present model. He not only taught them by what He said, but He also taught them through what He did. I guess you can say He taught them "audio-visually." Every location became a living classroom, every encounter a lesson. Jesus was not a theorist; He was a practitioner who caused people to marvel, who "taught as one who had authority, not as their teachers of the law" (Matt. 7:29).

I always marvel when I read the list of David's thirty men in 2 Samuel 23:37. It reads, "Zelek the Ammonite, Naharai the Beerothite, the armorbearer of Joab son of Zeruiah." I always wondered why an armorbearer would be included in the prestigious group of David's thirty men. Joab was the general of the army and probably had his choice of any armorbearer he wanted. Since an armorbearer in those days was like a wing man in an air squadron today, I would gather that he chose his companion with much care. I can just visualize Naharai watching Joab's every move; the way he handled himself defensively with his shield, his footwork, the way he used his sword and spear. Perhaps at night we could see Naharai out in the back yard practicing with Joab's weapons. He would thrust forward, then parry, and really work at copying the master fighter's techniques.

Then we can imagine this scene one day while the battle was waxing hot. David saw Joab and Naharai in battle and he questioned the man next to him, "Who is that next to Joab?" The man replied, "Why, that's Naharai, the Beerothite, Joab's armor-bearer." David then replied, "Why, he fights just like Joab used to when he was younger. Let's take him to be one of our thirty mighty men." How did Naharai become that proficient? By spending time with Joab—watching him, working with him, imitating him until he, too, became a mighty warrior.

At this juncture it would be well for us as models to ask ourselves two questions: One, "Whose armor am I carrying?" And two, "Who is carrying my armor?"[2]

We can only produce after our own kind. Jesus said in Luke 6, "People do not pick figs from thornbushes, or grapes from briers" (v. 44). Isaiah said, "A remnant of the house of Judah will take root below and bear fruit above" (Isa. 37:31). This is the key to our first responsibility as models to student leadership. The root must go downward before fruit can be borne upward.

THE CHOOSING

Selecting the correct people in any endeavor of leadership is a crucial process. Jesus could have chosen any number of men in all of Israel, yet He chose a certain twelve to transfer His vision and leadership to. Why did He choose these? What did He see in these fishermen?

There are many sections in the Scriptures that give guidelines on choosing leaders (Acts 6; 1 Tim. 3; Mark 4), but a simple and condensed guideline would be to look for F.A.T. people. This acrostic is not a dietary measure, but rather stands for "faithful," "available," and "teachable" people. These were the qualities Jesus looked for. He could foresee the development of these to leadership. To these He could say, "Come, follow Me."

Faithful

This first character quality to look for in the selection of leadership may be illustrated in John 6. Here Jesus told the multitudes who were following Him that if they did not eat His flesh and drink His blood, they could have no part in Him. Many of His disciples said that it was too hard a saying and left, and no longer followed Jesus. Then He asked the Twelve, "You do not want to leave too, do you?" To this Simon Peter answered, "Lord, to whom shall we go? You have the words of eternal life." Here we find a committed, faithful man. But how would this be applied to our youth groups today in selecting leadership?

This quality may be found in a student who considers his spiritual growth of enough priority to warrant a faithfulness to the church services and activities. I do not demean his other activities, but rather state that he is one who is willing to establish order and priorities to favor spiritual growth. He is one who is willing to give something up in order to be a consistent part of his local church or ministry.

This quality will be visible not only on a large scale; watch for the small things . . . faithfulness in small tasks or events. This is where the true quality of faithfulness is presented. Sometimes on a larger, visible scale, someone's "faithfulness" may be just a holy way of gaining recognition. Jesus said, "Whoever can be trusted with very little can also be trusted with much, and whoever is dishonest with very little will also be dishonest with much" (Luke 16:10).

Available

Peter was available—sometimes to the unwary reader of the Scriptures, too available. He was always ready to speak out, jump into the water, or to draw his sword. Pay close attention to the one who is always "hanging around." Every time you turn around, you almost stumble over him.

Availability goes right along with the faithful person. This is someone who does not parade his abilities, but rather lends his availabilities. He may be the one who will readily take a job or a responsibility no one else would have. In the Old Testament, Jonathan's armorbearer was a picture of availability. "Jonathan said to his young armor-bearer, 'Come, let's go over to the outpost of those uncircumcised fellows. Perhaps the LORD will act in our behalf. Nothing can hinder the LORD from saving, whether by many or byfew.' 'Do all that you have in mind,' his armor-bearer said. 'Go ahead; I am with you heart and soul'" (1 Sam. 14:6).

Be watching for students such as these. To the world's eyes they may only be a bother, but God's selections aren't always the ones we would make. Do you remember the instructions God gave to Samuel when he was to appoint a new king? "Do not consider his appearance or his height, for I have rejected him. The LORD does not look at the things man looks at. Many looks at the outward appearance, but the LORD looks at the heart" (1 Sam. 16:7).

Teachable

This quality is seen more in attitude than in action. This can be recognized as someone who has a heart for God. It is seen in the student's attentiveness and desire to learn all he can. This is someone who has an open and receptive spirit. Along with his teachable spirit, however, there is wisdom and temperance. There is a marked difference between a gullible spirit and a teachable spirit. A person with a gullible spirit is easily influenced by anything that sounds good, even if it isn't true. A person with a teachable spirit is able to discern the difference between right and wrong and weighs it in his heart.

Why did Jesus choose the Twelve? They contained these qualities: In Mark 4, Jesus gives a parable to the multitudes. Parables were used because they yielded up the truth gradually and gently, and only those who really wanted to know it would seek it out. After the parable was complete, the multitudes had left and Jesus was alone. His disciples quickly came around in response and questioned Him about the parables. To this the Lord replied, "The secret of the kingdom of God has been given to you." Why? They *wanted* to learn and they took the initiative to be taught. Ask yourself this question: "Who in my youth group exhibits these qualities?" Because much of this choosing is a very discerning process, always ask God to point these young people out. He is the One who does the choosing, and if you want to begin developing leadership, ask God to reveal and confirm these youth to you.

THE INVESTMENT

James Garfield, prior to becoming president of the United States, was principal at Hiram College in Ohio when an anxious father came in to enroll his son. The father came to Garfield asking if there was some kind of shortcut that would get his son through college more quickly and out into the world of money-making. Garfield's answer remains a classic:

"Certainly, but it all depends on what you want to make of your boy. When God wants to make an oak tree, He takes one hundred years. When He wants to make a squash, He requires only two months."[3]

There are no shortcuts to developing leadership in students, and this takes commitment. You as the model must be willing to pay a price. When we invest money in a purchase we ask ourselves, "What is the price? Can I afford it? Is it worth it?" These same questions must be asked again. "Suppose one of you wants to build a tower. Will he not first sit down and estimate the cost, to see if he has enough money to complete it?" (Luke 14:28).

Developing leadership in students takes a close working relationship with those we have chosen to take the leadership. We need to be willing to invest time in them, to study and prepare with them, to meet with them personally, to be open with them—available to them, to allow them to see us in the good times as well as in the pressure times, and to teach them; not only by what we say, but more by what we do. By doing this we teach them wisdom, and this quality is imperative in any leadership position. You will never be able to teach your young leaders how to handle every problem in every situation that may arise, but through imparting wisdom, their responses will be godly and their hearts right. This is what our aim should be. This is maturity.

The initial cost of developing a student-centered leadership is full commitment. Godly leadership of consistency is developed; it is not necessarily an inherent quality. Commitment must be required from both the adult and student leaders. It is only after this requirement is resolved that true development can begin.

After working with a group of students, God impressed me with certain students who had leadership potential. After much prayer, I approached each of them personally. "John, I believe God has placed much leadership potential in you and I would like to work with you on developing that. I would like to commit these next six months to just that. Would you commit yourself to that as well?" In almost every case the answer was an excited yes! and with that commitment we could begin working toward a student-centered leadership.

To get to know some students on a local campus where I was ministering, I coached the soccer team. There were many basics, teamwork, techniques, and plays to be learned, and you usually had only a few weeks to accomplish these before the league began. If I could accomplish these, I would be happy indeed. My job wasn't to make sure that the players were there on time, nor was it to constantly pump up their enthusiasm for the sport. That should have been resolved before they committed themselves to the team. If I had to be "riding herd" on them all the time just to keep their excitement up, I would be far from reaching my goal. But with our mutual commitment established, learning and progress could begin.

With this commitment established, developing leadership can begin. After potential leaders have been confirmed and chosen, it is important to let them know your commitment to them. With a mutual agreement an accountability is established. Without it there would be no standard of measure.

During this time, put these students in your "hip pocket." Begin to take one or more with you whether you're going to a Bible study or shopping, a baseball game, or just to study. In your youth activities, give them small responsibilities in the planning of the events, not in the upfront positions. Too many times we make the mistake of placing them in the "how to's" without teaching them the "whys." By giving them a part of the planning, they will be able to think through the purposes with you and then see you implement them in action. This builds confidence in the students and gives them a sense of ownership. To give the student upfront leadership without building confidence is only making room for premature failure, and to give a student techniques and methods without teaching them the principles and the whys brings only emptiness and inconsistency.

Jesus always built confidence in His disciples before He built responsibility. We find more situations in the Gospels where Jesus taught personal relationship than He did ministry outreach. One is the fruit of the other, and fruit never precedes maturity. As Jesus built them personally, His disciples were then able to minister relationally. It's also interesting to note that Jesus wasn't very anxious about them serving Him and expanding His base as much as He was willing to serve and to lay down His life to build them! I'm sure we can all agree as to how successful He was in reproducing consistent leadership.

> I'd rather see a sermon than hear one any day.
> I'd rather one should walk with me than merely show the way.
> The eye's a better pupil and more willing than the ear;
> Fine counsel is confusing, but examples always clear;
> and the best of preachers are the men who love their creeds,
> For to see the good in action is what everybody needs.
>
> I can soon learn how to do it, if you'll let me see it done.
> I can watch your hands in action, but your tongue too fast may run.

And the lectures you deliver may be very wise and true;
But I'd rather get my lesson by observing what you do.
For I may understand you and the high advice you give,
but there's no misunderstanding how you act and how you live.

—*Edgar A. Guest*

THE TRANSITION

With growing leaders, more of the youth program can be student-centered. As an adult leader, you need to ask the question, "What portions of the program can be delegated to these faithful leaders which will complement their gifts and abilities?" By giving them portions of the total program, their leadership can grow and have time to develop. To give them too much at one time will only frustrate the students and squelch any creativity they may have. A well-developed creativity is an important quality in a student-centered leadership. It must have the balance of complementing the total program as well as developing qualities of confidence, preparation, and wisdom in the student. Your desire must always be to serve these aspiring leaders, and you must never let it revert to their serving you. The delicate balance comes when the students feel an "ownership" in the program, but are committed to your blessings in each of their procedures and actions. This can be done only through a prior commitment, investment, and growth.

Another important aspect of a student-centered program is consistent monitoring. This may take the form of periodic reviews, weekly checkpoints, or term learning reports. Every student leader needs this monitoring for positive encouragement, praise, reproof when necessary, and just to know you care. During some of these weekly times, converse with them about their personal life without bringing in any "leadership" responsibilities or reviews. In this way they are reassured of your concern for them as persons and not just about their "performance."

With a student-centered program, you must "plan room" for error. If there is no room for failure, every mistake will be a wedge in your plans and a curse. On the other hand, if you preplan room for failure, you can use it as a learning opportunity. You will be much quicker to forgive and you will notice yourself responding rather than reacting. The student will learn tremendously about leadership from observing how you handle "malfunctions."

Although you plan room for mistakes, you program for success, and success can be measured only by the integrity of your heart. It is not measured only in numbers, nor is it measured by praise accorded to you. Always seek God's blessings alone. Our total and foundational motive should always be to serve the Lord. He cannot and will not honor anything less. "Am I now trying to win the approval of men, or of God? Or am I trying to please men? If I were still trying to please men, I would not be a servant of Christ" (Gal. 1:10). Although God calls us to be industrious, He does not call us to be manipulative. We are never to use others to fulfill our goals, but rather, we fulfill our goals by serving others.

There are no "sure-fire" methods of determining how much of a youth ministry is to be student-centered due to the vast array of unique programs and personalities, but concentrating on building leaders through discipling, love, and accountability, leadership and student-centered programs will emerge as the fruit of your labor. You will begin noticing these students taking the initiative to lead, and it is here that the full orb of discipleship takes its course.

FOOTNOTES

[1]Don Polston, *Living Without Losing* (Irvine, CA: Harvest House Publishing, 1975), p. 144.

[2]Gene Warr, *You Can Make Disciples* (Waco, TX: Word, 1978), p. 33.

[3]Jamie Buckingham, *The Last Word* (Plainfield, NJ: Logos International, 1978), p. 208.

ADDITIONAL READING

Gaines S. Dobbins, *Learning to Lead*. Nashville, TN: Broadman Press, 1968.

Walter Henrichsen, *Disciples are Made - Not Born*. Wheaton, IL: Victor Books, 1974.

Marlene D. Lefever, *Turn About Teaching*. Elgin, IL: David C. Cook Publishing Co., 1973.

J. Oswald Sanders, *Spiritual Leadership*. Chicago, IL: Moody Press, 1967.

II DEVELOPING AN ENVIRONMENT FOR MINISTRY

8

Developing a Unified Approach to Youth Ministry

George Evans picked up the dull pencil stubs his high-school students had used a few minutes before. As he scooped up the last eraserless pencil, George let his mind wander. "The kids were flat today," he thought. "It's too bad the youth group was out so late last night."

Then, without thinking, he walked over and retaped the sunset poster to the moveable partition that separated his room from the junior-high class.

George volunteered to teach Cold Creek Community Church's high-school Sunday school class six months ago. And most of the time he was pleased with the outcome of the lessons. But ever since Ernie and Mary Thompson started planning Saturday-night outings, the kids wanted to talk more about what happened the night before than about his inductive study of the Book of Mark.

"I'm doing okay," he said out loud, as he straightened the last folding chair and flipped the light switch. "Maybe I'll cut down on the Bible study part and add a few crazy games."

But for some reason, a sinking feeling in his stomach wouldn't go away.

Out in the church parking lot Ernie and Mary

Gary Richardson is the Associate Editor of GROUP Magazine, Loveland, Colorado.

Thompson smiled at each other through sleepy eyes. "Last night was fun, wasn't it?" Ernie said, matter-of-factly, as he tossed his crumpled church bulletin over the top of his bright yellow Toyota—the "banana car" the kids called it. "It *did* go okay last night, didn't it?"

Mary nodded her head. "Sure, Ernie, but don't you think we should be doing something a little more spiritual? I mean, bowling and movies and volleyball are great fun, but shouldn't we be doing more?"

"Okay, okay, I confess. I really wasn't sleeping in church today. I was thinking about cutting down on the fooling around and maybe starting a, you know, Bible study."

Both Ernie and Mary felt the frustration of seeing lots of needs, but not having the energy and time to go about meeting them. In one of his more open moments, Ernie said he felt as though he were trying to jog through a swamp.

A FULL-TIME SWAMP JOGGER

Eight miles away, Mike Bradley sat in the youth office, munching on a burger and fries. Since he'd become youth pastor, he'd planned two retreats, added a Bible study, put on a Christmas musical, and started a youth newsletter.

But Mike had that familiar sinking feeling too. Something needed to happen in his ministry. Each of the volunteer staff members more or less did his own thing in Mike's department. Some of the Sunday school teachers used Sunday morning as a time for expositional Bible study, while other teachers used the time to build relationships. Still other teachers discussed current events and popular movies. Mike sensed the tug of competitiveness between the different teachers and sponsors in his ministry.

He felt the pressure. How could he meet the different needs of the kids in the ministry while forging a team of volunteers who wouldn't quit at the drop of a philosophical pin? Mike too felt as though he were doing a little swamp jogging.

NO MORE SWAMP JOGGING

No one can deny it—both youth ministries were missing a solid foundation for a balanced ministry to youth. And without a unified, balanced, and organized youth ministry, the people involved in meeting their young people's spiritual, mental, physical, and social needs will probably get bogged down.

A church's programs, no matter how much time and energy dedicated youth workers put into them, will suffer from overlapping efforts, imbalanced programs, and differing philosophies that lead to needless competition if a common-sense plan of coordination doesn't keep everyone pointed in the same direction.

Whatever the programs, a youth ministry's effectiveness should be measured by what happens in the lives of young people attending that church; how many are leading Christlike lives and are involved in service to others.

WHAT IS UNIFICATION, ANYWAY?

The apostle Paul must have been youth director at several of Corinth's churches, for he described a unified and balanced youth ministry when he compared the church as Christ's spiritual body with man's physical body (1 Cor. 12). Just as Christ's spiritual body is singular, so a youth ministry draws its oneness—its togetherness—from the process of unification.

An academic definition of unification sounds something like this: "Unification is the adequate functioning of the various aspects of a youth ministry toward a single goal."[1] There *is* a way to stay away from that frustrated, no-accomplishment feeling that comes with trying to work through a swamp of conflicting goals, programs, and philosophies.

The way out of the swamp: "Whenever two or more people join together to pursue common goals in a ministry to youth, organization is needed to avoid overlapping and to avoid the oversight of particular areas of responsibility."[2]

This concept of unification is far from new or innovative. Christian educators were writing about it long before most people thought a church's youth ministry would ever be anything more than a Sunday morning experience. One such prophet said, "The church will not be truly unified educationally until all of its official family is united in a common educational purpose, and are willing to submit their program and administration to the educational method."[3]

In other words, using Youth Pastor Paul's analogy, the legs, arms, eyes, feet—even little toes—of a youth ministry need to be working together. Yet thousands of youth ministries have eyes looking in different directions, ears hearing different messages, and legs and arms that are getting tangled up with each other.

Unity is a fact for any successful organization, whether in a multinational corporation or in the churches in Cold Creek, Iowa. One Christian educator put it this way: "It isn't that the various programs in which our kids take part should each make a vital contribution to their lives. These several contributions must be worked into a single pattern which has unity." In other words, the whole is much greater than the sum of its parts.

Paul's "youth ministry" was unified to meet the needs of its people through programs. If contemporary youth ministries could determine the needs of their youth members and set about to meet those needs through a careful process of organizing, the youth would be more able to teach and train others as they've been taught and trained.

All this isn't to say that creativity, spontaneity, and variety are concepts that get stashed away with the mimeograph fluid and last year's volleyball net. Rather, flexibility and creativity in programing and ministry are key ingredients in meeting the unique and varying needs of the young people who make up your ministry. The solid ground a unified and balanced program gives you will make creativity and spontaneity easier goals to reach.

THE PEOPLE WHO MAKE IT HAPPEN

But since you can't dump all your existing programs, where do you begin? Start with your people—anyone who's a part of your ministry, whose life comes into contact with young people. Following is a list of the people who are traditionally involved in a church's ministry:

■ *The Leader.* (Commonly known as youth director, youth pastor, assistant pastor in charge of youth, youth coordinator, concerned lay person.) Whatever his or her title and qualifications, the leader in any Christian ministry is central, because in the biblical pattern he or she sets the tone for the rest of the ministry. The leader provides the example of leadership and demonstrates the realities of the ministry, even when the going gets sticky.

The leader's time should be spent in pouring his or her talents and abilities—life—into others, in motivating, encouraging, and helping other people in the ministry.[4]

The leader should be aware of the different resources and options open in terms of materials, activities, and structures for youth ministry. He or she should have a clear grasp of the principles and processes of youth ministry. Even though others will have different roles in the ministry (Sunday school teacher, Bible-study leader, fellowship person, poster putter-upper), they are still to function in the biblical servant-leader pattern. In other words, the leader is the skeleton that holds together the various parts and personalities of a youth ministry.

The leader, hired or otherwise, must avoid the two extremes of dictatorial, I'll-do-it-all kind of control and a do-whatever-you-want-to-do attitude. He or she is not a dictator who decides exactly what the group of leaders ought to do, nor a clown who woos and wins with great personality. The adult leader must be a guide, a director, a resource person, a facilitator. In short, the youth leader is a manager, but is behind the scenes most of the time—though seldom in front of the group, he or she is always there.[5]

■ *Anyone Involved in the Youth Ministry.* This includes Sunday school teachers, lay sponsors, Bible-study leaders, college students, young married couples—the list goes on. Each person should be kept informed of what's going on in other parts of the ministry. Every person who comes into contact with young people should have someone who provides encouragement, material, and prayer support.

■ *The Youth Themselves.* Young people gain a sense of belonging to something they feel a part of, contribute to, and have responsibility for.[6] Research indicates that youth prefer a group with a feeling of oneness, a sense of belonging and an atmosphere of warm friendliness.[7] One of a youth leader's goals should be to include the young people in all the processes of youth ministry.

■ *The Pastor.* Since the pastor is responsible for ministering to everyone within the church's overall program, he should at least be an ex-officio member of the youth planning team, or whatever team is developed or exists to plan and keep the youth ministry unified. The pastor should be a personal friend to the young people and have a feeling for their spiritual lives. He should also be kept informed of the ministry's progress and should be kept aware of any problems and needs that appear within the context of the overall ministry.

■ *Parents.* Parents who are kept informed and who help determine the general outline of the youth ministry can provide valuable support for the ministry. Use them by letting them serve on the youth board, maybe on a "parental rotation" basis. Keep them informed of different programs and prayer needs.

The process seems clear. Whatever the size, scope, emphasis, unique problems, and needs, a youth ministry can't be totally effective unless the people who are responsible for its success get involved in the nuts-and-bolts process of ministry together.

And "getting into the process together" requires some sort of overall structure or organization that provides for continuity and allows the development of communication between the differing areas of youth ministry. Though worded differently in various business, educational, and managerial texts, the following nuts-and-bolts principles should help keep you from a few swamp-jogging trips.

However you decide to organize, keep in mind that your structure:

1. *Isn't an end in itself.* The process of unification exists only to make communication and teamwork within your ministry more efficient. When the committee, task force, staff planning organization, whatever, ceases to help meet the needs of a unified program, it should go the way of hula hoops and white socks.

2. *Should allow everyone involved to take part.* The structure exists so that everyone in a ministry can work *together* in planning a ministry for youth. The do-it-all, Lone Ranger type rode off into the sunset years ago.

3. *Should be flexible.* Since a youth ministry is based on needs that change as the young people in the ministry change, a youth ministry structure should allow for future changes that are needed to make it more effective.

4. *Should reward creativity.* An effective structure encourages people involved in a youth ministry to be as creative as their ability allows. The structure should foster communication and a sense of freedom, but should never restrict anyone's attempts to meet needs through an endless variety of methods. And youth ministries need all the creative and innovative ideas they can get.

5. *Should include clearly understood channels of communication.* When a structure is working effectively, everyone involved gets the information and guidance needed to meet their goals. Communication channels that are open and sensitive allow for information to proceed efficiently between people working in different areas of the ministry.

THAT'S NICE. WHAT NEXT?

Okay, so now you see the importance of unifying your youth ministry. You know who's to help coordinate, balance, and unify. But some of your programs are going full tilt. And interfering with them or their leaders now could cause fatal problems, to you and/or to the programs.

It is likely that the people working with you have had bad experiences with slow and tedious committees that seem to start nowhere and end nowhere—with an infinite number of roadblocks and potholes in between.

Learning to work with different people (youth and adults) whose needs, interests, and way of expressing themselves differ, is an important skill. It's also important that the leader understand and cope with sharp-edged misunderstandings and wounded egos that could result as people become involved in their relationships with each other.

Yet, the very experience of helping to plan and knowing what's coming in the future means that people in the ministry are bound closer together in a singular purpose. The success of a planning and unifying session depends on everyone taking an active role.

How can this be done? Most people involved in a fragmented, overlapping ministry know that something's not right—it's sort of like jogging through a swamp. Remember?

If the group is to make decisions about its procedures and processes, then the entire group must assume responsibility for the evaluation of the ministry's strengths and weaknesses.

But don't present a plan of unifying the total youth ministry too soon. Don't blast into a classroom on a Sunday morning and announce your intentions to change the total youth ministry by the end of the quarter. Don't confess your dreams until the group members are seriously considering what they should do to improve the program and the youth ministry's effectiveness. The idea is best suggested during or immediately following the process of program or group evaluation. If your goal of a unified youth ministry is valid and touches the needs of the people involved in the ministry to youth, then you won't need to brush up on the soft-shoe, song-and-dance routines to "sell" the program.

WHERE IS YOUR MINISTRY HEADED?

Use this worksheet to help get everyone in your ministry thinking about the need for unification and balance in the total youth program.

1. List all the agencies of your church's ministry to its youth (Sunday school, Bible studies, Sunday evening youth fellowship groups, core groups, retreats, camps, youth clubs in the church, etc.).
2. Chart, in any way you wish, how you think those different agencies relate to each other.
3. Next, using the existing agencies, what would be the most effective and ideal ministry? (This can be the background for future discussion in goal setting.)
4. What are the needs of the young people in the church?
5. What agencies listed in number 1 are meeting those needs? How?
6. What's expected of me in my ministry with youth?
7. What do I expect from other people?
8. Where do the young people fit into the total church ministry?
9. How am I being trained?

The first meeting that includes youth ministry people and interested youth is exploratory. Everyone should feel free, if necessary, to suggest areas of concern that need attention. A sample first meeting agenda might be:

1. Snacks
2. A relationship-building exercise
3. What's-going-on-in-my-area reports from everyone involved in the youth ministry
4. Work through (discuss) the "Where Is . . ." worksheet
5. Bring up problems and tensions in the ministry or in someone's personal life that he or she feels free to share
6. Skill building or new input—group dynamics, discussion helps, creative crowd breakers, etc.
7. Discuss a basic strategy for getting organized. Set goals for the next meeting (to be held within the next month)
8. Praise and prayer
9. Fellowship and fun

Keep a watch handy and don't let this meeting go longer than two hours. Keep the meeting moving. A long, rambling first meeting will douse cold water on most sparks of interest and motivation.

WHAT DO I DO WHEN I DO IT?

In thinking through the process of unifying and balancing a youth ministry, here are a few of the major areas where the solid ground of communication and agreement are necessary.

Common Theological and Philosophical Roots

It only takes a quick survey of all the youth ministry junk mail and catchy magazine ads to get a wide-eyed look at how a youth ministry could end up with a smorgasbord of different programs using materials based on differing underlying philosophies of youth ministry.

One of the first baby steps in getting all the elements of a ministry to work without bashing into each other is coming to a consensus on basic theological and philosophical points.

Use these questions for starters:

1. What is the scriptural basis for your ministry with youth? How does that Scripture relate to the goals of your youth ministry?
2. How does that Scripture relate to your present programing?
3. If you could design the perfect youth ministry, what would you have as the central elements?

4. What should be the role of youth in a youth ministry?
5. What should be the role of the leader?
6. In your opinion, what should be the four most important outcomes of a ministry with youth?

KEEPING YOUR YOUTH MINISTRY BALANCED

It's not surprising to see four or five different youth ministries in the same city ministering to young people from the same high schools and neighborhoods with radically different programs. While there's nothing wrong with having different ministry emphases, there's always the danger of having one area of ministry out of proportion to other much-needed areas. It's sort of like having the world's most beautiful face and also the world's largest ears. Beautiful, but grotesque.

You can keep a youth ministry balanced by being aware of how your program fits into four areas: Instruction, Worship, Fellowship, and Service (or outreach or expression). See Matthew 22:37–40; Acts 2:42; Philippians 4.

There's nothing earthshakingly innovative about these concepts. Christian educators developed and refined these ideas before most of us were born. But keeping a ministry balanced in these four areas is critical to even the most avant-garde youth ministry. Let's take a brief look at what should be familiar concepts.

Instruction

By taking time to read, study, and apply the Scriptures to their own lives, young people can develop an understanding of who God is and what life is all about and learn to love God with their lives. Basically, biblical instruction is imparted through either a systematic study of Bible doctrines, passages, chapters, and Bible books, or through topics that are closely related to young people's felt needs and that show how the Bible best relates to those needs.

Worship

By setting aside specific times to be with God, listening, praying, and meditating (whether as a part of the whole church, in a small group, or alone) youth can develop the ability to see life from God's perspective.

While the corporate worship service may be

enough to keep your youth ministry balanced, consider working with your youth group in planning your own worship service. And the way to learn to worship is to worship. That means not just singing songs and listening to a speaker; it means having a part in the program, in the planning of it, and in the general outlining of specific plans. Though guiding young people in the planning of a worship service is often much more difficult than for the leader to do it himself, it can be the means of helping young people grow in worship experience and gain skill in leading others in worship.

The following questions may be helpful in building the worship program with the group:

1. What would you like your youth worship services to be like?
2. Who should be responsible for planning the worship sessions?
3. How can you make the most profitable use of Thanksgiving, Christmas, Easter?
4. How can you design unique and creative worship sessions?

Fellowship

The need to feel a sense of belonging is especially strong during the high-school years. During adolescence the group is all-important. The fellowship program must be carefully planned and integrated with the total youth program. Too often, the fellowship program is simply a social event unrelated to the rest of the group's activities. If possible, it should be an outgrowth of the unit of study and a means of fostering the specific goals of the group. For example, if the unit is "Developing and Building Friendships," then activities and outings designed to deepen friendships should be planned.

Service

Christian young people need to be actively involved in working through projects that apply Christian teachings to everyday needs. They should see that Christianity is expressed in a life of obedience to Jesus Christ. Instilling a sense of Christian responsibility in today's what-do-I-get-out-of-it youth culture is a necessary and critical part of making the gospel a part of your youth ministry. Look around you. The opportunities for service are numerous.

These four areas—Instruction, Worship, Fellowship, and Service—make up the ballpark for a total youth ministry.

Use the following basic procedure to see if your youth ministry needs to work on balancing its programs:

1. List all the programs that make up your youth ministry. (That is, if you haven't already done this in the evaluation process.)
2. List what you consider to be the goals of each program.
3. Then decide which of the four areas best fit each goal. Keep in mind that one program may have goals that fit into two or three areas.
4. If one or more of the areas of Instruction, Worship, Fellowship, or Service is lacking, consider developing a program or process that will best meet the needs of your young people through that area.
5. If an area is stuffed with goals and programs, you may need to reevaluate the goals of each program and determine which goals and programs can be revamped. If no alternatives are open for the excessive programs, you may need to let a program or two die peacefully.

THAT'S NOT ALL, FOLKS.

Putting a youth ministry on a solid theological and balanced program ground is a giant step toward a more effective ministry.

But the process of unification gives you more.

In an age where lukewarm relationships seem to be the norm for Christians, the process of unification can provide the framework for greater unity and better morale of everyone involved in the ministry.

By sharing experiences, needs, problems, victories, and even failures, the people comprising the youth ministry team will look on one another with new interest and appreciation.

At the beginning of each planning meeting encourage members who are experiencing problems in their areas of ministry to bring the matter to the group's attention so that the whole group can help analyze the problem together.

Emphasize the importance of the process as well as the accomplishment of the task of unifying your ministry so that members will realize that helping one another feel more closely knit as a group is just as important as getting the job done right or making the right decision.

ONE MORE WORKSHEET

After the first couple of meetings, you might want to ask yourself these questions:

1. What is our goal? Are we "on" or "off" target?
2. Where are we in our discussion? At the point of analyzing the problem? Suggesting solutions? Testing ideas?
3. How fast are we moving? Are we doing some swamp jogging of our own?
4. Are we using the best methods of work?
5. Is everyone working? Or just a few?
6. Is there an improvement in everyone's ability to work together?

If problems are shared, you can move the discussion along by asking questions such as:

1. Does anyone else have this problem? What did they do about it?
2. What makes __________ act this way? Is there anything we can do to help?
3. What things did you discover worked well with your group?

After the group's progress is evaluated, changes in future meetings should be made to keep the sessions at a comfortable pace—neither too fast nor too slow.

BALANCING A YOUTH PROGRAM: A CASE STUDY

It is possible to balance an existing youth ministry without scrapping the entire program. Take the Christian and Missionary Alliance youth program in Paradise, California, for instance. Curtis Nelson, a youth worker, who was trained through the church's youth ministry, tells about the change:

"Our goal was to build Christian young people, able to survive and make an impact on the world. We began with a youth group of ten regularly attending high schoolers, but after five years our youth group consisted of 150 young people. This growth took place as we developed a balanced program designed to not only meet spiritual needs, but also mental, physical, social, and other needs of the young person.

"Our balanced program began with changing the youth meeting from before to after the evening service. This allowed us more flexibility in programing. The Sunday evening meetings were designed to be interesting for both Christians and non-Christians. No two weeks in a row did we have the same type of meeting, but the meetings were always exciting.

"As we began to restructure our youth meetings we discovered we couldn't meet all the needs of young people with one meeting. So our program began to expand. Friday nights we planned around the school ball games. After the games we always had social activities. Then came the idea of a youth choir. Monday night became sports night for our church. During the summer it was the softball league, fall and winter was basketball season, and in the spring teams played volleyball. Tuesday night was Bible study night for our young people.

"After a couple of years the youth department discovered that Sunday school was just as important a part of the youth program as was the Sunday evening meeting. Sunday school teachers and youth staffers were not two unrelated groups, but part of the same team in providing a balanced program for our young people.

"After a couple of flops, we succeeded in beginning a weekly discipleship program. One staff person worked with two young people and worked through a series of sharing times centered on Christian qualities.

"Our program just kept expanding as we designed more and more regular activities to help meet the needs and get more young people involved. As the program continued to develop, the necessity of establishing a youth staff became apparent. The first staff people were chosen from the leaders of our young people, seniors in high school. Then interested adults were added to the staff. We later even approached some promising young people with the idea of being on the youth staff. An intern program was started to train high school graduates and college students who wanted to devote their lives to full-time Christian service. As things really got rolling, people began asking to be on our staff.

"A youth staff requires lots of communication and teamwork. Every other Sunday our interns and youth staff gathered from 8:00 A.M. to 9:30 for staff meetings. Many of us rarely saw each other except during the staff meeting and Sunday evening youth meeting, when we all tried to be present.

"For balanced programing you cannot do everything yourself—you need some help. Begin looking and training right now. Get the Sunday school teachers involved and train young people to be leaders. This idea is to build a group of people around you to help minister to young people. You will see exciting things happen."[8]

NOT-SO-FAMOUS LAST WORDS

The process of unifying and balancing a youth ministry does take time and effort. It is not a shortcut or overnight cure for swamp jogging.

But if your youth ministry is to be as effective as it can be, there are no alternatives.

Mark wrote, "Then the disciples went out and preached everywhere, and the Lord worked with them and confirmed his word by the signs that accompanied it" (Mark 16:20). This, in a nutshell, is the goal of a youth ministry—a united body going out, preaching with the Lord, confirming His presence by signs and miracles.

Have any miracles happened in your youth ministry lately?

FOOTNOTES

[1]Gunnar Hoglund, *Success Handbook for Youth Groups* (Chicago: Harvest Publications, 1978).

[2]Bob R. Taylor, *Youth in Church Training* (Nashville, Tennessee: Convention Press, 1969).

[3]Oliver Cummings, *Christian Education in the Local Church* (Philadelphia: Judson Press, 1951).

[4]Larry Richards, *Youth Ministry: Its Renewal in the Local Church* (Grand Rapids: Zondervan, 1972).

[5]Donald Aultman, *Guiding Youth* (Cleveland, Tennessee: Pathway Press, 1965).

[6]John L. Carroll and Keith L. Ignatius, *Youth Ministry: Sunday, Monday and Every Day* (Valley Forge: Judson Press, 1972).

[7]Merton P. Strommen, *Bridging the Gap* (Minneapolis: Augsburg Publishing House, 1973).

[8]Gary Richardson, *Where's It At? The Measure of Your Youth Ministry* (Wheaton, Illinois: Scripture Press, 1978).

9

"If This Is Sunday Night, It Must Be Youth Fellowship Time"

There are few things on earth that can generate as much enthusiasm and excitement as a room full of young people. And yet when they plant themselves in a chair for a church youth meeting they often seem to have little desire to be involved. Therefore, the words "youth fellowship time" often strike panic in the hearts of the individuals who have been charged with the responsibility of directing the youth program of a local church. As a result, their tour of duty usually consists of a few months of frustrating, unfulfilled involvement. Then they leave their post so that a "younger" or "more experienced" (they really mean "unsuspecting" person can have the opportunity to serve.

The natural tendency is to think that young people are not interested in a corporate investment of their time; but this is not true. Usually our struggles stem from the fact that we have not taken the time to ask questions like, "Why do we do it?" and "How does it fit?" Therefore, we often head into a program without a formulated plan based on a solid ministry philosophy. When this happens the corporate meeting of our group either ends up consuming our entire effort or it takes on the appearance of being a "wart"

Dave Mann is the National Director of Missionary Youth Fellowship International, headquartered in Fort Wayne, Indiana.

on the schedule with no apparent correlation to other segments of our program. The result is a flurry of activity with little or no ministry taking place.

WHY HAVE A LARGE GROUP MEETING?

When used in the context of a multifaceted ministry, the corporate session can and should accomplish several very important things:

A Rallying Point

Even though personal ministry is critical to the spiritual growth of individuals, each person needs to know that he has a part of something bigger than himself to aid in formulating personal identity. In addition to personal identity, group identity also develops. A person can say, "I am part of this; I belong."

Also, in serving as a rallying point, the group meeting plays a big role in creating an image for your total ministry. Whether we like it or not, the corporate meeting is the most visible part of what we do, and positive opportunities to be together with other young people can only increase our chances of reaching more with the gospel. It goes without saying that "If exciting things can be seen, people will be involved." A positive image with the adult community of the church is as important as a positive image with your young people. We must remember that without the support of the entire "body" we have little chance of succeeding in our ministry. A regular youth meeting with excited, growing young people communicates much to other members of the adult church community about what is happening.

A "Muscle Flex"

In addition to serving as the rallying point, the corporate meeting should also serve as a "muscle flex" for the group. There should be a feeling of strength and a sense of accomplishment as a group comes together. This can only happen when a group is involved in things that would be impossible outside of the corporate experience. The statement "There is strength in numbers" should be proven by the effects of our program.

Exercise of Community

The third and most important reason for the corporate meeting is the opportunity it creates for the exercise of community.

The building of strong, solid relationships between the peer group and the adult leadership is essential to an effective, ongoing ministry. Obviously, social experiences become vital in the establishing of this experience. Young people need opportunities to interact in a very informal setting in order that they might become transparent toward one another. As young people come together on a regular basis, the outgrowth should be the development of a caring community with knowledge of one another's frustrations and struggles. When this happens they will then have the ability to lend support to one another when and where it is needed.

Through these three items, which are so vital to a successful youth ministry, the corporate meeting can take on a positive role in the total scope of a ministry.

DEVELOP YOUR PHILOSOPHY OF MINISTRY

Behind any successful youth ministry is a solid ministry philosophy undergirding the objectives, goals, and strategy of the ministry personnel. Because of several misnomers concerning youth ministry, we often struggle to put together a philosophy that points us in the right direction.

- *"The meeting is the ministry."* As stated earlier in this chapter, the meeting is obviously the most visible part of our total youth ministry. Because of that fact, it is easy to feel that the ministry takes place there exclusively. When a person in a leadership position has this attitude, it becomes difficult to see beyond the program to realize the needs of individual people. A meeting is not the ministry, but rather a means to accomplishing it.
- *"The right curriculum is the key to success."* It seems that the first question that the youth sponsor asks after taking over the leadership of a youth group is, "What materials are available that will be of help to me?" What he actually means to say is, "What materials are available that will allow me to implement a program without investing my life?" It can't be done. The key to successful corporate meetings lies in those directing the program as opposed to written material. What you study is important, but even more important is the method used and the freedom you have in giving direction to the session. Curriculum does not accomplish youth ministry, people do.
- *"Youth don't want content, they want entertainment."* In a recent Gallup poll young people were inter-

viewed regarding their reasons for not being involved with traditional religious groups. One of the major problems they stated was that the ministry opportunities designed for them were very superficial. The youth interviewed went on to indicate that they desired to learn more about a personal relationship with God, concepts of faith and prayer, etc., through their involvement.[1]

We definitely need to offer social experiences; but, when the social portion of our ministry consumes all our efforts, we give our young people no more than they can obtain from many other places in our community. Social experiences build relationships that win us the right to have positive input in the lives of our young people. Let's not forget to move on to give young people the content they are looking for.

■ *"There is a right or wrong method of working with young people."* Whether a method is right or wrong depends totally on the circumstances and situations in which it is used. A method that works well with one group may fail miserably with another. There is no right or wrong way to do everything, but there is an appropriate method for a specific situation.

■ *"Everything I do has to be BIG."* For some youth leaders, bigger is always better. Exciting programs with large crowds of young people can do much for a youth ministry and they do have their place. But when someone is seeking an intense personal relationship with a young person that will lead to the opportunity of dealing with his or her needs in an individual manner, a constant diet of large events and meetings only serves to allow the young person with the needs to become lost in the crowd.

■ *"Youth know exactly what they want."* Most young people realize that they have needs, but they have difficulty pinpointing them. Here is where the adult youth sponsor can play a vital role in assessing those needs and helping young people realize their gifts.

■ *"The kids will accept me because I'm in charge."* Many youth directors expect instant acceptance from the group—"After all, I'm in a position of leadership." But it doesn't seem to work that way. Youth respond to what works—not necessarily the authority figure. As a result, time must be invested in building the type of relationship that will also build confidence.

This holds true not only of people, but also pertains to the use of Scripture. Just because we say "the Bible says" does not mean that young people will necessarily respond in a positive way to the directive. We must make every effort possible to point out how the principle we are dealing with fits practically and logically into their lives. The efforts we exert to present a logical, practical approach to our faith only add credibility to the Scripture in the minds of our young people. And we need not be afraid to deal with Scripture from this basis unless we fear that the Scripture is not practical or logical.

■ *"A good youth leader is very young and full of enthusiasm."* The older, more mature adult who could supply a stable model of a Christ-like life to the young people of the church are often overlooked. Communication with young people is not a matter of age, but rather one of desire and concern for their spiritual welfare.

A good philosophy for our total ministry, including the corporate meeting, is to keep individuals at its center. When that is the case the corporate meeting becomes a tool for reaching and developing young people as opposed to being an end in itself. We must keep in mind that our job is not to implement programs, but to minister to people.

DETERMINE THE BEST METHODS FOR YOUR GROUP

Following the formulation of a solid ministry philosophy, we need to gather one other piece of information that will give our meeting the direction it needs. That piece of information is an honest evaluation of the situation in which we find ourselves. "What are our young people like?" "What resources, both physical and human, do we have at our disposal?"

Take a look at the needs of individual young people to whom you are going to be ministering. Not only will you need to deal with the actual needs in their lives, but also the felt needs. In fact, the felt needs must be dealt with before any opportunity to deal with the actual needs will present itself.

Many youth leaders are prone to implement a slick-looking curriculum with many gimmicks and audio-visual pieces, and have very little success because they haven't taken the time to find out if the topic with which they are dealing relates directly to the needs of their group.

After isolating the needs of individual young people, you will need to spend some time evaluating their culture. Ask yourself such questions as "What priorities exist in the lives of the young people in the community in which I am ministering?" "What avenues of recreation and entertainment do they most enjoy?" "What is their general social attitude?"

In addition to evaluating the young people of your community prior to formulating plans for youth meetings, it is also wise to examine the resources, both physical and human, that are available to you.

As far as the physical facilities are concerned, it is easy for us to see them being used only as they have been in the past. Whereas, with a little creativity and elbow grease an old storage shed or garage can be transformed into a Rec Center or, with the addition of a few couches and overstuffed chairs, carpet, and a new paint job, the formal classroom can be changed into a living room-type setting. And that vacant lot full of weeds next to your church can be turned into a recreational field for volleyball or softball. In reality, the facilities that we think are counterproductive to our ministry can turn out to be tremendous assets.

Another asset that is often overlooked in the planning of weekly youth meetings is the human resource available to us through our local congregation. Every congregation is full of interesting people with varied interests, abilities, hobbies, and occupations, most of whom are waiting for opportunities to be involved with others. Why not give them this opportunity? Here our creativity in being able to utilize people will not only give the young people of our youth group variety in programing, but will also give other adults of our congregation the chance to minister along with us.

After drawing some conclusions about your young people and your resources, it is then a good idea to think through the most appropriate night and time, as well as the right setting for your meeting. Churches often assume that a certain night and time is appropriate for their young people without taking into consideration any other responsibilities their young people might have in the community or at their school.

Other churches intentionally schedule youth meetings to run concurrently with community events that they do not feel promote a Christ-like lifestyle. The result usually is that the individuals they are trying to reach never become involved because of the inconvenience. Our youth meetings not only need to be interesting, exciting, and educational, but also convenient. When a young person must make a choice between attending a church youth meeting or a social, school, or community activity, he finds himself in a difficult situation. If he chooses the youth meeting, he often attends out of a sense of duty or guilt that leads him to believe that church involvement is something that a person "must do" as opposed to something that he does out of desire to have a growing relationship with Jesus Christ. When this happens, the youth meeting becomes a counterproductive factor in the spiritual growth process.

The setting of the session is also vitally important. Young people need to feel at home and at ease if they are going to be able to honestly and openly share their needs with the youth leader and their peer group. If this type of open atmosphere cannot be achieved in the church building, another setting should be sought, possibly a community building or someone's home. This is especially true when you are attempting to accomplish outreach to a nonchurch-oriented group of young people.

In choosing the room that will be used for the meeting, the youth leader should find one that will keep the young people in one tight, contiguous group. This will definitely add to the excitement and enthusiasm of the meeting, as well as promote a sense of community.

As we stated earlier, the method employed depends totally on the needs of the group. But in any case, there are five criteria that should be used in the selection of the proper method.

First, does the method promote solid interpersonal relationships among the young people present? Through their involvement will they be developing a caring, concerned attitude for one another? For this type of relational experience to take place you will usually need to implement methods that offer young people the opportunity of interacting with one another; initially in some very light, nonthreatening areas. Interpersonal relationships form the base and act as the cohesive agent for the group and, as a result, are of utmost importance.

Second, our methods must be as honest and as Christian as our message. At times it becomes easy to rationalize the use of some very unchristian methods because they seemingly are very effective in leading young people to committing their lives to Christ. Decisions usually made through the use of manipulative techniques are not lasting, and in fact only prove to young people later on as they think through what they have done, that becoming a Christian is not a valid experience.

Third, our methods must be logical and practical. They need to make sense. As young people think through all the principles that we share with them, these principles need to come together in a logical form that relates to their lives in the situations with which they are confronted.

Fourth, we need to create trust in our young people. Somehow we must break down their stereotypes of the Christian. Not that we become phony or have to be like them to win them over. On the contrary, we must present a caring, honest model of what the Christian life is all about.

Fifth, our methods must promote involvement. Young people need to be a part of what is happening. This is not the easiest way to handle a youth meeting. It creates many situations where problems may arise when the youth do not follow through on their commitments, but it is a learning process for them and we must give them the opportunity to fail as well as to succeed. In fact, during those moments of failure we may have the greatest opportunity to have input into their lives.

Most of the programs that we plan need to be an entity to themselves and not be dependent on preceding or following sessions. This is especially true when we are dealing with a nonchurch-oriented crowd. Because of their level of commitment and involvement in activities outside of the church, they may not be able to be involved with us on a regular basis. Therefore, a great number of sessions that build on one another will give a fragmented picture of the content being covered. This often leads to a distorted view of Christianity. If a series is planned, it should consist of about four or five sessions and be announced well ahead of time so that all the young people are aware that when they miss a session they are getting only a part of the picture.

PROGRAM FOR RESULTS

When planning and implementing programs there are four sequential phases that need to be kept in mind.

Create a Nonthreatening Atmosphere

This phase should involve much activity, interaction, and fun. Young people are social beings and need the opportunity to interact on this level with one another. They need to laugh together and enjoy being a part of the group. Many methods can be utilized to aid in the creation of a wholesome atmosphere. Crowdbreakers, short humorous films, games, experiential games, and skits will all help do the job.

This programing phase needs to be taken seriously. We often look at it as a meaningless part of the session, but in many respects it is one of the most important parts. What takes place during this initial phase often determines how successful we will be in the presentation of content later on.

In choosing the proper method for accomplishing this first phase of programing, we always need to be harmless and at the same time looking for ways to involve as many young people from the group as possible. In fact, we should always have at least one function that involves the entire group.

Breaking your group into smaller random units for competition always aids in the building of new relationships and the strengthening of old ones; to say nothing of the help it gives in breaking up unhealthy cliques that often fragment the group.

If a stunt is being utilized, the person responsible for implementing it should rehearse it to the point that he knows what is happening and when it should happen. The group should be surprised, not the person leading the stunt.

Any humorous films that are used should be very short and very humorous. A five- to ten-minute film is ample. Anything longer than that, especially if it is not as funny to the group as it was to you when selecting the film, will create a long, agonizing introduction to the meeting.

Internalize the Problem or Issue

After setting the stage by working through phase 1, we should begin the process of helping our young people in this second phase to be dealt with during the meeting. Before young people will listen to the Christ-centered solution that we present, they need to understand the situation to be dealt with to the point where they not only can talk about the situation, but also can feel its magnitude and intensity. This needs to be accomplished so that they can see it as a problem or an issue even if it does not affect them directly, but touches only others. Methods such as role plays, experiential games, small group buzz sessions, etc., become vital to the accomplishing of our aims. No matter which one of these methods we implement, interaction and discussion need to be part of it. Otherwise we leave out the personal aspect that only defeats the purpose of this phase.

Leading a discussion effectively is something that is developed through experience. A person needs to be vulnerable and transparent before the group as he serves as facilitator. He must hold his opinion as long as possible, be very shockproof no matter what is said, and never put anyone down for their stated feelings.

When there is a long pause, many individuals facilitating a discussion become frightened and step in with a comment. Periods of silence are a vital part of a discussion. People need time to think before they react. Also, seldom should a facilitator begin calling on people who have not indicated a desire to speak to the issue. When this happens, it has a tendency to move the discussion away from an honest sharing of one's feelings to a point where individuals are forced to say something, even if they have not formulated any individual feelings on the issue.

External Application

After the internalization process has been covered, the third phase needs to be implemented. During this phase content is presented giving a positive means, through biblical principles, of dealing with the problem or issue being focused on in the meeting. The content should be presented concisely, logically, and practically. If the stage has been set properly and we have been successful in implementing the first two phases of our programing, we will not need to give time to anything outside of comments that speak directly to the issue.

For some topics, such as theological issues,

which your young people know very little about, phases 2 and 3 should be dealt with through an extended presentation. But again, as was just stated, the presentation needs to be well thought out and very organized.

We need to take great care to purge our presentation of clichés and pat answers that are so easy to rely on in these types of situations, and which also tell our young people that we have not devoted much time or thought to our preparation. Remember, they have heard them before. We need to give them something that will affect their lives.

Internal Application

Following our third phase of external application we need to move to phase 4—internal application. After giving them directives as to how they can positively deal with the problem or situation that we have discussed during the meeting, they need to be asked to do something with what we have shared with them. This may come in the form of an assignment, a challenge or commitment, or the opportunity to react to what has been said during the external application phase. Without this final phase we have only a program. But when young people can allow facts to become a life-changing experience, we have accomplished ministry.

Another aid in the internalization of the application can be the structuring of the program so that young people will remain after the session for unstructured activities. This will offer you and other youth ministry personnel from your congregation the opportunity to talk with individual young people in an informal setting about their personal relationship with God and how it relates to the area dealt with during the session. Refreshments or informal recreational activities are good methods to implement for this purpose.

What we have been trying to present through this chapter is the fact that having an effective, regular youth meeting depends on much more than proper programing technique, creative ideas, and innovative methods. All of these help, but ultimately if our methods, ideas, and techniques are all we have, then we will only be running programs and not accomplishing ministry. If our regular youth program is to be successful and is to meet the spiritual needs of our young people, it must have a solid relational base of helping our young people better understand their relationship to themselves, their peer group, the adults of the congregation, and of course, God.

The weekly youth meeting is only one tool available to us for our ministry, but it is a good one when used properly and when based on a proper ministry philosophy. The ultimate test of success for our weekly meeting will be when we hear young people of our group make comments like, "I never thought I could talk with anybody about this, but here people care." And, "I can share it with them openly," or "Here people not only hear what I say, they listen too!"

FOOTNOTE

[1]Princeton Religious Research Center, *Religion in America 1979–80* (Princeton, New Jersey, 1979), pp. 63–73.

ADDITIONAL READING

Bill Ameiss, *Oop's!* Wheaton, Illinois: Victor Books, 1979.

Rich Bimler, 77 *Ways To Involve Youth in the Church*. St. Louis, Missouri: Concordia Publishing House, 1977.

John L. Carroll and Keith L. Ignatius. *Youth Ministry: Sunday, Monday and Every Day*. Valley Forge: Judson Press, 1972.

Mike Frans, *Are Junior Highs Missing Persons From Your Youth Ministry?* Wheaton, Illinois: Victor Books, 1979.

Pat Hurley, *The Magic Bubble*. Wheaton, Illinois: Victor Books, 1978.

______. *The Penetrators*. Wheaton, Illinois: Victor Books, 1978.

______. *Penetrating the Magic Bubble*. Wheaton, Illinois: Victor Books, 1978.

Lawrence O. Richards, *Youth Ministry: Its Renewal in the Local Church*. Grand Rapids, Michigan: Zondervan Publishing House, 1972.

Gary Richardson, *Where's It At?* Wheaton, Illinois: Victor Books, 1978.

J. David Stone, (General Editor). *The Complete Youth Ministries Handbook, Volume One*. Shreveport, Louisiana: Creative Youth Ministry's Models, 1979.

10

Junior High—A Building Program for the Senior High Ministry

If you could be placed in a time machine and go back to any age you would like, would you choose 12, 13, 14, or 15? I doubt it. Why? Because of pain—the pain of growth. Junior high is not an easy period in a person's life. Remember your first rash of pimples? Those misunderstood feelings of passion? During adolescence an adult is emerging from a child. A once-in-a-lifetime metamorphosis is taking place. A larva is becoming an imago. The in-between stage in insects is called a pupa. In humans it is called adolescence.

Jesus went through adolescence. Luke 2:51 and 52 sum up the earthly life of Jesus from age 12 to 30 by stating that He was subject to His parents and that ". . . Jesus grew in wisdom [mentally] and stature [physically], and in favor with God [spiritually] and men [socially]."

This multifaceted and complex growth we see in the life of Jesus is typical of the growth that takes place in all adolescents and is at a peak during junior high. Therefore, ministering to them at this time can be very difficult.

As I meet and talk with youth ministers, youth workers, and school teachers, I realize that junior highers are usually avoided like a plague. Those who

---

Craig Clapper is an Assistant Pastor of The Chapel in University Park, Akron, Ohio, specializing in the junior high ministry.

do get "stuck" with them have a tendency to handle them in one of two ways: The first is the "hang in there" way. The junior highers are treated like sixth graders and are expected to "hang in there" until they "grow up," that is, become senior highers. But junior highers are not very good at "hanging in there"; instead, many "fall out" and never return. There is also the "get in there and go" way. Junior highers are treated like senior highers and are expected to "act" like senior highers. Junior highers also are not very good at "acting," and many "get out" and never return.

Is there an alternative to these two ways? Is it possible to effectively minister to a person who is going through such drastic change? In his best seller, *Future Shock,* Alvin Toffler states that with dramatic change comes an adaptability breakdown. People just cannot cope. However, Toffler goes on to say that if a person understands what is going on and establishes "stabilizing zones" such as living in the same home, driving the same car, or keeping the same mate, then that person can remain stable in a changing world. Junior highers need a "stabilizing zone." Their lives are full of dramatic change. I believe that the person and power of Jesus Christ and the principles of His Word provide the only "way" to effectively minister to junior highers. Only Jesus Christ can provide the love, patience, wisdom, and understanding that adults so desperately need if they are going to work with junior highers. And, only He can provide junior highers with the stability they so desperately need.

JUST WHAT IS A JUNIOR HIGHER?

Junior highers are, in a sense, imperfect specimens of the human race. They are half child and half adult; half grade-schooler and half high-schooler. Even the terms "early" adolescent and "junior" highers seem to imply that they have not yet arrived.

As we noticed in Luke 2:52, Jesus grew in four basic areas. The first area mentioned was wisdom, or mental growth. Although we cannot see it, an early adolescent's mind is changing as quickly as his body. He is beginning to see the world through his own eyes instead of through the eyes of his parents. He used to pretty much believe what was fed into his computer. In the junior-high stage he reexamines all past and present information so as to establish his own ideas about life. His mind can now think abstractly, and think about thought. If it is not understood, this time of reexamination can be frustrating to parents and teachers. However, this reexamining and questioning period is good and necessary. Without it a person's beliefs are not his own. Junior highers may shock you by stating that they no longer believe in God. They are actually saying, "My whole life I have been taught and I have believed that God does exist. For some reason I am no longer certain I believe it. Please help me believe it!" The junior-high years should be a period of reaffirming the truths taught in childhood. I review familiar Bible stories, but go deeper and explain the "why" behind the story. I allow them to freely ask questions. I try not to be shocked at their doubts, and I am learning not to be afraid to say "I don't know," when I do not know an answer.

The next area of growth mentioned in the life of Jesus was stature, or physical growth. Physical growth can be seen easily in an early adolescent. It is not uncommon for a junior higher to grow six inches in one year. However, the growth often is not proportionate overall. I have seen 120-pound junior high guys who are 5′10″ tall and wear a size 10½ tennis shoe! Some girls will be fully developed while their friends have not yet begun to develop. The rapid growth causes the pores to secrete too much oil and pimples appear just when physical appearance is most important. Puberty sets in and the surges of passion generate feelings that they have never known and do not understand. This can all add up to a pretty trying time for a junior higher.

The third area of growth we saw in the life of Jesus was favor with God, or spiritual growth. Each summer we run three junior-high camps of one week each. All week long we study, play, sing, work, laugh, and cry together. Then on Friday evening we top the week off with a very moving campfire service. About half the campers either commit or recommit their lives to Jesus Christ. They go home all fired up and ready to win their school to Jesus. However, in a few weeks their "revival fires" begin to fizzle. Each year they return to camp and by their last junior-high summer they are ready to recommit a recommitted committal. And what do I say? I say Praise God! Junior-high years are a time of high temporary commitment. We do not expect an early adolescent to commit himself to a vocation or mate, so why expect him to become a mature Christian during a time of such turmoil. I do not mean that they should not accept Jesus Christ as Savior. I believe early adolescence is the most crucial time to make that decision. What I do mean is that a "total" commitment that proves itself in a consistent Christian life will be very difficult for them to maintain when nothing else in life is consistent. They will flounder and fail, they will become disappointed and feel like giving up. They will sometimes frustrate their teachers. Because of this, teacher continuity is highly desirable. One of the benefits of staying in the same location for five years has been the ability to see down the road. My first ninth graders are now sophomores in college. The recommitted committals are now committed for life! Be patient, hang in there; and look down the road.

The fourth and final area of growth we saw mentioned in the life of Jesus was favor with man, or social growth. Not only do junior highers suffer from pimples and passion, but they also suffer from peer pressure. Peer approval is of utmost importance during junior-high years. The child within the junior higher wants to break away from his parents and become independent. This, however, is a big and scary step. So the junior higher first steps into dependence on a peer group. That is why junior highers are so into fads, friends, cliques, and basically just being "cool." It is a horrible experience to be "out of it" in junior high. Junior highers can be very cruel to the "uncool" person.

However, a desire for independence is healthy. We as youth workers should provide opportunities for our youth to develop proper peers. Instead of "tightening up," we should "let out" a little rope. It is very helpful to have a number of activities that will enable them to build strong friendships within the youth group. It is also important to have programs with parental involvement designed to pull the junior higher closer to his parents, when the tendency is to drift apart. Remember, youth ministry exists as a supplement, not a substitute, to the home. A youth worker who endeavors to build close relationships between junior highers and their parents will be a blessing to both.

I believe the key to working with junior highers is understanding the mental, physical, spiritual, and social growth that is taking place. This rapid and varied growth is what distinguishes early adolescence from any other time. A great asset to working with junior highers is remembering that we were junior highers once. We have gone through the change. It is best if we do not repress our own memories of early adolescence. Sometimes the most painful memories provide the best source of empathy for the youth worker.

WHAT IS IT THEY NEED FROM US?

With great expectation I recently ordered a steak dinner at a fine restaurant. The warm rolls were great, the baked potato was piping hot, the salad bar had almost everything you wanted, but the steak was tough and gristly. Therefore, the meal was a great disappointment. We too can serve great retreats, rallies, fun, food, and fellowship, but ruin it by not serving a proper main course—a proper spiritual emphasis. A proper spiritual emphasis is essential to a well-rounded youth program. Without it our youth program offers nothing a school or social club cannot match. In the Sermon on the Mount, Jesus taught us how to live life with a proper spiritual emphasis. Jesus concluded the sermon with an illustration that teaches us that the person who builds his life on the person and principles of Jesus Christ will remain stable in the midst of the storms of life.

Junior highers are in a storm; the rains of self-doubt are pouring on them. Floods of peer pressure are flowing about them. The winds of change are beating on them. They need to know Jesus Christ and His Word. They need to know that He cares and that His Word is dependable. Retreats, rallies, fun, food, and fellowship are great and necessary, but only Jesus Christ and His Word can give stability in the storm. His Word tells junior highers of their worth, how to choose and make friends, and how to get along with parents. All these are clearly taught in Scripture and are some of the key needs of junior highers.

HOW DO WE EFFECTIVELY MINISTER TO THEM?

The children of Israel were about to enter the Promised Land and Moses knew that drastic changes were awaiting them. The problems and people in the new land could easily lead them astray. This generation had not personally experienced the crossing of the Red Sea or the giving of the law at Sinai. They were the wilderness wanderers. Moses called a meeting and reviewed God's past dealings with their nation. He reminded them of God's promises and power. Then He told them how to pass this information to their youth. "Hear, O Israel: The LORD our God; the LORD is one. Love the LORD your God with all your heart and with all your soul and with all your strength. These commandments that I give you today are to be upon your hearts. Impress them on your children. Talk about them when you sit at home and when you walk along the road, when you lie down and when you get up" (Deut. 6:4–7).

I believe this portion of Scripture teaches us when, where, and how we too can pass on what we know to our youth.

Notice first, that the teacher must know and love the true God. There is no better teacher than a good example. We must realize that we are God's advertisement to our junior highers. Our relationship to God is of utmost importance. We must also have the Word of God in our hearts. Head knowledge is not enough. His Word must penetrate our total being and dictate our behavior.

Next, notice the methods of teaching. There is to be diligent teaching. I believe this is referring to classroom or formal teaching. It can be done in various ways but it must be done. Junior highers must have sound doctrine to stand on. Make certain the classroom teaching is not boring or too long. Remember that their attention span is shorter than senior highers and they are just now beginning to grasp abstract thought. Make learning exciting, put your whole self into it; use real-life illustrations. In order to have real-life illustrations I ask God to bring relative-life situations about during the week so that my next lesson will be alive and fresh. Invariably it happens. Something happens during the week that becomes the main illustration for the next lesson. It is much like fishing with a net; you catch whatever is passing by because you have your net out.

I use Sunday mornings and evenings for formal teaching. On Sunday mornings I teach books of the Bible. I lecture about 20 minutes, then the junior highers break into small discussion groups with a youth worker to discuss how the lesson applies to life. On Sunday evenings I teach 3 ten-week incentive courses per year on various subjects geared to needs. I require homework, tests, and Scripture memorization. I am able to offer substantial rewards in the form of retreats. This has been extremely well-received.

Another type of teaching we notice in this passage is informal teaching. Sitting at home, walking along the road, going to bed, and getting up are all opportunities to see how classroom teaching relates to life. Wednesday evenings, social activities, and one-on-one time are what I term "informal teaching." On Wednesday evenings we dress very casually, play games for 40 minutes, and then have sharing and praying for 20 minutes. Junior highers really believe in prayer and are eager to present prayer requests. However, it does take time for them to feel comfortable praying in front of others. At every social activity we have an evangelistic appeal.

Junior highers are excited about "friendship evangelism" if they are confident that their friends will have a great time and not get bored stiff when it comes to the Bible study. Sometimes we show a Christian film or have a special singer, but usually we just stop on the way home from the activity for a "pit-stop" Bible study. We may stop at a roadside rest area, a park, schoolyard, or even a graveyard to have a 15-minute sermonette. Several junior highers can point back to a "pit stop" as the time they or a friend they brought accepted Jesus Christ. I always try to speak personally to the visitors. I invite them back and give them a gospel tract. I also praise the junior higher who brought a friend for caring so much. I explain that this gives a prime opportunity to question the friend's relationship to Jesus Christ and share Christ with the friend.

An effective teacher must also spend informal one-on-one time with his junior highers. Go to their ballgames, play their favorite sports with them. Find out what their interest is and do it with them. Show a personal interest in individuals. Whenever I check out a location for a future activity I take a few junior highers with me and we spend the day together. Sometimes we even spend the night somewhere. In this way they see that Jesus Christ lives in me twenty-four hours a day; and that I am fallible!

An effective ministry is not run by one individual. I attempt to work through a group of about 20 co-workers in the junior high ministry. College students and young married couples seem to work out best. A junior-high worker does not have to be a Superman or Wonder Woman to be effective, but he or she does have to be loving, patient, and kind. In essence, the junior-high worker must be Christ-controlled and cannot be a phony.

WHY A JUNIOR HIGH MINISTRY?

I have a 5-year-old son. He likes to make things out of Play-Doh. Sometimes he forgets to put it away when he has finished playing. Soon the Play-Doh begins to dry out. If it is found soon enough it can be worked with and most of it will still be good. However, if it sits out too long it will dry out and no longer be pliable enough to use.

I believe that junior highers are soft and pliable and offer us a unique opportunity to mold a life. At our church we begin in the Cradle Roll Department building the principles of God's Word into a child's life. We continue right on through the difficult junior-high years building stability into their changing lives. Then in senior high we begin to see a unique person unfold—a person whose power for living is from God, whose principles for living are from God's Word, and whose "stabilizing zone" is the Lord Jesus Christ.

ADDITIONAL READING

James Dobson, *Hide or Seek.* Old Tappan, New Jersey: Revell, 1979.

______. *Preparing for Adolescence.* Santa Ana, California: Vision, 1978.

Ruth Hummel, *Wonderfully Made.* St. Louis: Concordia Publishing House, 1967.

A. J. Bueltmann, *Take the High Road.* St. Louis: Concordia Publishing House, 1967.

T. Omar and E. Robert Clark, *Understanding People,* Wheaton: Evangelical Teacher Training Association, 1972.

Wayne Rice, *Junior High Ministry: A Guide Book for the Leading and Teaching of Early Adolescents.* Grand Rapids: Zondervan Publishing House, 1978.

Mike Frans, *Are Junior Highs Missing Persons From Your Youth Ministry?* Wheaton: Victor Books, 1979.

Tim Stafford, *A Love Story.* Grand Rapids: Zondervan Publishing House, 1977.

Paul D. Meier, *Christian Child-Rearing and Personality Development.* Grand Rapids: Baker, 1977.

11

Alternatives to Traditional Youth Programing

The word "traditional" evokes a variety of responses from people. To some, tradition is synonymous with words such as "heritage," "roots," "stability," and "proven." To others, the word means "old," "boring," and "archaic." When the word is applied to youth ministry, the same variety of responses occurs.

Speaking of tradition and denominations, Bishop Festo Kivengere of the Anglican Church (which knows something of tradition) has observed, "Traditions in themselves are not bad. But traditions fail badly when, instead of becoming bridges across which we can meet and know each other, they become means by which we are isolated."[1] If we can apply his statement to youth ministry, the principle seems to be that traditions in youth ministry are not bad as long as they enable us to effectively build bridges of personal growth and do not in themselves become barriers to growth and progress.

Just as people's responses to tradition and the traditional are varied, so are the concepts of what is really meant by "traditional youth programing." For the purposes of this chapter, it will be helpful if we can develop an operational definition of "traditional youth programing" for use as a frame of reference in

---

Dave Zehring is Senior Pastor of Covenant Baptist Church, Mesa, Arizona.

the discussion of alternatives. "Traditional youth programing" will then refer to a program within a local church consisting of a Sunday morning Sunday school, a Sunday evening "youth" program, perhaps a midweek Bible study, and special activities, e.g., socials, camps, and concerts.

THE NEED FOR ALTERNATIVES

At the beginning of this discussion it is possible that you are asking yourself, "Why should an individual or group consider alternatives to the present program?" If present programing is not "working," the questions would appear to be irrelevant and any alternatives would be welcome. However, if what we are presently doing is "successful," then the question would seem to be more appropriate, "Why *should* we change?" There are two factors that create a need for alternatives. The first factor is our goals and the standards by which we measure success. Typically, success tends to be evaluated in terms of quantity, rather than quality. That is to say, if a program has a sufficient number of students involved, it is successful. But just because a program produces numbers of students does not mean it is successful from a biblical perspective. It may, in fact, fail to produce enduring personal growth and sustained movement toward a balanced Christian life in spite of being quantitatively successful. On the other hand, the failure of a program to "work" almost inevitably stems from a lack of definition of biblical goals for youth ministry on the part of both adult and student leadership, but many "successful" programs suffer from the same lack of definition, a problem that eventually takes its toll in the lives of both the students and the adult leadership.

There is a real pressure in our society, and particularly in large metropolitan areas, to attempt to compete with the entertainment industry. Churches who fall victim to this pressure by trying to provide activities solely for entertainment create an impossible situation for themselves because they have neither the financial resources nor the manpower to entertain as effectively as the secular industry. In addition, the "entertainment youth ministry" model fosters an unbiblical attitude of self-centeredness among Christian students. Without a definite understanding of our goals, youth ministry can become subject to the whims of the students and be evaluated solely in terms of their personal pleasure and response.

A number of years ago in Los Angeles two towers were constructed as monuments of progress in the Watts District. In 1979 the city of Los Angeles denied a petition for funds to refurbish the dilapidated metal spires on the grounds that the towers served no useful function. As in architecture, so also in youth ministry, form of program *must* follow function. Much energy is spent in churches when they attempt to refurbish forms that have lost their function and now only create frustration!

A reevaluation of the goals of a local church's youth ministry may bring about a realization that alternatives to present programing are necessary in order to achieve those goals.

The second factor that creates a climate for alternatives to traditional programing is change in our cultural milieu. Someone has noted in reference to the horse and the transportation revolution of this century, that the horse had definite limitations inherent to it that could not be overcome. No matter how much time people spent redesigning saddles, improving training techniques, and developing better types of feed, as long as they limited themselves to the horse they never traveled any faster than a horse could take them. It wasn't until men discarded the horse as the sole means of transportation and began to explore totally different alternatives that the revolution in transportation was made possible. Youth ministry has faced a similar challenge in the past as well as in the present. The innovations of the past have rapidly become the traditions of the present and are subject to their own limitations, just like the horse. Our culture demands change. Unless we continue to experiment and develop innovative alternatives to ministry, we run the risk of being relegated to the horse-and-buggy era.

RESISTANCE TO ALTERNATIVES

A certain amount of resistance can be anticipated when contemplating alternatives to traditional programing. Adults, as well as students, tend to prefer forms with which they are comfortable. The amount of resistance generally corresponds to the extent of change being proposed. The greater the change, the more resistance. Resistance may come from a variety of quarters. For example, if the alternatives being proposed call for more involvement and commitment from the adult leadership presently in charge, strong opposition may come from them, or if the alternatives involve a change in the times and days students are asked to come, both parents and students may protest. Students may also balk if the changes proposed represent a departure from an "entertainment youth ministry" model to which they have become accustomed. Use of contemporary forms of communication such as multimedia, drama, or music may create apprehension or questions in the minds of the church staff or boards and spur resistance.

Proposing change may trigger varying degrees of intimidation from those in opposition. Often those initiating change have been forced to back away from their ideas or resign. Therefore, it is critical for the youth leader to be able to discern when to "fight" and when to "flex" with the prevailing mood. Early in my ministry the Senior Pastor, Dr. Edward B. Cole of Pomona First Baptist, took me aside and gave me some excellent counsel when he told me that just as in the military, battles are conceded in order to win wars, so in the church, smaller issues must be surrendered in order to win the major ones. Compromise should not be thought of as a dirty word when we initiate change. There is a time when we must stand by our principles no matter what the consequences, but not until all the compromises have been thoroughly examined! All too often the issue with the youth leader is not one of *principle* but one of *pride.*

While some resistance can be expected, it can be reduced and change can be initiated with the excitement and support of the church if we plan well. One of the keys is the evaluation of our goals for youth ministry. If goals are biblically defined and our proposed methods are consistent with these goals, much concern can be countered. Poorly defined goals foster fear and resistance.

Another key in winning the support of the church is to work through the established channels of leadership in the church. Taking the time to explain the goals, the changes, to answer questions, and to listen to concerns of those in leadership positions is always a wise investment. We found that one additional key to initiating change with the support of the church was to use a transition period of several months. During this time we introduced some elements of the alternatives we were suggesting. This allowed both students and adults to get a feel for the direction we were heading and eliminated much of the shock associated with change. As time passed, we gradually introduced additional elements of the alternative style of youth ministry we were proposing. As a result, we have experienced positive support from the total body.

AN ALTERNATIVE SUGGESTION

In November of 1977 I was exposed to an alternative to traditional approaches known as "Son City." For several months prior I had been convinced that the "weak" spot in our high-school ministry was in the area of evangelism. Our students were demonstrating some of the same attitudes in their spiritual lives that are sometimes evident when people become physically overweight and out of shape. We were providing opportunities for worship, Bible study, and fellowship, but still the students were bored, easily discouraged, lethargic, critical, and negative. I struggled, along with other adult leadership, trying to "improve" the existing programs until I finally came to the conclusion that the problem was not one of getting enough spiritual "calories" but getting too many and not being able to burn them off. In short, our students were spiritually *fat*. Evangelism, the primary means by which Christians exercise their spiritual muscles, was almost nonexistent. It was shortly after making these discoveries that the Lord prompted me to renew my friendship with Dan Webster, who is High School Pastor at Garden Grove Community Church. It was there I was introduced to "Son City." Dan shared how Son City had been developed in Chicago in the '70s by Rev. Bill Hybels, now pastor at Willow Creek Community Church in Palatine, Illinois, and how Garden Grove had come to adopt it. Watching the program, I immediately knew that this was an approach that would enable our students to love their friends to Christ. As I began to meet with Dan in order to gain a better understanding of the Son City program, I also began to pray and to plan for its introduction into our church. I was excited, and wanted to initiate the change at once. However, it was not until January of 1979, thirteen months later, that we began "Thursday Nite," our own Son City approach.

The philosophy behind Son City is biblically practical. For Christian students it is designed to provide an opportunity for them to give themselves away to those who do not know Christ. It enables them to carry out the Great Commission, that is making disciples, which Christ gave His disciples in Matthew 28:19. The program serves as a resource for Christian teen-agers as they love their friends to Jesus. It is not intended to do the work of evangelism for them; simply to assist. The Christian students are taught to view Son City as a "process of evangelism" rather than as an "act." This removes much of the pressure commonly associated with "one shot" evangelism and builds perseverance and faithfulness in the lives of Christian students. For college students, Son City offers opportunities to utilize leadership abilities as they disciple key high-school students each week. This is in keeping with Paul's mandate to Timothy to take the things Paul had taught him and "entrust [them] to reliable men who will also be qualified to teach others" (2 Tim. 2:2). Adults involved in Son City are allowed to employ technical abilities with which God has gifted them and thereby participate in the ministry as they produce the program weekly. The thrust of Son City, then, is evangelistic, but not in the traditional sense. It is the Christian students who are responsible for the spiritual welfare of their friends. Decisions are made as they live and share Christ, not as the result of a "hired gun's" ability to win souls. The philosophy of this approach assumes that Christian students are building and maintaining relationships with non-Christian friends. That proved to be a false assumption for the majority of the high-school students in our youth group. Many of them had come to believe that they were to avoid contacts with non-Christians instead of initiating them. Some students could not name one person with whom they were acquainted who was not a Christian. Consequently we spent several months talking and teaching about the privilege Christ has given to us as "signposts" to a lost and dying world. The task is still not complete; we are finding it necessary to frequently review our mission as Christians on planet earth.

With regard to nonbelievers, Son City is designed to be a creative, relevant, and uplifting experience in which they are exposed to God's love. The program seeks to communicate the meaning and purpose Jesus Christ can bring to their lives in terms they can understand. Each week a topic relevant to the needs of the non-Christian student is selected as the theme for the evening. The topic may be on loneliness, friendship, the character of God, or building self-esteem. The subject is always approached from a biblical perspective, yet in terms the secular students can understand. Son City uses contemporary mediums of communication in order to reach secular students at their level. Son City strives to avoid the stereotypes commonly associated with "church" programs. It is not a "church service"; there is no sermon, no offering, no hymns. There is a "talk" but the speaker does not "preach." Every effort is made to put the non-Christian at ease so that he may respond freely to God's love as it is channeled to him through the Christian students.

Son City seeks to combine the best methods and techniques from organizations such as Campus Life and Young Life, along with ideas from other sources, in order to provide a creative experience for high-school students. The basic ingredients of Son City include team competition, live contemporary music, multimedia, drama, sound, staging, and lighting. While the basic ingredients are commonly shared by all Son City programs, each local Son City adapts and tailors the program to suit its particular needs, facilities, and resources.

Developing a Son City program, or any other alternative to traditional programing, is not an exercise in total originality. Borrowing and adapting ideas from other ministries is an essential practice every youth minister should follow. J. Daniel Baumann gives the rationale for this practice in his book, *All Originality Makes a Dull Church*. He says, "Lessons learned by any local fellowship of believers ought to be common property of the entire body of Christ. Not to learn by the lessons of others is a waste of time and energy."[2] Initiating and developing an alternative approach is a study in continual refinement. However, whatever the stage of refinement, the program should always seek to achieve the highest quality possible in the overall production in order to build and maintain credibility with the secular student.

The use of teams in the Son City approach reflects an attempt to meet the social needs of high-school students. The teams are designed to create not only enthusiasm, but also a warm and accepting environment in which new students can get acquainted with others. The teams are the setting in which the students receive personal recognition, attention, and affirmation. Each team is led by a spiritually mature male and female captain, who are responsible for the organization and general welfare of the team. In addition to the leadership the captains give their teams at Son City, they are also involved in meeting with and discipling the key people on their team with the goal of reproducing themselves.

The team competition used each week provides the students with an opportunity to enjoy a fun activity that usually calls for very little athletic ability. The object is to allow as many students as possible to be involved in the competition and to foster a feeling of personal ownership in each team member. The competition is kept in check and is not allowed to overshadow the ultimate purpose of Son City, which is to love people to Christ.

The formation of teams is an important step in developing a Son City approach. Each team should be formed around a core of committed students, and the spiritual maturity of the core of each team is of vital concern. A high level of maturity is necessary in order to build a strong foundation. In fact, the growth of the team depends largely on the spiritual maturity, commitment, and faithfulness of the core members. In some cities the teams are related to campus ministries and therefore each team is made up of students drawn primarily from a given high school. However, other Son City programs have teams that are heterogeneous in terms of school make-up.

The use of live contemporary music, multi-media, and drama as media of communication simply reflects the creative forms available to the church today. As technology advances, other forms may be developed that will allow further innovations in communicating Christ's love. These media are not used randomly in Son City but rather are designed to specifically address the theme of each week and enhance the message of hope presented in the talk. The exact style and amount of music, multimedia, and drama employed by a particular Son City depends on the sociological make-up of the community, as well as on the talent and financial resources in the local church. Styles of music, for example, vary from Son City to Son City around the country. The important idea is to make every effort to communicate in terms to which the secular students can relate. This does not imply a compromise in our Christian commitment or testimony, but simply an attempt to remove unnecessary communication barriers. It has been our experience, in the area of music, that frequently secular songs point out the *needs* and problems associated with a particular theme, while Christian songs present the hope available in Christ. Son City attempts to reflect the attitude of Paul who said, ". . . I have become all things to all men so that by all possible means I might save some" (1 Cor. 9:22). Sound, lighting, and staging are also valuable assets for communication. The amount utilized, again, depends on the resources of the local church.

These media of communication, along with the technical sound and lighting equipment, give the Son City evening a certain amount of entertainment value. Yet, entertainment is not the primary purpose of Son City, nor can a Son City evening, by any stretch of the imagination, compete with the entertainment offered in the secular world. While Son City attempts to present a quality program using contemporary technology and art forms, the reason students return week after week is because of the care and concern—the love—they are given by the Christian students.

Son City is not designed to replace the balance of programing for students in the local church but rather to complement it. In many cases a creative alternative will stimulate interest and point out a need for other existing or additional programs. Because Son City is an evangelistic thrust, it is imperative that opportunities for Bible study, worship, and fellowship be made available to the Christian students. It is essential that a balance is maintained in the total program between these elements. It is also important that the students recognize their relationship and responsibilities to the rest of the body of the local church.

Can we assume that adopting an alternative to traditional programing will not affect other areas of programing? Obviously, the answer to that question depends on the alternative. After adopting the Son City format in our church, we found that some programs were affected directly, while others were not. Actually, all of our programing has felt the impact of Son City's presence and growth. This is because God has used this approach to challenge and stretch the high-school students in ways they had never before experienced. While Sunday school and choir are two programs that have remained the same externally in structure, both have benefited from the growth of the students involved in Son City. Son City did make it necessary to restructure the midweek Bible study and move it to Monday evening. It is now designed for the Christian core members of each team and has taken on new significance in their lives. Consequently we now have more students involved in Bible study than ever before. The social needs of the high-school students are now met through the Son City evening as well as additional team activities. These have replaced the traditional monthly social.

Because of the introduction of Son City and the restructuring and moving of the midweek Bible study, the Sunday evening youth program was suspended. However, all of the purposes formerly served by the Sunday-evening program are now being met by the other programs.

The camping programs of the high-school ministry have remained intact, but we now have more students involved and a greater percentage of them are non-Christians.

Some churches have utilized special activities such as athletic tournaments (i.e., softball, basketball, track, and field) or talent contests (i.e., music, drama, cheerleading) in conjunction with Son City in order to reach particular subgroups of the general high-school population. These have proven to be effective bridges for evangelism.

As the church moves toward the end of the twentieth century, it finds itself faced with more challenges and opportunities than ever before. If the church is to be a significant influence at the local level, then we must continue to focus and refocus our eyes on the objectives Christ has placed before us. We must not allow ourselves to think in terms of traditional vs. alternative styles of youth ministry, but rather in terms of how we can best reach our objectives. Therefore, let us continually reaffirm our commitment to the timeless principles of God's Word, while recognizing the creative innovations and applications of His Spirit.

FOOTNOTES

[1]Bishop Festo Kivengere, Quoted from message given at Pomona First Baptist, July 1978.

[2]J. Daniel Baumann, *All Originality Makes a Dull Church* (Santa Ana: Vision House Publishers, 1976), p. 21.

ADDITIONAL READING

Don Cousins, *Tomorrow's Church Today! (Son City)*. Elk Grove Village, Illinois: Kukla Press, 1979.

12

Ministering Through Core Groups

The technological society in which we live has given birth to impersonality. The contractions and accompanying pain had been growing with increasing rapidity and intensity over the last two or three decades. Now, at last, our fully developed babe has arrived. As if this child were royalty of sorts, the effect has been ubiquitous. Our all-too-familiar slogans, "Have a nice day" and "How are you doing?" have become mechanical dispatches to give the appearances of warmth and concern. Our neighbors are no longer the people who reside next door or on our block. Husbands and fathers have opted to provide material gifts for their families instead of giving themselves in meaningful dialogue and sharing together. Honest responses to the following questions will perhaps further prove the point.

- How many families do you know in your immediate neighborhood?
- When was the last time you asked someone "How are you doing?" and they responded other than "Fine" or "Great"?
- How many *close* friends do you have with whom you can share your innermost thoughts?

John Musselman is the Minister of Youth, Coral Ridge Presbyterian Church, Fort Lauderdale, Florida.

- If you had a very serious problem and needed help, to whom would you go?
- Do you generally keep your thoughts to yourself?
- Do you wish you had deeper relationships?
- If you were to die today, who would come to your funeral?

If, by some ingenious invention of modern technology, you were enabled to peer into the hearts of the students God called you to minister to, what do you suppose you would find? Would they have some of the same thoughts you have? How would they answer those questions? Are the so-called "popular people" secure in themselves? Do the beauty queens have it all together? Do athletes really feel tough? Do some have painful periods of loneliness and even despair of life? Do still others have periods of self-doubt and discouragement? Are they fearful of a nuclear holocaust, euthanasia, abortion, communism, deformity, death, or pain? Do they worry about exams, finances, college plans, or a date for the coming weekend? And don't leave out the trivial things that are important to them. As your technological scanner probes the hidden closets of these hearts, would you be surprised to locate upset over a small mole or a broken nail that took months to groom? Does someone in your ministry want to be larger or smaller, taller or shorter? Would we ever be shocked at our findings!

Our findings would be encouraging to us. Gloating over their trials or personal difficulties is not exactly what we have in mind here. We would simply have our eyes opened to the startling discovery of rampant personal fear, weakness, and difficulties. By God's grace we could then minister to them in deeper, more significant ways.

Many students sense that though life is complex, it nonetheless does not have to be shallow. These same students sense that they need one another. They want someone to care about them, to notice when they achieve something of significance to them, to miss them when they could not be at a certain program or function in the ministry and to show a bit of compassion when they are not feeling so well. We have found that one of the most meaningful environments in which a student can have his needs met is the small group.

Small groups in the local church are nothing new. For a number of years now many skilled and scholarly authors have written and taught about the importance of developing small-group contexts for people within the local church. They have sensed that there is greater growth and a deeper understanding of biblical fellowship when there is a small number of people who meet together on a regular basis for fellowship, prayer, and the study of God's Word. But we certainly should not limit those who would have fellowship in a small group to adults only. We have found that high-school students meeting in a small group with an adult leader over a given period of time have experienced deeper relationships and have understood more of what it means to grow spiritually in the context of honesty and a supportive fellowship.

We have stated our purpose in this way: To gather high-school students into small clusters to foster spiritual growth through discussions, fellowship, prayer, and the maintenance of a daily quiet time. These students learn to pray for one another, to weep with those who weep in their group, to support one another through trials, to encourage one another when a fellow student is in the pit of despair, and to laugh together in the joy of the Lord. The groups are never structured in such a way that inflexibility is the watchword. The groups have their own personalities because every individual created in the image of God comes to the group with his own agenda of the needs that he feels must be met. When you multiply these needs by the number of people in a group you have a group personality that is unique and complex. The adult leader will be sensitive to his group and seek to shepherd in an individual as well as a corporate manner.

THE NEED FOR CORE GROUPS

There are small youth ministries and large youth ministries, just as there are small and large churches. When a youth ministry begins, normally it is small and the fellowship level of this particular group is good. But once numerical growth begins to come to this young ministry because new people are finding new life in Jesus Christ and others are transferring into the community, certain students begin to feel that there is a largeness on the horizon that frightens and even threatens them. They would like to maintain the smallness of the group and yet they realize the kingdom of God is increasing and must increase. We found students in our ministry like this at the beginning when we began to grow. Some were unwilling to invite their friends or to become involved in an outreach ministry to win the lost because they were afraid they would destroy the vitality of the fellowship of their small group. They had a legitimate concern. But this means of dealing with the problem was not biblical. We do not have to substitute smallness for largeness or largeness for smallness. Both should coexist because both are biblical. The church must continue to grow, including our ministry to youth. But at the same time the quality of the ministry must not suffer with numerical growth. If small groups are developed when numerical growth begins to occur, then students can be made to feel that they are still loved and cared for all the while new students are finding new joy and new life in our Lord Jesus Christ.

When does a youth ministry start small groups? Most small-group specialists would indicate that from six to twelve people is the number for an effective small group. We have found this to be true in our ministry. So the logical answer to the question is that small groups should begin when the group size exceeds twelve. This, of course, is assuming that all twelve are actively involved in the ministry and would like to participate in some kind of a small group. If the total youth ministry in the local church consists of twelve people, then obviously you already have a small group and the youth minister or lay leader in the church can be the facilitator in this context. If you have a larger youth ministry of, for example, between 25 and 300, then you can have any number of small groups within the large group structure. It is recommended that the number of students in a small group not exceed twelve, whatever the size of the large group in the youth ministry. What tends to happen in such a situation is that the students find themselves clamming up because they are afraid to take time away from someone else who may in their opinion have a more important matter to bring before the whole group. Also, other students feel left out when there are that many people. They feel there is not enough personal contact with the adult leader, which is something almost all want to have.

One further point in terms of group size needs to be made. It is paramount that the group leader have input as to the size of his or her own group. After structuring our small groups for some time and telling the group leaders what their size should be, namely twelve, we discovered that some leaders were not functioning as effectively as we knew they could. We began asking each leader to specify in the beginning of the formation of his new group what size he wanted. This helped him not to feel guilty about not taking twelve students, which may in all probability have been too much for him. Many of these leaders come from heavy work loads and do not have the time to invest in that many lives in a given week, particularly when they are involved in other aspects of ministry. This insight has cut down tremendously on tension in the adult leaders and has not made them feel guilty if they take a smaller group of say five or six. It would be far better to have an adult leader take five students per year for five years than it would be to give twelve students to a leader for two years and burn him out.

SELECTION OF YOUR ADULT LEADERS

Each group has a young adult leader who has committed himself to the students. These leaders are carefully chosen on the basis of their Christian commitment, their love for students, and their ability to relate well. They are not there to lecture, but to facilitate discussion, to interact with students, to foster an atmosphere conducive to spiritual growth, and to make themselves available for personal counsel and guidance.

Because we believe this is a very important position in our ministry, we ask each of these leaders to sign a covenant. This covenant follows:

> Having received Jesus Christ as a personal Savior, and now living in fellowship with Him, I realize that ministering Christ and His Word to others is a high calling. In view of my commission as a small-group leader, and relying on the help and guidance of the Holy Spirit, I promise to fulfill my responsibilities and agree to the following covenant:

1. I subscribe to the doctrinal statement of my church, and will teach nothing that is in conflict with its position.
2. I will daily set aside time for communion with my Lord in prayer and Bible study.
3. I will earnestly pray for the spiritual growth of my group members.
4. I will faithfully prepare myself each week for ministry through prayer and by living out the Bible truths I teach.
5. I will faithfully attend and promote the services of our church, and will support the church financially and with my prayers.
6. I will attend each month's worker's conference, and any meeting of the staff of my department, unless hindered by some reason I can conscientiously give to God.
7. If for some reason I cannot fulfill my responsibilities, I will consult with the youth minister and will surrender my group if that seems advisable.

Name ______________________________
Date ______________________________

This covenant is signed on a yearly basis and covers the school year from September 1–May 30 of each year. The covenant is more of a commitment to the Lord Jesus than it is to us personally. Our leaders have taken this seriously and it has helped produce solidarity in the leadership of our ministry that has been stable for some time. The kind of commitment on the part of leaders has made for more security among the students themselves who often come from very unstable home environments.

QUALIFICATIONS OF SMALL-GROUP LEADERS

Because this position is so vitally important, we have specified eleven qualifications that we like to see in our youth staff:

■ *A Willingness to Learn.* Anyone who is beyond learning is beyond growing. As ministry is dynamic (not static), so each leader must be committed to submitting himself or herself to a multiplicity of learning experiences. This eliminates a stagnant ministry. If leadership is growing and maturing in Christ, this will filter down to the youth of the ministry.

■ *A Desire to Utilize the Principle of Association.* To effectively minister to the real needs of youth the leader must understand the absolute necessity of being with them. Ministry does not take place in a vacuum or through program orientation.

■ *A Willingness to Pay the Price.* Late-night phone calls, counseling, and other personal interruptions could almost be considered the norm of youth ministry. Ministry is not concluded after the program.

■ *Filled With the Spirit.* True ministry is wrought by the supernatural workings of the Spirit of God in the hearts and minds of people. Spiritual individuals experiencing the daily appropriation of the Holy Spirit will overflow in ministry to the youth. The church for too long has been recruiting entertainers and/or recreational leaders for youth. Those are the responsibilities of Hollywood and the YMCA, not the church.

■ *Christian Lifestyle.* The lay staff must model the Christian life before the students on a consistent basis. Therefore, each must be above reproach, rejecting those things that could cause a person to stumble.

■ *Persistence.* Youth need the faithful oversight of a diligent leader to assist them in their work and ministry. This monitoring factor will assure that the assigned work will be completed in the stipulated time. Also, because of some ambivalence among adolescents, lay leaders will find themselves working overtime (in many cases) to stay abreast of current trends in particular youth. Youth need to know who will not give up on them.

■ *Reproduction.* The lay leadership is called to reproduce. Like produces like. Youth will become like their teachers and models. On account of this, a nonproducing adult leader must "turn in his badge."

■ *A Good Listener.* Students do not want to be talked "at." They are people with emotion and sensitivity to be talked "with." One-way communication will not get the job done.

■ *Creative.* Each adult must be willing to discover and utilize the gifts and talents God has given for the building up of the body of Christ. We must avoid the practice of boring students through repetition and the lack of innovative spirit.

■ *A Servant's Heart.* We are not called to be masters, but servants. Lording it over the youth is not only a practice forbidden in the Scripture, but one that fails to produce growth. There is only one master. We are the servants of Christ called out of the world to minister as His ambassadors.

- *Love.* Ministry without love is like a football game without the ball. The team cannot play and one cannot minister at all. Constant criticism of youth will insure one thing: they will live up to your expectations. Love is the motivating factor for involving students in real ministry.

Of course, we do not expect every leader we have to measure up to these qualifications perfectly. But we do expect that each leader will seriously take each one of these and make it a personal goal for his or her own spiritual growth. We feel that the better they attain these qualifications, the stronger a leader of young men and women they will be.

BECOMING A MEMBER OF A SMALL GROUP

A successful small group is one in which each student makes a serious commitment to Jesus Christ and to the other members of the group. Obviously, if eleven students are committed to growth together and one is not, the growth will be somewhat stifled and the caring community will not emerge as rapidly or as deeply. To preserve the quality in Christian character of each group, each student is requested to meet the following criteria for participation:

- A personal commitment to Jesus Christ as Savior and Lord.
- A commitment to the other students in the group—to be faithful in attendance, participation, and confidentiality.
- A personal commitment to spiritual growth through studying God's Word, prayer, worship, and partaking of the sacraments.

Because we take the small group ministry seriously, we also like the students to take it in the same way. Therefore, we have devised a helpful tool that is simply a small-group covenant for each student. As the covenant was signed and dated by the adult leader so the student takes this particular covenant and does likewise. The covenant reads as follows:

1. I have trusted in Jesus Christ alone to forgive me of all my sins and give me eternal life.
2. As a responsible member of God's forever family I am committed to my own personal

spiritual development as well as helping my brothers and sisters grow in Christlikeness.

3. Understanding that as believers in the Lord Jesus Christ we are called to minister to one another by God's grace, I commit myself to show care, concern, and love to the other members of the group.
4. I will actively seek to serve Christ through the use of my gifts and ability that the Holy Spirit has given to me and I have discovered.
5. I will make every attempt to be present with my group each week to be ministered to and to minister.

Signed ______________________________

Date ________________________________

OPERATING THE SMALL GROUP

Each small group meets once a week on a regular basis for a 45-minute period. During this time any number of things may take place within the group. The Lord may have laid a particular issue or biblical truth upon the leader's heart that week and he or she would like to get the reaction of the students to that particular truth. Another leader may sense that there is a student who is going through a difficult time because his parents are on the verge of getting a divorce. Still another may have come up with some exciting new game that fosters a greater depth of biblical koinonia among the students and he wants to use this on that evening. Still another may want to take student requests and spend the evening praying together in a small group.

Sometimes the groups are not just used to build koinonia, but they can become task-oriented groups. By that we mean that certain groups will take on a particular project that will have a beginning time and a completion time. This task may be supporting a missionary financially on the mission field, or it may be providing Thanksgiving baskets for the needy in their own home town. These projects should be decided on by the students themselves in the small group so that there is goal ownership for each individual project. We try to make sure that the project does not overshadow one of our main purposes for the establishing of the small groups and that is the building of fellowship and a caring community among a small number of students. Again, we do not have to opt for one or the other. We can have a fellowship and prayer-centered small group that periodically assumes a project that will help them not to become inbred in their relationships. These projects also help them to follow the biblical mandate to be service oriented and to give of themselves and the things that they have to those who are in greater need.

The length of time over which a group of students meets in a small group is vitally important. If the time framework is too short, say two or three months, then the students find themselves wanting to know other students more and they're whisked away to another group without ever having built the depth of fellowship they had anticipated. On the other hand, if the length of time is too long, say two years, then the group can become ingrown and the students begin to become disinterested in some of the "boring" things they have done from time to time. They need a fresh experience in their life. We have found that the school year from September until May is a good time parameter to place on the existence of the small groups. So each September we begin new small groups and those stay intact until May. On occasion a new student may be added to a group if it has the total group's consent. It must be understood that the addition or subtraction of one member of a small group changes the dynamics of that group. So the ideal situation is that between five and twelve students meet together with one leader for a period of nine months. It is during that time that we pray that the Lord will mend hearts together in a mutual ministry of love and concern.

Not only do the students meet together for that nine-month period, but also the adult leaders meet together themselves once a week for that period. The adult leaders share together what God is doing in their groups, they share ideas of what has been successful and what has not worked in their groups. There is the sharing together or prayer requests and a genuine concern for each leader that builds the community among themselves.

THE RESULTS OF IMPLEMENTING SMALL GROUPS IN THE LARGER GROUP

Once small groups become integrated into the youth ministry of the local church, students begin to feel a sense of caring and fellowship they had not experienced before. The pressure is taken off the youth minister as the one who by many standards is supposed to do all the visiting and the caring for each student in the ministry. By training and equipping young adult leaders to disciple students, there is more of a personal dimension that occurs in the youth ministry. By increasing the number of adult leaders working in the ministry, the base and foundation for expansion of ministry is increased.

We are convinced. The implementation of the small groups in our ministry has revolutionized it from within. Never before have students had a feeling of well-being that their personal needs are a concern of another adult in our ministry. To be sure it is not the totality of a youth ministry that should include an evangelistic outreach, Sunday school classes, home Bible study groups, prayer groups, and many other dimensions of ministry that they need to learn for their life's work in the Lord's field. But when this dimension is neglected there is the feeling that the machinery of the ministry is moving without the personal touch. And we have found this dimension in implementing small groups to have placed the icing on the cake whereby students are genuinely ministered to in love. Many of the groups are not without their struggles because they are growing. And that is what these are intent on doing.

13

Bible Studies in the High-school Program

> So is my word that goes out from my mouth: it will not return to me empty, but will accomplish what I desire and achieve the purpose for which I sent it. (Isa. 55:11)

Isaiah wrote that God's Word will not return empty. Scripture is that sharp-edged sword of the Lord that changes people's lives, young and old alike. It must be taught with accuracy and relevancy to our teen-agers.

Bible studies therefore are a much-needed part of a church's youth program, for through them we can teach and preach God's Word to evangelize and edify people. We must be about the task of proclaiming the gospel to win young people to the Lord and preparing them to serve Him. Christian teen-agers will dare to be different from their peers if they are properly trained in the adventure of Christian living. This evangelization and edification can occur more effectively outside of the church setting, in the neutral environment of a home Bible study. However, these studies must be a supplement to your youth programs; they cannot replace them. If they are used properly, they will revolutionize your ministry.

STRATEGIES

Purpose

Determine the spiritual strength and felt needs of your youth group. Decide whether they would

Rory Wineka is an Assistant Pastor responsible for the senior high ministry at the Chapel in University Park, Akron, Ohio.

benefit more from: 1) a study for personal edification because you have many new or immature Christians, 2) a study for evangelization because many non-Christians are in your group, or 3) a study for evangelistic outreach because your group is a fairly bold witness for Christ to their peers and will persistently invite their friends to the study. All studies should be designed initially to touch all three of these areas until you see who's coming regularly. Center your attention on the core group of teen-agers, but also try to reach the minority. Always encourage teens to bring their friends.

Within this design, develop a long-range plan. For example, when I began leading high-school studies in my church eight years ago, they were small edification studies. All of the youth who initially came were young Christians. I consequently taught them principles of Christian growth. Whenever they responded to my invitation to invite unsaved friends, I slanted the study (often on the spot) evangelistically.

As more of our young people developed a stable, daily walk with the Lord, they began inviting their peers. Then the studies became evangelistic and edifying.

Today more than 150 different teens attend our studies (50 from outside our Sunday school class) because of the strong witness our high schoolers have in their public schools. This changeover took a long time because Christian maturity is a long process. So today the studies are heavy on evangelism and light on edification. However, you always should concentrate on having each of these two principles in your studies (according to group needs). In addition to these, fellowship must play an important role.

Young people listen more to their peers than they do to adults. When unsaved teen-agers see Christian teens walking daily with the Lord and participating in a Bible study, it has an effect. Teens learn from teens, good and bad. It's our responsibility as youth leaders to provide these valuable learning opportunities for youth.

Choosing Location

Provide this opportunity in the home of one of the key young people in your high-school program, and God will use that neutral environment to change more lives than you will see changed in your church building and Sunday school classroom. Make sure that the family, including their teen-ager, has a good testimony for the Lord. For example, it would be tragic to assume that the young person's family is committed to the Lord, when the father could be an alcoholic who might walk in drunk at one of your sessions some evening.

If you have a large class, determine the central locations of most of your youth and plan strategic studies accordingly.

Schedule

My experience has taught me that the Bible study should:

- Begin in October after the young people are used to school homework and end in April before "spring fever" and exams hit.
- Meet weekly except for holidays.
- Start at 7 P.M. with a time for prayer requests and prayer. From 7:15 to 8:00 have Bible study and from 8:00 to 9:00 fellowship.
- Be brief. For example, don't spend seven months on one book of the Bible. The longest segment should be two months.
- Have variety by adding one- to three-week units on "hot topics," e.g., dating, rock music, prophecy, witnessing, etc.

Materials

Make sure you use workbook type studies that demand personal preparation for each participant prior to each week's meeting. Make them pay for their own books. That adds responsibility and builds commitment.

Use materials that are current, relevant, and that meet their *felt* needs. This is where you must know your youth and must "shop around" for good workbook studies on their level.

Always have a broad-tip magic marker and an art pad, 24 inches square, for the purpose of creating visuals. An important supplement is to plant the Word in their minds via illustrations. If you're a poor artist, have someone else make your drawings beforehand, or buy overheads when they're available with your materials.

Other valuable items are 3 x 5 cards and pencils.

After a study, have the teens write out: "I learned . . . ," "I relearned . . . ," "I would like to learn. . . ." This provides valuable evaluation information for future reference and for measuring your effectiveness. Tell them to make the cards anonymous whenever they choose.

Encouragement

Tie your studies in with your Sunday school class. Challenge your young people on Sunday morning to fellowship and learn together during the week, and bring their friends. Stress the importance of the need to know and share the Word of God. If this study is important to you, it will be important to them.

Also correlate your study subjects with your Sunday school subjects. Have these programs complement each other, e.g., if you have a large Sunday school class that disallows discussion, teach subjects on Sunday and have the groups discuss them during the week.

Preparation for Leaders

The studies will be no more successful than the prayer that precedes them, especially in choosing and preparing the leaders. If there is only one study, the youth pastor should lead it. However, as the studies multiply, the youth pastor's role will become administrative. The youth pastor leading only one of several studies causes several problems:

- The other leaders have to compete with him and this creates undue pressure.
- The youth will flock to the pastor's study, normally.
- It tends to show favoritism, whether intended or not, to a specific home, family, or geographical group of teens.

Therefore, when there are two or more studies, the youth pastor should avoid leading one, unless he leads them all. Most youth pastors have enough to do without leading two or more weekly Bible studies.

Discipleship

One of the best supplemental aspects of a study is discipleship. Take one or two key young people who are committed to the study and have your leaders meet with them in a one-on-one discipleship program for one-half hour preceding the study. This is convenient and it builds the leadership of your class as you concentrate specifically on edifying and training young people to grow in serving the Lord. This will do more for your youth program than anything else—creating a strong *positive peer pressure* as these young people assume leadership positions in your group.

Rallies

After your studies progress, plan exciting and challenging bimonthly Bible study rallies, inviting all who attend the studies to bring their friends for a minimal fee ($1.00).

Play some mixer games, have special speakers, films, multimedia presentations, etc. Plan a time of small-group sharing of testimonies and prayer. Afterward have refreshments.

Always divide your young people into groups with teens who do not attend the same study, e.g., if you have four studies, choose one from each study to be in respective groups. Have name tags for easy identification. Let lay leaders or class leaders lead discussion.

During the summer, after the studies are over, plan monthly evangelistic rallies in neutral settings, i.e., public parks, individual homes, camp, etc. Keep the momentum going once it begins to roll! Keep challenging your young people to grow and reach out in love. They'll respond, although it will take time to build this program. Be patient!

Fellowship Together

Encourage your young people to socialize together on weekends. Stress how much the members of the body of Christ need each other. Positive peer pressure builds character by example. It is imperative that they concentrate on building and encouraging each other in the Lord, and that they avoid fellowshiping with the world.

The youth leader cannot run their lives and plan all their activities. Challenge them to plan together creatively within their studies to socialize on weekends, especially to date other Christians in their class. (You cannot overstress the importance of their dating within their Christian peer group.)

The individual units must be designed to develop discussion of the Word of God. Discussion leads to personal discovery, which is the way people learn best.

Preparing Study Lessons

Larry Richards' book, *Creative Bible Teaching* (Moody Press), gives an effective, yet simple, lesson plan format for teaching teens. He concentrates on a "hook-book-look-took" format in which the teacher follows a process of discovery that leads to practical application of biblical truth by the young people.

Application is imperative for young people to grow in the Lord. This discovery process meets personal needs and allows the person to be conformed to the image of Christ according to God's plan for his individual life. Without application, all you have is biblical knowledge, which is a sorry substitute for spirituality. I've seen too many Christian teens who confuse spirituality with biblical knowledge. As J. I. Packer says, "You can know a great deal *about* God without knowing Him personally."

The leader (not lecturer) must direct the young person's attention to:

- Observe scriptural truth. "What did it say?"
- Interpret that truth. "What did it mean?"
- Apply that truth to their own felt needs. "What should I do about it?" (Often we as leaders have to help teens *feel* their needs.)

The leader should prepare clear, relevant, and stimulating discussion questions, written on 3 x 5 cards. Use these questions to guide your young people through spontaneous interaction. Guide them through the discovery process of learning as the Holy Spirit leads them.

The leader must remember that the authority is the Word of God, the teacher is the Holy Spirit, and the leader (himself) is merely a megaphone of the Lord's truth. The Bible is the focus of attention, not the leader.

The leader's prayer preparation must lay the foundation for any study that is to be successful according to God's plan. Each individual should be prayed for by name, that God would open his or her mind and heart to be receptive to the revealed truth. The lesson should be labored in prayer, so God may teach the leader, granting him the wisdom to rightly divide the Word of truth, to God's glory. As someone once said: "To give people a cup of cold water from the well of God's Word, you must dig deep!"

So, be prepared. Know the Word. Use memorable, relevant illustrations. Listen to your young people. Love them. Be transparent as you show personal, sincere interest in them. Be enthusiastic. Make them think! Challenge them with questions that do not have yes and no answers.

Recognize the privilege and responsibility God has granted you regarding the teaching of His Word to change young lives—then rise to the occasion, by His grace. And to Him be the glory!

FINE POINTS

1. Keep the group under ten when possible.
2. Use role play situations.
3. Teach the group to pray conversationally.
4. Let your group summarize the lesson.
5. Use the same homes and leaders for the six months of the study.
6. Don't do anything to break the momentum of the study (unless it's negative momentum), e.g., changing homes or leaders during the course of a year's study.
7. Make the first session informal, with name tags, a mixer, sharing, and refreshments.
8. Let teens take turns bringing refreshments weekly.
9. If you have more than one study, hold them different nights of the week, e.g., Monday, Tuesday, Thursday to allow flexibility for different schedules of teens.
10. Survey your group to discover their felt needs so you may plan mini-units accordingly.
11. Evaluate the studies and adapt according to need. Young people are different. Build your program according to the people in it. Never concentrate on program to the neglect of people. Have the young people and leaders submit evaluations to you at year's end. Evaluation will be the key to building next year's studies.
12. Have your junior-high classes stress Bible learning to prepare them for senior-high

studies. Do not allow junior highers to attend these studies. If your junior highers are ready for it, plan monthly devotional type studies for them to lay the foundation for their high-school studies to come.

SPECIAL PROJECTS

The design of high-school Bible studies should incorporate some special project ideas that will add extra life and stability to the overall program. I have tried several projects. The following have been the most successful in changing young people's lives and in building strong, consistent studies:

Contact Program

The major problem the first two years I led studies on the high-school level was inconsistent attendance on the part of the teen-agers. In an attempt to change that situation, I developed a geographical contact program.

This program is designed for positive peer pressure, by assigning key young people in the class to be responsible for their geographical areas. When a person has been absent from the study, the leader will contact him or her by phone. The procedure we use is as follows:

1. Identify yourself.
2. "We missed you at the study."
3. Prayer request?
4. "Thanks for your time; just calling to show we care and that we miss you!"
   Comments: ______________________________
   ____
   ____

This procedure has been very effective in getting teens to encourage their peers to be involved. It is an excellent way to develop sincerity of Christian love in young people, as they have an opportunity to challenge and encourage others through the love of Christ. This program has built consistency and commitment into our young people. It is also of a great help in this contact program to stress the fact that the study is *their* study, not the church's, and only the individual commitment of the teens will "make it happen."

To implement this program, it's essential to pick key leaders to do the calling, have study leaders keep accurate weekly attendance records, and set up a master list of all young people according to geographical area.

Before the first week of the study, have your key leaders call all young people in the class to invite them to the study in their area. Or, the youth pastor could send personal invitations to each person.

This personal contacting has been beneficial to the tremendous growth of our studies this past year from 35 to 115 people average per week. It builds responsibility into your key leaders and commitment into your youth.

Bible Reading Journal

One of the key objectives in having a weekly high-school study is building the desire into young people to study God's Word so that their lives might be changed. They need to learn to feed themselves. They must *want* to learn.

The first phase of accomplishing this task is to get them to *daily* study their lessons for the next week's study. We need to establish patterns of Bible study in their lives *now,* or there's a good chance they will never discipline themselves later in life.

After the studies are over, I stress that they continue their consistency in having a set devotional time in the morning with the Lord. "Our Daily Bread" by Radio Bible Class is a good starter for this.

A chart I developed to aid this effort of establishing their patterns of study is shown in Figure 1.

Prayer Sheets

There are two major emphases in each of our studies and our Sunday school class: Bible study and prayer. A person cannot get to know anyone, including God, unless he communicates with Him.

I stress a pattern of Christian maturity with our young people that looks like this:

- You cannot serve or love a God whom you do not know. Get to know Him through study and prayer.
- Your concept of God determines your confidence in Him.
- Your confidence in God determines your conduct (daily obedience).
- Therefore, your study and prayer life lead to your *concept* of God, which leads to your

Figure 1

Bible Reading Journal

Sunday Date ____________
Scripture I read today: ____________
What I learned today: ____________
____
____
____
What I'm going to do about it: ______
____
____
____

Monday Date ____________
Scripture I read today: ____________
What I learned today: ____________
____
____
____
What I'm going to do about it: ______
____
____
____

Tuesday Date ____________
Scripture I read today: ____________
What I learned today: ____________
____
____
____
What I'm going to do about it: ______
____
____
____

Wednesday Date ____________
Scripture I read today: ____________
What I learned today: ____________
____
____
____
What I'm going to do about it: ______
____
____
____

Thursday Date ____________
Scripture I read today: ____________
What I learned today: ____________
____
____
____
What I'm going to do about it: ______
____
____
____

Friday Date ____________
Scripture I read today: ____________
What I learned today: ____________
____
____
____
What I'm going to do about it: ______
____
____
____

Saturday Date ____________
Scripture I read today: ____________
What I learned today: ____________
____
____
____
What I'm going to do about it: ______
____
____
____

confidence in God, which leads you to *conduct* of a daily walk of obedience with God. (See Figure 2.)

As our young people follow this formula for Christian maturity and growth, God builds into their lives a commitment to service and self-sacrifice, to His glory.

In our studies, we stress keeping prayer sheets (Figure 2). These sheets are used to take weekly requests. We also stress the memorizing of the verses regarding prayer, which are typed onto the sheets. This prayer sheet has helped stabilize the prayer lives of many of our young people.

Without this prayer emphasis, your studies will go nowhere, and neither will the lives of your youth. They *must* want to learn to pray (Luke 11:1) and to study God's Word (Ps. 1:1–2).

Visitation

Another key project that has been used in our studies that has built both our Sunday school class and Bible-study attendance is home visitation.

If after two phone calls from our contact program the young person doesn't come, I have my key leaders visit him in his home.

Before we visit, we call and ask permission to come. The visits again are positive peer pressure designed to encourage active participation in our program. The visit is a "love visit," very low-key to show we care about the individual.

We visit by geographical areas, just like our contact program, so you have peers visiting those they usually go to school with. The contacts may even be made in the schools if necessary and convenient.

Discipleship

The last project that we have implemented into our Bible studies is discipleship.

The reason I began this discipleship process is because three years ago, whenever we had an activity, especially a service project, ten girls showed up for every guy! The young men lacked leadership development. I then decided to hand pick a group of five young men to train them according to 2 Timothy 2:2, "And the things you have heard me say in the presence of many witnesses entrust to reliable men who will also be qualified to teach others."

Figure 2

Prayer Concerns

DAILY

"Evening, morning and noon I cry out in distress, and he hears my voice" (Ps. 55:17).

"But seek first his kingdom and his righteousness, and all these things will be given to you" (Matt. 6:33).

REQUESTS:

1. ____________ 4. ____________
2. ____________ 5. ____________
3. ____________ 6. ____________

SUNDAY

"Seek the LORD while he may be found; call on him while he is near" (Isa. 55:6).

"Let us then approach the throne of grace with confidence, so that we may receive mercy and find grace to help us in our time of need" (Heb. 4:16).

REQUESTS:

1. ____________ 4. ____________
2. ____________ 5. ____________
3. ____________ 6. ____________

MONDAY

"Do not be anxious about anything, but in everything, by prayer and petition, with thanksgiving, present your requests to God. And the peace of God, which transcends all understanding, will guard your hearts and your minds in Christ Jesus" (Phil. 4:6–7).

"Delight yourself in the LORD and he will give you the desires of your heart" (Ps. 37:4).

REQUESTS:

1. ____________ 4. ____________
2. ____________ 5. ____________
3. ____________ 6. ____________

TUESDAY

"Trust in the LORD with all your heart and lean not on your own understanding; in all your ways acknowledge him, and he will make your paths straight" (Prov. 3:5–6).

"We will give our attention to prayer and the ministry of the word" (Acts 6:4).

REQUESTS:

1. ____________ 4. ____________
2. ____________ 5. ____________
3. ____________ 6. ____________

Etc.

Today those five young people have multiplied into a program of 75 (50 youth, 25 lay leaders)! Our male-female ratio is 50–50 and we have *strong* male leadership in the class now.

This discipleship—training young men to serve the Lord and to dare to be different—has revolutionized our class. These young men exert most of the positive peer pressure in the class. I simply cannot say enough about the importance of discipling young men for the Lord.

As Isaiah 55:11 says, "God's word . . . will not return . . . empty." Lives are changed. And now these young men are changing others' lives, according to Proverbs 27:17, "As iron sharpens iron, so one man sharpens another."

I keep an evaluation form on our discipleship activities. It is shown in Figure 3.

CONCLUSION

Having spent eight years working with high-school Bible studies administered through the local church, I am convinced of their validity in building youth programs and in changing young lives. Our studies have gone from an edification emphasis to an evangelism emphasis because our young people have been prepared to penetrate the public schools with the gospel of Jesus Christ. As you train young people in church to serve the Lord with their lives, use Bible studies to supplement that process.

ADDITIONAL READING AND RESOURCE MATERIALS

Ed and Bobbie Reed, *Creative Bible Learning*. Glendale, CA: Gospel Light Publications, 1977.

The Navigators. *Lead Out*. Colorado Springs: Navpress, 1974.

Larry Richards, *Creative Bible Teaching*. Chicago: Moody Press, 1970.

G. Coleman Luck, *The Bible, Book by Book*. Chicago: Moody Press, 1955.

Merrill F. Unger, *Unger's Bible Dictionary*. Chicago: Moody Press, 1973.

Figure 3

Discipleship Evaluation Form

1. Leader's Name ______________________________
   Date ______________________________
2. Disciple's Name ______________________________
3. Present Material Being Used ______________________________
   ____
4. How often have you met in the last month? ____________________
5. On a scale of 1 to 10, evaluate the disciple in these areas:
   a. Being teachable ________
   b. Consistency in:
      1) prayer ________
      2) study of Word ________
      3) meeting with you ________
      4) memorizing Scripture ________
      5) walk with Christ ________
   c. Building relationship with peers (making friends) ________
   d. Having an attitude of servanthood ________
   e. Humility ________
   f. Witnessing (concern for lost souls) ________
   g. Knowing the Word ________
   h. Self-discipline ________
   i. Self-confidence ________
   j. Overall responsibility ________
   k. Submission to authority (obedience) ________
   l. Attaining an attitude of glorifying God at any cost ________
   m. Living out a life of love, giving ________
   n. Being a follower, in general ________
   o. Being a leader ________
   p. Balanced Christian character ________
   q. Fearing God ________
   r. Willingness to serve ________
   s. Trusting God ________

III PROVIDING ACTIVITIES WITH PURPOSE

14

Planning an Event

Being elected the vice-president of his freshman class in college was supposed to be the easiest job in the world. After all, Wally's only responsibility was to look political and he was good at that. As good as he was at looking political, Harvey, the class president, was equally adept at sounding political. In fact, when Harvey decided to transfer to a state school after first semester, Wally inherited a list of campaign promises that included, among other fantasies, the initiation of a radio program produced and sponsored by the freshman class. The sum total of Wally's radio experience included starring as a Bible quizzer on "Kiddies Kollege" at age 10 and sitting with the engineer as "Grace and Glory" was broadcast from his dad's church. How in the world was an 18-year-old freshman supposed to plan such an event?

Whenever he went to retreats with other groups, Tom's group, or so it seemed to his sponsors, was always the largest, noisiest, most energetic, and creative. This year it was going to be different. The sponsors would plan and execute their own retreat! But guess who received the job of pulling the whole event together? Right! The Youth Director! But where was he to start?

Mark H. Senter III is Assistant Professor of Christian Education at Trinity Evangelical Divinity School, Deerfield, Illinois.

Christmas programs at church had always seemed like an exercise in mediocrity, until one year the pastor envisioned turning the front of the sanctuary into a Disneyland of Christmas festivities—five life-sized houses representing different countries, 250 children bedecked in lively costumes, a 10-piece orchestra, special lighting effects, and microphones to pick up the speaking parts of even the tiniest kindergarten child. Again the question arose, how does one go about planning for such an event?

Though each of the above situations is unique, there is a common strain that runs through all of them. Each was an event that had to be planned in order to be executed. As I have evaluated the procedures that were used in these and hundreds of other "events," it would appear that there are a number of basic and, for the most part, uncomplicated procedures that can be taken in order to adequately plan an event.

STEP 1: PROPOSE

In any group of people, three distinct types can be found: creators, organizers, and doers. The smallest group is the creators—those who can take an old idea, add new or different elements, and come up with a concept that appears refreshing and meaningful. Organizers, the second category of people, are those who are quite willing and even eager to work with the creators in order to get an idea into working order. Doers, by far the largest group, are those who enjoy doing what they are asked to do in order to accomplish a larger task to which they are committed.

Figure 4

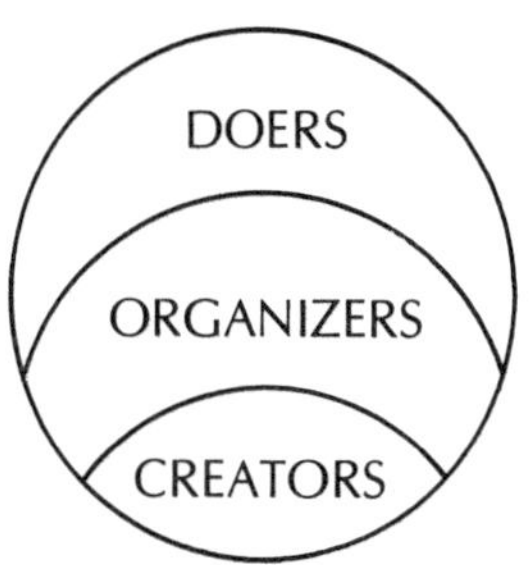

Though a youth minister may have more than one of these ministry strengths, he may find himself frustrated in other areas of his ministry. Actually this is quite normal. To ask a creator to organize may frustrate him to distraction. To ask an organizer to do a job may be the death knell for that assignment. Conversely, to ask a doer to organize may frustrate everyone involved, and to ask an organizer to create may merely insure a continuation of whatever has happened in the past.

Fortunately, the body of Christ was not designed for every youth minister to be the creator of every ministry event for young people. Nor does it require that he organize every event. However, the leadership position in which he finds himself does require that he adequately perform one or the other of these functions. In so doing, the wise youth minister will draw on the strengths of other believers in order to accomplish his objectives in the most effective manner possible.

The proposal stage of planning tends to be part of the creator's function. It begins with the *identification of a need* in the lives of people to whom he ministers. Through a parent or the senior pastor, a student or club leader may observe the need and bring it to the attention of the youth minister; usually it is the youth minister who is among the first to identify a need in the lives of the students and takes steps to meet that need. At times these steps may even include a large event such as a retreat, seminar, missionary trip, program, or concert.

In order for real needs to be met or partially met through an event, specific *purposes* for the event need to be clearly established at the outset. The purposes should be clear, concise, and measurable. For a winter retreat the purposes might be:

1. To provide an outdoor winter activity for 60 high-school students in a setting away from home.
2. To confront the students with the lordship of Jesus Christ and its implications for their lives.
3. To provide at least one cross-country skiing experience for each student attending.

It will be on the basis of the purposes established at the outset that the event will be evaluated in STEP 5.

If the event in any way varies from the past program, there will probably be the necessity to *sell* the concept to certain key people before the idea ever gets off the ground. This may take time.

Several years ago I came up with the idea of bicycling around Lake Michigan on a concert tour. As you can imagine, I had to do a lot of selling. First, I had to convince a reluctant music director that it was a realistic possibility; then, the Christian Education deacon had to be persuaded that it could pay for itself; next, the executive committee of the youth group had to be challenged to think and act in a way greater than they had ever acted before—the youth group as a whole and specifically the musical group had to be sold on the idea; finally, parents had to be convinced that this activity was in the best interest of their children.

Other churches will have differing procedures through which the youth minister will have to go to "sell" the event, but seldom will the event succeed if it has not been properly explained to the people who are involved in the decision-making process.

The final step in the proposal stage is that of *approval*. Who does the approving will vary from organization to organization, but the event is doomed to failure without clearing the idea with the proper authorities ahead of time. Seldom do you sell everyone on a new idea. Thus the key issue becomes, did you sell the right people—the people who can make or break the event? This approval nearly always includes the blessing of the senior pastor or the area director of a parachurch organization. It usually includes influential persons on the Christian education committee or youth council. Invariably, approval must be obtained from the opinion leaders in the church who may force an informal veto to ideas in which they do not have confidence. Practically, the funding body must grant permission. If any funding will be needed from the sponsoring organization, even as backup support, those who are financially responsible must be adequately informed.

The first time the youth minister attempts to plan an event, the proposal stage will seem endless. However, if he does his job well and does not attempt to short-circuit the process, he will find that in succeeding attempts to plan major events, the confidence that people have placed in him because of the way in which he conducted himself previously, will greatly reduce the time needed for the selling process.

STEP 2: ORGANIZE

Last spring I was asked to put together a thirteen-week television program focused on one aspect of the educational process. It was a task I had never undertaken before, nor had I ever taken a course or even read a book on the subject of television programing. Though the task seemed incredibly large, my experiences as a youth minister had taught me how to take the large assignments and break them down into manageable parts. So I took the six interrogatives that I would have used to prepare for a retreat and applied them to an entirely new "event" and put together a well-received program.

The organization stage of the planning tends, logically enough, to be the function of the organizers. It is the organizer's responsibility to take the idea of a creator, be it himself or someone else, and make it happen.

The first question that the organizer must ask is, *Why?* This is the same question that was raised by the creator as he tied the needs of the students to proposed event in STEP 1 of the planning process. The organizer has to be sure that these purposes are firmly fixed in his mind or the activity may fall far short of the expectations of the creator, as well as of those who have given their blessings to the event.

Traditions are established quickly in a youth ministry. An activity that is well-received one year suddenly becomes an expected part of the next year's program. In his desire to have a ministry similar to that of the previous year, or in the case of a new person on the job, a ministry as meaningful as that of the previous youth minister, the *Why* question may be assumed and therefore never clearly defined. The result could easily become activity for activity's sake with little or no lasting spiritual impact. Thus it is essential that the *Why* question be clearly answered in the minds of each of the organizers and doers, as well as in the mind of the creator.

The second question that the organizer should ask is, *Who?* Who will be needed to staff the event? Who are the people that can provide the specialized expertise that will be required to enable us to obtain our stated goals? This could be a special speaker, a drama coach, a ski instructor, an outfitter, a cook, or a number of others in leadership roles essential to the whole activity. The next logical step is to put names beside each of those responsibilities. In order to discover who is available, the mature youth minister may have to beat the bushes asking everyone available for suggestions as to who could accomplish these tasks for purposes of the event that is being planned. Then people must be approached to see if they would be available to use their abilities in this particular ministry. If adequate personnel is not available, the wise organizer will be well advised to postpone any further planning until a complete staff can be assembled.

It should be noted here that seldom does the organizer have his ideal staff. In fact, if he is able to recruit his ideal staff each time, there is a distinct possibility that his ideals are not high enough. The organizer must determine therefore which staff members are essential to accomplish the stated goals and be sure that those people are available.

When the organizer is confident that he will be able to adequately staff the event, the next question that must be asked is, *What?* What will each of these people be expected to do and in what way will they be expected to get their job done? Perhaps the best way to explain to one's staff what is expected of them is to give them in writing a list of their responsibilities. This is commonly called a job description. Its purpose is to eliminate misunderstandings and to keep all participants working as a team.

Task descriptions may also prove to be helpful when the organizer would like to have a responsibility performed in a specific manner. It may save a lot of grief on the part of very capable people if they know ahead of time exactly how high the props must be for the play, or what criteria should be used for making assignments of roommates, or how much can be spent for the program at the spring banquet.

Where? is basically a question of facilities. There will be no ski trip unless there is a ski lodge of some description. There will be no spring banquet unless someone has signed a contract with the restaurant that the committee has selected. It can be an awful feeling to come into the church gym, psyched for an all-night volleyball game, only to discover it decorated for a wedding reception because no one had bothered to clear the event with the church calendar.

As a general rule, the more desirable the facility and the more appealing the time of the year, the further in advance the facility will have to be scheduled. This is, if for no other reason, an incentive for starting the planning process early.

The fifth major question that must be asked is, *When?* It is a question of both time and timing. The time aspect of the question may seem painfully obvious, but there is more than meets the eye at first glance. For example, suppose that a graduation banquet is being planned and the date is set for Saturday,

May 23. It is the intent of the banquet committee to have the junior class honor the graduating seniors. However, overlooked is the fact that the SAT (Scholastic Aptitude Test) is being given that day and most of the juniors attending the church are planning to take the test. The result may be a banquet that lacks the support of the very people who are essential to honor the seniors. And why did this happen? It was probably because someone did not take the *When* question seriously, especially in light of the purposes of the event.

The timing portion of the question may be equally important if the stated objectives are to be reached. Do you have enough time to adequately put together the proposed event? The best way to determine this question is by outlining everything that must take place before the proposed event can happen and then placing a calendar beside the outline in order to determine if the work can reasonably be done in the time allotted.

For more complicated events such as a denominational conference, retreat, or a television program, the planners may want to use a PERT (Program Evaluation and Review Technique) chart in order to diagram and sequence everything that must take place in the preparation process. The PERT chart shown in Figure 5 is an example of how the planning for a retreat might appear.

The last question that needs to be asked in the organization step of preparation is the question, *With What?* It is essentially a question of cost and equipment. Before the event is announced to the students who will be involved, the question of financing must be answered. How much will the students be expected to pay? How much will youth group leaders and/or sponsors be encouraged to contribute? Will there be financial backing from the sponsoring organization? Are there any other sources to which the organizers could go in order to raise money for the activity?

In most communities, the resources of the students are limited and therefore the question must be asked, "What is the most that the students, sponsor, or church can pay without pricing the event out of range?" In order to answer this question, the organizer would be wise to develop a philosophy of

Figure 5

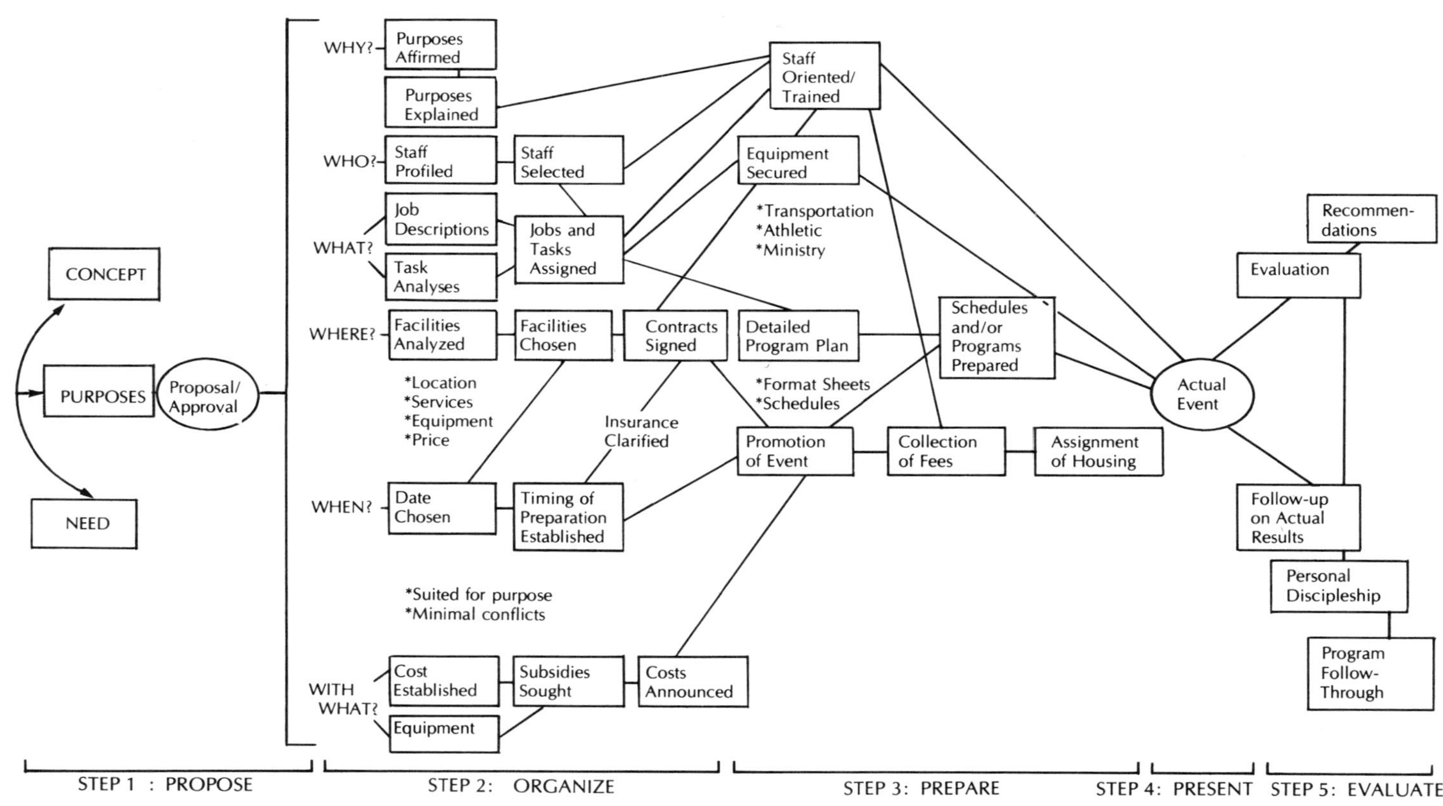

CONCEPT
PURPOSES
NEED
Proposal/ Approval
WHY?
Purposes Affirmed
Purposes Explained
WHO?
Staff Profiled
Staff Selected
WHAT?
Job Descriptions
Task Analyses
Jobs and Tasks Assigned
WHERE?
Facilities Analyzed
Facilities Chosen
Contracts Signed
*Location
*Services
*Equipment
*Price
Insurance Clarified
WHEN?
Date Chosen
Timing of Preparation Established
*Suited for purpose
*Minimal conflicts
WITH WHAT?
Cost Established
Equipment
Subsidies Sought
Costs Announced
Staff Oriented/ Trained
Equipment Secured
*Transportation
*Athletic
*Ministry
Detailed Program Plan
*Format Sheets
*Schedules
Promotion of Event
Schedules and/or Programs Prepared
Collection of Fees
Assignment of Housing
Actual Event
Evaluation
Recommen- dations
Follow-up on Actual Results
Personal Discipleship
Program Follow- Through
STEP 1 : PROPOSE
STEP 2: ORGANIZE
STEP 3: PREPARE
STEP 4: PRESENT
STEP 5: EVALUATE

how major events will be funded. There are three primary models for funding youth events:

- Self-supporting: Each event will be funded by the fees paid by the students. Thus ministry expense, transportation, sponsor expense, as well as room and board, will be paid by the student.
- Partial Support: Each student will be expected to pay for his own room, board, and fun while the sponsoring organization will pay for the ministry costs and at least part of the transportation costs.
- Scholarship Approach: Each student will be asked to pay an amount that is attainable for his family's budget and the sponsoring organization will secure scholarship money to cover the difference between income and actual costs.

For some events a free-will offering would seem to be a sufficient means of raising the needed financing. However, it should be kept in mind that students tend to be notoriously poor givers when it comes to offering time. If this method of financing is chosen, the youth minister would be well-advised to instruct his students that a minimum donation of a specified amount will be expected from each student at the offering time.

In order to accurately project the cost of an event such as a retreat, one church developed a budget activity planning sheet. The purpose of the sheet is to estimate, as accurately as possible, the costs of the event and then compare actual expenditures with projected expenditures. In the first section of the sheet, the expected expenditures are listed. This includes everything from room and board and honorariums to the cost of whipped cream for the skit night. The second part of the form is used to list the expected income. This is generally tabulated by multiplying the price charged to the students by the number who could reasonably be expected to attend. In that the church's policy allows for the subsidy of ministry and transportation expense, the third section of the form is designed to indicate the budget account from which the difference between expense and income will be drawn. (See Figure 6.)

Figure 6

Activity Budget Form

Activity ______________________ Date ______________
Location ______________________ Distance ______________
Number involved ______________________ Leader ______________

EXPENDITURES		Projected	Actual
Transportation	______	______	______
Meals	______	______	______
Lodging	______	______	______
Insurance	______	______	______
Special equipment	______	______	______
Program expense			
Fees	______	______	______
Transportation	______	______	______
Rentals	______	______	______
Miscellaneous	______	______	______
	______	______	______
TOTAL EXPENSES		______	______

INCOME		Projected	Actual
Fees (no. and rate)	______	______	______
Other sources	______	______	______
	______	______	______
TOTAL INCOME		______	______

CHURCH SUBSIDY		Projected	Actual
Account Number	______	______	______
Account Number	______	______	______
Account Number	______	______	______
TOTAL SUBSIDY		______	______

Waiver forms used

____

Budget Approval ______ ______

Though a primary answer to the *With What?* question lies in the area of money, a second part to the answer must be answered in terms of equipment. Adequate sound systems, props for skits, athletic equipment, movies and projectors do not just materialize when retreat time rolls around; they have to be secured in advance. Follow spots, special sound effects, scenic backdrops, and appropriate costumes for the youth-night play must be planned for far enough in advance to allow the equipment to be borrowed, rented, or built. All of this needs to be identified and planned by the organizer.

STEP 3: PREPARE

With the task of organizing the event well in hand, the preparation phase of the event is primarily the responsibility of following through on the plans that have already been set in motion. Though in many ways the preparation phase is where the work is done, many youth ministers find that following up on the details that will mean the difference between just another activity and an excellent event is anything but challenging. At this point the organizer may want to call on a gifted "doer" to follow up on these essential details. The fortunate youth minister may be able to call on his secretary to handle these tasks. For others, a sponsor or parent gifted as a doer may be the perfect answer. However, the wise youth minister will keep in close contact with his assistant to make sure that the important preparations are taking place.

In STEP 3 four essential functions will take place, each of which is an extension of the questions answered in STEP 2. The first function is that of programing. The organizer will probably want to stay in close contact with the creator at this point as the whole flow of the event is committed to paper. This is especially crucial when a dramatic presentation or a program using a variety of participants is envisioned. For a banquet, or an annual review of ministries, a talent show or a Christmas program, the wise youth minister will draw up a format sheet that designates timing, location, sound, and lighting so that little is left to guesswork (Figure 7).

The second function in the preparation phase is that of training. The organizer himself will probably want to perform this activity, for it is the orientation

Figure 7

Program Format Worksheet

Event ____

Day ______________ Date ____________________ Time ________ AM PM

Time	Program Item	Personality	Sound	Lights	Misc

and/or training of the doers to actually bring the proposed event to a desired conclusion. The training may be as simple as a meeting for all the participants in a monthly youth night at which time each person actually walks through his activity in the program. (Who do I follow? Where do I stand? When do I start? Where do I go when I'm done?) Or it may include a series of meetings or rehearsals as determined by the nature of the event.

Equipping is the third step. Simply stated, all of the equipment identified in STEP 2 needs to be gathered and taken to the location where the particular event will take place. A check list might be helpful in order to assure not only that equipment gets to the location, but that it gets home after the event is concluded. Figure 8 is an example of a list that might be designed for a retreat.

The final aspect of the preparation stage is that of promoting. It is very important that the purposes of the event be kept clearly in mind as publicity is being created. There needs to be "truth in packaging" and at the same time a flavor of excitement about the event. Without going into a long explanation of how to publicize an event, perhaps a list of helpful promotional ideas would expand the thinking of the promoter. These could include:

1. Word of mouth
2. Attractive brochure
3. Direct mail
4. Announcement by pastor
5. Announcement by youth minister
6. Bulletin-board feature
7. Bulletin announcement
8. Skits
9. Any of the crazy ideas from the promotion section of the Ideas Books, published by Youth Specialties.

STEP 4: PRESENT

Take heart! The time has now come for the actual event to take place and if anything can go wrong, it will. During the infamous flight of Apollo 13 when the American Space Program nearly lost three astronauts in outer space due to an explosion in the space capsule, a television commentator sagely remarked as the safe recovery of the astronauts seemed

Figure 8

Retreat Checklist

MINISTRY EQUIPMENT	Going	Returning
Slides and trays	______	______
Song books	______	______
Movies	______	______
Handouts	______	______
Extension cords	______	______
Pencils	______	______
Screen	______	______
Musical instruments	______	______
Movie projector	______	______
Sound system	______	______
Slide projector	______	______
Ice breakers	______	______
Overhead projector	______	______
Overhead transparencies	______	______
Other items		
______	______	______
______	______	______
______	______	______

ATHLETIC EQUIPMENT	Going	Returning
Indoor games		
______	______	______
______	______	______
______	______	______
______	______	______
Outdoor games		
______	______	______
______	______	______
______	______	______
______	______	______
Game books/file	______	______

ACTIVITIES	Going	Returning
Props		
Awards		
Book table		
Reading materials for loan		
Other items		

ADMINISTRATION	Going	Returning
First-aid kit		
Permission slips		
Home phone numbers		
Room assignment list		
Schedules		
Rules		

FOOD	Going	Returning
Cooking Utensils		
Plates		
Napkins		
Eating utensils		
Food supplies		

Disposal bags	______	______
Detergent	______	______
Wash pads	______	______
Wash cloths	______	______
Towels	______	______
Stoves	______	______
Fuel	______	______
Matches	______	______

HOUSING	Going	Returning
Tents (No. ______)	______	______

imminent, "Well, you can't plan for everything, but nothing substitutes for planning."

I used to be on a church staff with a man who would pray for everything from the straps on the luggage racks to the plugs on the microphone cords prior to an event. His reasons, based on years of experience, were simple: It is usually the little things that go wrong and stymie months of preparation and prayer.

The actual presentation or execution of an event contains many of the same components as a football game.

Stick to the game plan!

It is very easy for the talented and ministry-oriented minister of youth to completely scuttle several months of planning because he senses that the flow of the program is not what he had anticipated. Though there is a time to deviate from the plans developed over a period of team planning, it should be considered an action of last resort rather than an initial reaction. Similarly, the changing of the game plan should be a group decision participated in by all of the key leaders in the event that time allows for such a discussion. It should be noted that the longer the program (retreats, trips, conferences) the more possibility there is to participate in the decision-making process. For short events (rallies, plays, concerts, services), one key person should be entrusted with the responsibility of determining when and how the game plan will be altered.

Communicate!

Though the quarterback is calling the signals in the huddle, he has received a wealth of information from various sources prior to making that call. The scout in the press box has given information to the coach, the coach has spotted a weakness in the interior line of the other team, the split end has discovered that the injury of the free safety limits his ability to cut to the left and so the quarterback (or coach if he is calling the plays) takes all of this information into consideration before calling the next play.

A system of communication must be established before the event is under way. Frequently this is the part of the process that is discussed least during the preparation time and desired most during the presentation time. Longer events may merely require staff meetings at least once a day. Shorter events may require a set of hand signals such as might be used in a broadcast studio or, for more elaborate productions, a set of producer's headsets in order to ensure a smooth flow of the program toward the conclusion to which the Lord has directed through your weeks and months of preparation.

Concentrate!

In the well-planned event, everyone has a specific task assigned to him and if he does not execute his assigned responsibility, then someone else will have to carry an extra load. Two dangers are always present here. First, a person can become so caught up in the flow of the program that he is caught off guard when his time to participate occurs. The second problem is found in the opposite direction. He can become so involved in the details of the event that he ceases to be aware of the working of the Holy Spirit in the process. It can become similar to the surgeon who performed successful surgery to replace a faulty heart valve, but due to other complications the patient died.

Expect the best!

After all, to the best of your knowledge, your "game plan" is in harmony with the God of the universe, so why should it not result in the best possible response? For too long evangelicals have settled for mediocrity in the name of piety. Perhaps it would be wise for the youth minister to bring his expectations in line with his theology—"God saw all that he had made, and it was very good" (Gen. 1:31).

STEP 5: EVALUATE

The final stage of planning for any event and the first stage in planning for the next event is the evaluation step. Evaluation is based on the goals that were established before the event began.

In light of the goals, only three questions need to be asked: "What did we do right?" "What did we do poorly?" "What should we change if we do the event again?" These three questions will cover most of the elements that need to be analyzed before the next event is planned.

Five words should characterize the evaluation: broad, prompt, specific, written, and follow-up.

The evaluation should be *broad* enough to reflect the thinking of a healthy cross section of the people involved. Ideally, the cross section should include input from planners, participants, and spectators.

The evaluation should be *prompt.* It might be a wise idea to ask the participants to provide a preliminary evaluation of the event as the program draws to a conclusion. This is best done by providing the participants with an evaluation form that will facilitate the process. The final evaluation, however, should be postponed for at least three days in order to allow the evaluators to recover from the elation or discouragement of the event and regain an objective perspective. It is not wise, on the other hand, to allow the evaluation to be separated from the actual event by too great a time because then the effectiveness of the process may be diminished by the fact that the evaluators may have forgotten some of their key impressions.

The evaluation must also be *specific* if it is to be effective. Such statements as, "The speaker was excellent," or "Discipline was handled poorly," do not tend to be very helpful when the next event is being planned. Perhaps the key phrase in the evaluation process is "as evidenced by. . . ." The evaluators may choose to make the general evaluation, "the speaker was excellent," but then amplify it by providing a personal observation, "as evidenced by the hours that I saw the speaker and the counselors spend in follow-up appointments," or "as evidenced by Toni Johnson when she commented that the lordship of Jesus Christ had never made much sense to her until she heard Bill speak on Saturday night."

The specific evaluation should be done in the light of the objectives stated at the outset of the planning process. Many times the Lord will choose to work directly through the entire event as it was conceived and executed. On such occasions the evaluation process might even become a praise meeting. On the other hand, the Lord may have chosen to work in spite of the planning (or lack of planning) or to have totally surprised the leadership by doing something quite unexpected and entirely apart from the objectives as originally conceived. These, too, should be praise times, but in addition, the evaluation should focus on how the event might be made more conducive for the Holy Spirit to work the next time a similar event is planned.

The evaluation should be *written.* Even though

Figure 9

Conference Evaluation Sheet

To be turned in at the business meeting on Sunday evening.

GENERAL EVALUATION (Please check one answer for each question.)

	Great	Better Than Expected	So-So	Weak	Forget It!
1. How would you rate the week as a whole?					
2. How would you rate the Bible hour (8:45 A.M.)?					
3. How would you rate the workshop, seminar, or fellowship module that you attended?					
4. How would you rate quizzing this year?					
5. How would you rate music competition this year?					
6. How would you rate oral communication this year?					
7. How would you rate written communication this year?					
8. How would you rate projected communication this year?					
9. How did you enjoy the evening features? (8:00 P.M.)					
10. How did you enjoy the banquet?					
11. How did you like the location of the conference?					
12. How did you like the dates of the conference ? (fourth week in June)					

SPECIFIC EVALUATION

1. What changes would you make if you were planning the conference for next year?

2. What workshop, seminar, or fellowship module would you like to see included in next year's conference?

3. What workshop, seminar, or fellowship module did you attend?

4. Did the fact that the conference met the week after another conference provide any hardship for you?

5. Please use the reverse side for further comments.

all of the people involved in the evaluation process may seem to agree as to what their evaluations of the event were, a year from now when the next activity is being planned, it is unlikely that the same group will totally agree on what they had said or on the course of action suggested for future events. To complicate the picture, youth ministry is plagued by a high rate of turnover, so unless the evaluation has been committed to writing, the planning process for the next event may have to start from ground zero.

Finally, the evaluation should suggest a course of *follow-up*. This may involve recommendations as to how the ministry of the event could be extended in the most effective manner or why such events should be discontinued. It may suggest organized follow-through activities or individualized contacts by youth workers. It may mean immediate activity or a preparation process for a similar type activity for the following year. It may involve the altering of ongoing programs in order to adequately respond to the newly discovered needs or merely continuing the existing program with new enthusiasm. Whatever is suggested, it should be done with the conscious effort to bring glory to God by purposeful activity rather than by ecclesiastical default.

CONCLUSION

The principles of preparing for events presented in this chapter could apply to anything from a political rally to a band boosters' club. The reason these concepts have been included in this book is not to supplant the work of the Holy Spirit but to provide the Spirit of the living God the most effective tool available for His use. After all, why should the hosts of darkness have a corner on the market of effective planning and presentation?

On the other hand, there may be the tendency for the people who are preparing for an event to become so caught up in the process that they begin to trust more in the system than in the Lord of the system. This danger is equally grave, if not more so, than the danger of sloppy planning, for the polished producers can easily slip into the mold of the religious manipulators.

The key to avoiding these two extremes is a pure heart dominated by the qualities of love found in 1 Corinthians 13; submission to the Holy Spirit as described in Ephesians 5; and a lifestyle that seeks first the kingdom of God and His righteousness as described in the words of the Lord Jesus Christ in Matthew 5–7.

15

Ministering in the Wilderness

Today's young people are being bombarded from every side with hedonistic values. They are fed a diet of predigested secondary experiences and, living inconsequentially, they find themselves too involved at the moment to examine these experiences and are compelled onward by their peers. It is no wonder that youth workers investigate every new program and ministry tool on the market that could possibly enhance their work with this complex age group. Some discover that the wilderness is such a tool.

The wilderness has been used as a training ground for young people throughout history. It is here that young men and women alike make the transition from childhood to adulthood by confronting the dangers and challenges inherent in wilderness living. In many cultures, this experience is a rite of passage into adulthood.

Many biblical characters fled to the wilderness to seek refuge and gain a new perspective—Moses, Elijah, David, and the children of Israel spent much time there. Even Jesus went to the wilderness to confirm His true character and at various points in His ministry for renewal.

Bud Williams is Associate Professor of Physical Education at Wheaton College. He coordinates the recreation ministries program and helped initiate and direct the Vanguard and Wilderness Learning Seminars for over fifteen years.

WHAT IS THE WILDERNESS?

It is that which is in direct contrast to what has been domesticated by man. The wilderness is that area of life yet to be tamed by him, is uninhabited by him, and is capable of overpowering his best efforts. God has made the wilderness, and only He has complete control over it. It presents a challenge to the supremacy of man. There are many situations in which man can confront the wilderness and learn, but for the purposes of this chapter we will confine ourselves to the wilderness of nature.

God used the wilderness *to isolate His people* so they could reflect on their values without the pagan culture influences that inhibit the development of godly moral values. He used the wilderness *to teach new values.* God used the wilderness *to test His people.* For each of His promises, He provided tests so that the children of Israel could prove Him faithful and respond in obedience to Him. Finally, God used the wilderness *to demonstrate His love* for His people. He always met their needs, revealing Himself as the powerful Creator and the all-sufficient Provider.

USING THE WILDERNESS AS A TOOL FOR MINISTRY

The wilderness can still offer isolation from pagan cultural influences. Because it is an unfamiliar setting to most people, it often has a neutralizing effect on them, and here we can introduce a Christian value system based on biblical concepts. The support of Christian peers and the example of leadership models, combined with exposure to Christian values in a community life setting, can have a powerful impact on the participants. Rather than simply hearing someone expound on Christian values, they have the opportunity to see these values "fleshed out" in life. The primary experiences and consequences of wilderness living place learning on the behavioral level: young people are confronted with unavoidable real-life situations where their values are put to the test and their actions have immediate feedback.

Isolated in the wilderness, members of a small group soon realize the necessity of being self-sufficient. They begin to understand their accountability for decisions of immediate consequence. This sense of personal accountability provides motivation for right action and helps raise the "creative tension" of the individual in the group. As this tension rises, hidden needs are revealed and the individual feels a strong desire to have these newly felt needs met so that he can become part of a successful functioning group. Real-life conflict becomes the catalyst through which real growth can occur.

There are few other forms of ministry in which the leader has the opportunity to see a problem through to the end relatively quickly, observing and supporting the individual as he attempts to make changes in his own life. In these shared experiences, the leader is brought into the group as a fellow participant, enhancing the effectiveness of his ministry. The role of the leader is that of an active participant in the learning process, to be vulnerable and open to learning himself, to be sensitive to the needs of each member of the group, to plan activities that motivate the participants to meet their needs, to provide input when needed, to clarify, to lovingly support those in the process of growth and change, to confirm, to accept those who fail and emphasize God's grace, and in all these roles to be sensitive to the leading of God's Spirit. This shared experience provides an opportunity for him to be a powerful influence as a model, and he is provided with an ideal vantage point for assessing individual needs. As a result, he is able to more efficiently plan activities to motivate the participants to deal with their needs.

Christian values and principles for the resolution of needs will come from a variety of sources. In a group of Christian young people, Christian values and principles are already understood but may not be applied. Members of the group will usually bring these up. In a non-Christian group, the leader becomes the primary source of this input, introduced when it will have a direct, immediate application.

One of the most important aspects of the growth cycle is reflecting and recording. After the group has struggled with a real-life problem and each member has come to grips with his or her own needs and values and faced the consequences of his or her actions, the group needs to sit down and talk through the experience. Why did they succeed or fail? In what ways did each contribute to or hinder the group's efforts? What values came into conflict? What needs were exposed? What healing must take place? What gifts need to be confirmed? What motives need to be clarified? What misunderstandings need to be cleared up? What has each learned about him/herself, his/her relationship to others, to his/her tasks, to God? What changes need to be made within each person to become successful next time? In what ways did God display His faithfulness? Which other attributes of God were revealed? At this point, confirmation of these advances should take place. Each participant needs time alone to think through and record his/her involvement and the growth that is a result of the experience.

This growth cycle is an ongoing one that takes place for each activity, as well as throughout the total program.

How does a leader go about assessing needs and planning the program based on needs? The more we mature as Christians, the more we are able to see within us the qualities of our Lord, as the Spirit helps us conform to His likeness. These qualities are most exemplified or seen lacking in us as we are thrust up against the struggles and trials of life and the wilderness can provide many of these tests. Beyond those qualities of the Christian life there are also social, mental, and physical skills and abilities that each one has attained to a certain degree. Through the demands of living in a challenging environment, social, mental, and physical skills and abilities are further developed or shown lacking. As the leader attempts to live out these qualities and values of a mature Christian and maximize his social, spiritual, and physical capabilities, he becomes a model for his group, against which they can compare their own lifestyles and values. Through the leader's close involvement he is able to sense those points of tension that test him, and likewise test those in his group.

This ongoing assessment of needs leads to program planning that provides additional challenges to further expose and test those needs. The key to programing is thorough familiarity with a variety of activities, and planned flexibility to introduce activities at a time that can best test and meet individual and group needs.

A MODEL FOR PROGRAM PLANNING

In order to create a program based on meeting the needs of group members, it is first necessary to look at a system for organizing those needs. Abraham Maslow's hierarchy of needs theory states that before a person can concentrate on deeper needs (such as safety), his basic psychological needs (such as minimal amounts of food, sleep, clothing, and shelter) must be met.[1] He is then free to concentrate on his safety and security. Love shown to him allows him to seek self-acceptance. All three of these needs must be met before his needs for self-esteem can be met, often through personal or interpersonal achievements. Once self-worth is attained, he can move on to the deeper needs for self-actualization (or self-fulfillment).

Basic Safety Needs

If we are going to have a program for ministry, we must have people, and we must see to their safety and security if we want their continued participation. It would be inhumane and immoral to endanger the lives of those for whom we are responsible. We must make their health and safety our number-one priority.

Health and safety are always based on attitudes of ultimate concern for the welfare of those placed under our leadership. We should treat each person as we would want to be treated and guard their well-being.

An important factor in the planning of a wilderness experience is the constant assessment of individual capabilities, both before and during the event. Each individual must be deemed to be in good health, physically able to be part of the group, and able to maintain the group's level of stress and endurance. If injuries occur during the event, the leader must determine whether or not the group member is physically able to continue without endangering his own safety or that of the group. There must be a contingency plan for handling serious injuries. In planning for the event, situations should be structured so that they do not exceed the capabilities of the individuals involved. It may push them to a level they've never before achieved, but should not force them beyond what they are truly capable of doing. The event should be planned for the average developmental level of the group and the members of the group should be of a similar developmental level. The leader and staff for the event should be familiar with all aspects of the experience, whether through advance research or contact with an expert who knows the area to which the group will be going. Generally speaking, the experience should be well-planned, with all situations anticipated, but should occur spontaneously.

Beyond being aware of what *could* happen, the leader must be *prepared* for unexpected situations. Weather can change from hot to cold, wet to dry. Health problems and injuries always seem to occur when most inconvenient. An emergency medical kit and someone with a thorough knowledge of first aid and lifesaving are essential, along with a contingency plan for emergencies. Spare equipment is important too.

Good supervision is an important safety factor for wilderness experiences. Don't exceed your limit of how many participants you can *really* supervise at one time.

The ideal ratio of leader to participants is 1 to 9. The group should not exceed 12 or be less than 6 for the sake of safety. An assistant leader is also highly recommended.

Program activities chosen should meet general safety standards. The American Camping Association, Bradford Woods, Martinsville, IN 46151, and Christian Camping International, Box 646, Wheaton, IL 60189, provide basic guidelines and safety checks for activities. Standards for wilderness camping are also available from the U.S. Forest Service and National Park Service. Booklets setting standards for specific wilderness activities such as whitewater canoeing, caving, mountaineering, and backpacking are available at no charge from the U.S. Department of Health, Education and Welfare (Center for Disease Control, Atlanta, GA 30333). This source can also provide suggested statutes for youth camps.

The leader should not only be highly skilled in the activities, but also in dealing with emergencies inherent to each activity. If there is water present (this includes 95% of all wilderness programs) the leader should be qualified as a lifeguard and lifesaver. Extensive first aid and rescue training is important for wilderness leadership . . . much wilderness travel takes place in rugged and isolated terrain. The leader should never be solely dependent on a local rescue group for his emergency needs. The group itself should be the primary source of rescue, with knowledge of available emergency resources a part of the planning process.

There is no excuse for poor planning or inadequately trained leadership. Recent court cases have repeatedly emphasized the leader's responsibility to know all standard safety practices, and to exercise his best judgment. In most cases, the law of precedent or acceptable practice is the deciding factor. Other group leaders who are using similar activities will most likely be brought into court as expert witnesses to determine the common procedure. These expert testimonies then become the standard by which others are judged; therefore, it is important to keep abreast of current practices and safety measures in order to do our best to protect our participants. As Christians, this goes beyond legal obligations to our moral responsibility for others.

Acceptance Needs

After meeting the needs of health and safety, we can then focus on meeting participants' needs for a sense of belonging and acceptance. A person will naturally begin to feel wanted when he sees that his basic physical needs are being met. But he needs more, and the display of deeper interest on the leader's part can expand the participant's perception of his needs being met.

Wilderness living provides many opportunities for the development of a caring relationship. Little things like help in putting on gear, sharing basic knowledge in food preparation, finding and building a shelter, direction finding, and other helps all go together to form an interdependent, caring atmosphere. Structuring activities that require a total group contribution for success encourages group members to follow the leader's caring, helping example. Later, group sharing of how each member contributed to the entire group's success brings greater awareness of the importance of each member to the group. Also, sharing individual interests and expectations can focus attention on individual goals in which all can become involved.

There is a delicate balance between demonstrating a caring attitude and taking away the opportunity for self-discovery and personal achievement by doing too much for individuals and the group. It is easy to go overboard either way. To be aloof or extremely nondirective can stifle the development of a counseling relationship which is necessary for the leader to have input into the growth process. However, to do too much for the individual defeats the ultimate objective of the program, which is to produce maturing persons capable of solving their own problems and appropriating needed resources themselves.

Overprotection is a problem of our affluent culture. As youth leaders and parents, we wrongly protect our youth from the struggles of life. By doing too much for them, we have sheltered them and allowed them to become soft. We have showered them with the rewards earned as a result of our struggles, as symbols of our love, not realizing that it is this very struggle that has made us what we are.

Self-esteem

Success and failure are the means by which a person discovers who he is. Self-esteem is the result of finding and achieving a balance between one's capabilities and limits.

In our society, a few challenges remain that permit the discovery of abilities at a most important time, the transition into adulthood. "Rites of Passage" have existed for past generations, but now they are found less and less frequently. Few young people find it necessary to contribute to the family's economy, or to help with family needs—a farm or business, or caring for ill or dependent family members.

Our society has segregated us by age and ability, and turned much of our responsibility over to institutions—schools, hospitals, nursing homes, governmental agencies, businesses. Young people are *directed* rather than allowed to exercise their own judgment to be responsible for the consequences of their actions. Their very achievements are recognized with abstract symbols, like the letter grades and certificates of the educational world.

The wilderness can set a person against difficult, challenging experiences that measure the limits of his or her capabilities and bring immediate, tangible rewards, and a sense of self-esteem through achievement. As the person learns new skills and develops latent abilities that meet the new demands, he learns about his God-given talents and becomes a more complete and capable person.

Even failure has a place. When a person's limits are exceeded and he fails, he sees his finiteness in a new light. He is reminded of his need for a humble, dependent relationship with his Creator. This realization is difficult to attain in our humanistic culture. God often used the wilderness to make man recognize his limits and, in contrast, the limitless power of God.

Self-fulfillment

As self-esteem is developing through achievement and failure, the opportunity for a deeper level of self-fulfillment and maturity begins to be apparent. Once a person becomes aware of his abilities and develops a sense of self-worth, he can direct those abilities toward the glorification of God through service to others. Matthew 10:38–39 illustrates the paradox of self-fulfillment, "Anyone who does not take his cross and follow me is not worthy of me. Whoever finds his life will lose it, and whoever loses his life for my sake will find it." The wilderness, with its demanding tasks that necessitate cooperation, is an excellent place to discover this truth.

God gives gifts to individuals to help strengthen the body of Christ. These gifts are evident in any group, and help the group member reach a higher level of maturity. The leader should affirm these gifts, and guide the group members in their proper use for the service of others.

LEADERSHIP STYLE

Hersey and Blanchard[2] have popularized "situational leadership," a style often used by successful leaders.

The leader's initial involvement with an immature group is highly task-oriented, with very little emphasis on relationship. As the group matures, the leader gradually shifts to a greater concentration on relationships. The leader continues to emphasize relationships as task leadership eventually shifts to the group. Finally, as the group reaches full maturity, even relationship direction is given over to the group. It is at this point that the leader can withdraw and become an observer, leaving the group on its own, in what he knows will be a successful struggle with real-life problems. The isolation of a wilderness living experience is an ideal environment in which groups can grow through this entire process.

It is important that, in releasing the group for its own struggles, the leader be sure that the group is ready for its independence, operating within manageable safety limits and capable of coping with emergencies.

WILDERNESS ACTIVITIES

Backpacking, canoeing, rafting, climbing, kayaking, caving, mountaineering, snowshoeing, cross-country skiing, and winter camping are just the beginning of the list of wilderness activities. Some offer a means of travel. They provide opportunities for learning through close living in the isolation of the wilderness. Other activities provide the "high adventure" needed to confront some young people with new challenges—fear, frustration, the need for cooperation, their need for self-control, and most of all, their need for God.

These activities must be measured in terms of their potential effectiveness and their safety. They must be matched to individual abilities and needs. If the activities are used as gimmicks to get people to participate, they are of limited value. If they are used as tools, as part of a growth process to confront people and bring them closer to God, they are of great value.

In planning any activity, a distinction must be made between actual and perceived risk. Man has an inherent need for adventure which, by definition, includes risk. However, we must anticipate the amount of actual risk and keep exposure to it to a minimum. Activities can be hazardous and not be perceived as such, or they can be very safe and feel threatening to the participants. A roller coaster is an excellent example of this; it is thrilling, and riders believe it will be dangerous when, in fact, it has been proven very safe in terms of actual risk.

In the wilderness, a well-planned rappel can seem to put the participant in a precarious position, but it can have an exceptionally low risk factor. However, canoeing in a slow-moving river can seem very safe to a canoeist, but be highly dangerous because of rocks or currents below the surface. Even a slow current can pin a swamped canoe or a person.

Selection of all wilderness activities should be on the basis of low actual risk.

Finding wilderness areas to use in your ministry is not as difficult as it sounds. Public lands are easily located on state or county maps. The local administrator of these lands can provide you with information about the site and any special policies governing its use. You will find additional detailed information on topographic maps available from the U.S. Geological Survey. These maps give accurate details of land features, exits to safety, danger areas, and emergency resources.

Plan a trip for yourself and your staff before you take your group out. Become familiar with suitable locations for program activities. Set up a detailed program based on your own experience at the same site. Arrange supervisory and safety procedures in advance and be ready to implement them if necessary.

Proper ecological practices must be followed in order to preserve the wilderness. These vary from place to place, but a common guideline is to leave only your footprints, and no further trace that you have been there. Trash must always be carried out. Fires are permitted in some areas and you may dispose of burnable refuse in such places. Human waste must be disposed of properly, usually buried in 6–8 inches of soil, at least 100 feet from water, trails, campsites, or rest areas. If the environment is not capable of handling decomposition (i.e., above the timberline or in heavily used areas) it is carried out for disposal.

Drinking water should always be treated unless it has been declared potable by governmental testing. It is unnecessary for someone to become sick from bad water that could easily have been treated by boiling, filtration, or with chemicals.

The law requires that you follow all standards set by the state in which you operate the activity. A copy of these standards can be obtained from the state's health, social services, or natural resources departments.

Wilderness ecology practices and safety standards are constantly being reviewed and updated. Be sure your program meets *current* rules. Wilderness camping magazines and contact with nationwide camping and recreational organizations will help you stay informed.

Basic equipment can be obtained from a local sporting goods store or an outfitter. Most of the cooking gear needed can be made from #2½ or #10 cans with wire hoops attached. A light-weight frying pan and one eating/drinking cup and spoon per person are all that is really needed for cooking and eating.

Each participant should bring his or her own sleeping bag and backpack. For winter camping, two sleeping bags per person, one inside the other, with a foam pad underneath for warmth, will be quite comfortable.

A plastic sheet makes an excellent ground sheet. A 10′ by 12′ nylon tarp or plastic sheet can serve as a four-man shelter.

Hypothermia, or lack of heat, is the number one killer of people in the wilderness. It occurs when body heat is lost faster than it can be replaced, and usually strikes people who are not prepared for an emergency or sudden changes in the weather. It is easily avoided when a person remains warm, dry, and rested. Wool or synthetic clothing, in layers appropriate for the climate, helps pull moisture away from the body and keeps it dry. Since most heat loss is from wetness or an uncovered head, prevent sweating by controlling layers of clothing and wear a hat when cold. Footgear that is broken in prior to the trip, and good rainwear are also necessary for an enjoyable trip.

Most grocery stores carry some nonperishable foods that are both lightweight and nutritious. Bring along plenty of snack foods and encourage participants to eat and drink frequently. This helps to restore lost fluids and provides extra energy.

With a strong philosophical base for knowing what we want to accomplish and how we will do it, and with the many tools and resources available to us, we are now ready to explore a rewarding ministry with young people in the sanctuary of God's great outdoors.

FOOTNOTES

[1]Abraham Maslow, *Motivation and Personality,* 2nd Ed. (New York: Harper, 1970).

[2]Paul Hersey and Kenneth H. Blanchard, *Management of Organizational Behavior,* 3rd Ed. (Englewood Cliffs, New Jersey: Prentice-Hall, Inc., 1976).

ADDITIONAL READING

(All Colorado OUTWARD BOUND School books may be obtained from Colorado OUTWARD BOUND School, 945 Pennsylvania, Denver, Colorado 80203.)

Recommended Pre-program Readings for Participants

David Augsburger, *Caring Enough to Confront.* Glendale, CA: Gospel Light Regal Books, 1973.
Viktor Frankl, *Man's Search for Meaning.* New York: Pocket Books, 1973.
Alfred Lansing, *Endurance.* New York: Avon Books, 1959.
J. B. Phillips, *Your God Is Too Small.* New York: The Macmillan Company, 1967.
John Powell, *Why Am I Afraid to Love?* Chicago: Argus Communications Co., 1967.
Francis A. Schaeffer, *The Mark of the Christian.* Downers Grove, IL: Inter-Varsity Press, 1974.

Recommended Leader Preparation Readings

General Camping

Graham B. Blaine, Jr., *Youth and the Hazards of Affluence.* New York: Harper and Row Publishers, 1966.
Donald Conrad and Diane Hedin, *How to Learn from Nonclassroom Experiences.* Denver: Colorado OUTWARD BOUND School.
Gerald L. Golins, *A Resource Document on Designing and Managing OUTWARD BOUND Courses for Delinquent Populations.* Denver: Colorado OUTWARD BOUND School, 1975.
Walter A. Henrichsen, *Disciples Are Made—Not Born.* Wheaton, IL: Victor Books, Scripture Press, 1974.
Michael Jeneid, *Adventuring OUTWARD BOUND—A Manual.* Australia: Lansdowne Press, 1967. (Write to OUTWARD BOUND, Inc., Reston, VA 22070.)
Kenneth R. Kabich, *The Role of the Instructor in the OUTWARD BOUND Educational Process.* Three Lakes, WI: Ken Kabich, 1979.
Dennis L. Gibson, *Live, Grow and Be Free.* San Bernardino, CA: Here's Life Publishers, Inc., 1982.
David W. Johnson, Frank P. Johnson, *Joining Together: Group Theory and Group Skills.* Englewood Cliffs, NJ: Prentice-Hall, 1975.
Richard Katz, *A Solo Survival Experience.* Denver: Colorado OUTWARD BOUND School.
Lois E. LeBar, *Education That Is Christian.* Old Tappan, NJ: Fleming H. Revell Co., 1953.
Joel F. Meier, Talmage W. Morash, George E. Welton, *High Adventure Outdoor Pursuits: Organization and Leadership.* Salt Lake City, Utah: Brighton Publications, 1980.
Lawrence O. Richards, *A Theology of Christian Education.* Grand Rapids, MI: Zondervan Publishing House, 1975.
______. *Youth Ministry, Its Renewal in the Local Church.* Grand Rapids, MI: Zondervan, 1972.
Victor Walsh and Gerald Golins, *The Exploration of the OUTWARD BOUND Process.* Denver: Colorado OUTWARD BOUND School, 1976.
Em Griffin, *The Mind Changers.* Wheaton IL: Tyndale House, 1976.

Philosophy

David Brower, ed., *The Sierra Club Wilderness Handbook.* New York: Ballantine Books, Inc., 1971.

Ricki McLeod, *A Planning Guide for Short Backpacking and Ski Touring Courses with Colorado OUTWARD BOUND School.* Denver: Colorado OUTWARD BOUND School, 1976.

Dan Meyer, Arlene Ustin, and Peter Bryant, *The Instructor's Handbook.* Morgantown, NC: North Carolina OUTWARD BOUND School, 1974.

OUTWARD BOUND in Corrections. Denver: Colorado OUTWARD BOUND School.

Bill Riviere, *The Camper's Bible.* Garden City, NJ: Doubleday & Co., 1961.

Backpacking

Gerry Cunningham, *How to Enjoy Backpacking.* Denver: Gerry Division of Outdoor Sports Industries, Inc., 1972.

Colin Fletcher, *The Complete Walker* (2nd ed.). New York: Random House, 1974.

Dennis Look, *The Joy of Backpacking.* Sacramento: People's Guide to the Wilderness, Jalmar Press, Inc., 1976.

Harvey Manning, *Backpacking One Step at a Time.* Seattle: REI Press, 1972.

R. C. Rethmel, *Backpacking.* Minneapolis, MN: Burgess Publishing Co., 1974.

Denise VanLear, *The Best About Backpacking.* San Francisco: Sierra Club Totebook, 1974.

Robert S. Wood, *Pleasure Packing: How to Backpack in Comfort.* Berkeley, CA: Condor Books, 1972.

Wilderness Areas

Thomas Avery, *Copper Country—God's Country.* Au Train, MI: Avery Color Studios, 1973.

David Bohn, *Glacier Bay—The Land of the Silence.* New York: Ballantine Books (Sierra Club), 1967.

Harvey Broome, *Faces of the Wilderness.* Mountain Press Publishing Co., 1972.

Peter Browning, *The Last Wilderness.* Chronicle Books, 1975.

Michael E. Duncanson, *A Paddler's Guide to the Boundary Waters Canoe Area: Detailed Maps and Descriptions of 31 Wilderness Canoe Routes in the Superior National Forest of Northern Minnesota.* Virginia, MN: W. A. Fischer, Co., 1976.

Eric Morse, *Canoe Routes of the Voyageurs—The Geography and Logistics of the Canadian Fur Trade.* St. Paul, MN: Minnesota Historical Society, 1962.

Nick Nickels, *Canoe Canada.* New York: Van Nostrand, Reinhold, 1976.

Bob and Jody Palzer, *White Water; Quietwater, A Guide to the Wild Rivers of Wisconsin, Upper Michigan, and N.E. Minnesota.* Two Rivers, WI: Evergreen Paddleways, 1975.

Counseling Skills

Gary Collins, *How to Be a People Helper.* Santa Ana, CA: Vision House Publishers, 1977.

Richard S. Doty, *The Character Dimension of Camping.* New York: Association Press, 1960.

William Glasser, *Reality Therapy.* New York: Harper and Row Publishers, 1965.

George H. Harvey and Daniel C. Jessen, *Understanding and Reaching Boys for Christ.* Wheaton, IL: Service Brigade, 1972.

Map and Compass

Be an Expert with Map and Compass: The Orienteering Handbook. La Porte, IN: Silva, Inc., 1961.

Hans Bengtsson and George Atkinson, *Orienteering for Sport and Pleasure.* Brattleboro, VT: The Stephen Greene Press, 1977.

Donald E. Ratliff, *Map, Compass and Campfire.* Portland, OR: Binfords and Mort, 1964.

U.S. Superintendent of Documents, *Map Reading Catalogue.* N.D. 101.20: 21–26/1. Washington, D.C., Government Printing Office, 1961.

Climbing

Kenneth A. Anderson, *Handbook of American Mountaineering.* San Diego: Conklin Litho, 1969.

C. W. Casewit and D. Pownall, *The Mountaineering Handbook.* New York: J. B. Lippincott & Co., 1968.

Peggy Ferber, ed., *Mountaineering: The Freedom of the Hills.* Seattle, WA: The Mountaineers, 1974.

Chris Jones, *Climbing in North America.* Berkeley, CA: University of California Press, 1976.

Tom Lyman, *Bouldering and Outcrop Climbing.* Brattleboro, VT: The Stephen Greene Press, 1978.

______. *The Field Book of Mountaineering and Rock Climbing.* New York: Winchester Press, 1975.

Henry L. Mandolf, ed., *Basic Mountaineering.* San Diego: Conklin Litho, 1969.

Ruth and John Meadenhall, *Introduction to Rock and Mountain Climbing.* Harrisburg, PA: Stackpole Books, 1969.

Royal Robbins, *Advanced Rockcraft.* Glendale, CA: La Siesta Press, 1973.

______. *Basic Rockcraft.* Glendale, CA: La Siesta Press, 1973.

Anne and Steven Schneider, *The Climber's Sourcebook.* Garden City, NY: Anchor Press, 1976.

Walt Wheelock and Royal Robbins, *Ropes, Knots and Slings for Climbers.* Glendale, CA: La Siesta Press, 1967.

First Aid,
Search and Rescue

Fred T. Darvill, Jr., *Mountaineering Medicine.* Mount Vernon, WA: Skagit Mountain Rescue Unit, Inc.

B. Kodet and Angier and Russel Bradford, *Being Your Own Wilderness Doctor: The Outdoorsman's Emergency Manual.* Harrisburg, PA: Stackpole Books, 1968.

Theodore Lathrop, *Hypothermia, Killer of the Unprepared.* Portland, OR: The Mazamas, 1970.

Dick Mitchell, *Mountaineering First Aid* (4th ed.). Seattle, WA: The Mountaineers, 1978.

U.S. Superintendent of Documents, *National Search and Rescue Manual.* Washington, D.C.: Government Printing Office, 1973.

James A. Wilkerson, ed., *Medicine for Mountaineering* (2nd ed.). Seattle, WA: The Mountaineers, 1975.

Equipment

Basic Canoeing. American National Red Cross, 1965.

Gary Cunningham and Meg Hensson, *Lightweight Camping Equipment and How to Make It.* Boulder, CO: Mountain Sports, 1962.

William Kemslei and the editors of *Backpacker Magazine. The Backpacking Equipment Buyers Guide.* New York: Macmillan Publishing Co., Inc., 1977.

Tent, Canvas, and Webbing Repair: Maintaining Manual for the Outdooring. New York: Drake Publishers, 1978.

You Want It When? Logistics Handbook. Colorado OUTWARD BOUND School, 1976.

Canoe-Kayak

Ray Bearse, *The Canoe Camper's Handbook.* New York: Winchester Press, 1974.

Jay Evans and Robert K. Anderson, *Kayaking; The New Whitewater Sport for Everybody.* Brattleboro, VT: The Stephen Greene Press, 1975.

Herbert I. Gordon, *The Canoe Book.* New York: McGraw-Hill Book Co., 1978.

Bev and Fred Hartline, *A Sketchy Introduction to Whitewater and Kayaking.* Seattle, 1974.

John Malo, *Canoeing.* Chicago: Follett Publishing Co., 1969.

Robert E. McNair, *Basic River Canoeing* (3rd ed.). Martinsville, IN: American Camping Association, Inc., 1972.

Bill Riviere, *Pole, Paddle & Portage.* New York: Van Nostrand, Reinhold Company, 1969.

William Sandreuter, *White Water Canoeing.* New York: Winchester Press, 1976.

Peter Dwight Whitney, *Whitewater Sport: Running Rapids in Kayak and Canoe.* New York: The Ronald Press Company, 1960.

P. F. Williams, *Canoeing Skills and Canoe Expedition Techniques for Teachers and Leaders.* Pelham Books, 1967.

Standards

Camp Standards with Interpretations for the Accreditation of Organized Camps. Martinsville, IN: American Camping Association, March, 1980.

Safety in Outdoor Adventure Programs. 4-H Adventure; Cooperative Extension; U. of California, P.O. Box 34066, San Francisco, California 94134.

Outdoor Cooking

Hasse Brunnell, *Food for Knapsackers* (2nd ed.). San Francisco: Sierra Club Totebook, 1971.

Hasse Brunnell and Shirley Sarvis, *Cooking for Camp and Trail.* San Francisco: Sierra Club Totebook, 1972.

William W. Forgey, *The Complete Guide to Trail Food Use.* Pittsboro, IN: Indiana Camp Supply, 1977.

Dorcus S. Miller, *The Healthy Trail Food Book.* Wiscasset, ME: Coastal Business Center, 1976.

Fred Powledge, *The Backpacker's Budget Food Book: How to Select and Prepare Your Provisions from Supermarket Shelves.* New York: David McKay Co., Inc., 1977.

Dian Thomas, *Roughing It Easy.* Provo, Utah: Brigham Young Press, 1974.

———. *Roughing It Easy—Two.* Anderson, IN: Warner Books, 1977.

Survival

Bradford Angier, *Color Field Guide to Common Wild Edibles.* Harrisburg, PA: Stackpole Books, 1976.

———. *Free for the Eating.* Harrisburg, PA: Stackpole Books, 1966.

______. *More Free for the Eating Wild Foods.* Harrisburg, PA: Stackpole Books, 1969.
Gerry Cunningham, *How to Keep Warm.* Denver: Gerry Divison of Outdoor Sports Industries, Inc., 1971.
Edible Plants in the Wilderness, Vol. 1. Beaverton, OR: Life Support Technology, Inc., 1972.
Edible Plants in the Wilderness, Vol. 2. Beaverton, OR: Life Support Technology, Inc., 1972.
Joe Freitus, *160 Edible Plants Commonly Found in the Eastern USA.* Lexington, MA: Stonewall Press, 1975.
Alan Hall, *Wild Food Trailguide.* New York: Holt, Rinehart and Winston, 1973.
Fred Lanoye, *Drownproofing—A New Technique for Water Safety.* Englewood Cliffs, NJ: Prentice-Hall, 1963.
Larry Dean Olsen, *Outdoor Survival Skills.* Salt Lake City: Brigham Young University Press, 1969.
Primitive Medical Aid in the Wilderness. Beaverton, OR: Life Support Technology, Inc., 1972.
Poisonous Plants in the Wilderness. Beaverton, OR: Life Support Technology, Inc., 1972.
Survival in the Wilderness. Beaverton, OR: Life Support Technology, Inc., 1972.

Winter Camping

John Henry Auran and the editors of *Ski Magazine. America's Ski Book.* New York: Charles Scribner's Sons, 1966.
Ned Baldwin, *Skiing Cross Country.* New York: McGraw-Hill Ryerson, Ltd., 1977.
Steve Barnett, *Cross-country, Downhill and Other Nordic Mountain Techniques.* Seattle, WA: Pacific Search Press, 1978.
M. Michael Brady, *Ski Cross-Country.* NY: Dial Press, 1974.
Raymond Bridge, *The Complete Snow Camper's Bible.* New York: Charles Scribner's Sons, 1973.
John Caldwell, *Cross-Country Skiing Today.* Brattleboro, VT: The Stephen Greene Press, 1977.
______ . *The New Cross-Country Ski Book,* 4th Edition. Brattleboro, VT: The Stephen Greene Press, 1974.
Cortland L. Freeman, *Steve Rieschl's Ski-Touring for the Fun of It.* Boston: Little, Brown & Co., 1973.
Clayne R. Jensen, *Winter Touring: Cross-country Skiing and Snow-Shoeing.* Minn., MAL: Burgess Publishing Co., 1977.
William J. Lederer and Joe Pete Wilson, *Complete Cross Country Skiing and Ski Touring.* New York: W. W. Norton & Co., 1972.
Robert McQuilkin, *Comfort Below Freezing.* Mountain View, CA: Anderson World, Inc., 1980.
William Osgood and Leslie Hurley, *The Snowshoe Book.* Brattleboro, VT: The Stephen Greene Press, 1971.
Gene Prater, *Snowshoeing.* Seattle, WA: The Mountaineers, 1974.
Ray Stebbins, *Cold-Weather Camping.* Chicago: Henry Regnery Company, 1975.
Lito Tejada and Allen Speak, *Wilderness Skiing.* San Francisco: Sierra Club, 1972.

Ropes and Initiatives

Robert Lentz, *Adventure Curriculum: Physical Education.* Hamilton, MA: Hamilton-Wenham Reg. High School, 1974.

Doris Nielsen, *The Houghton College Highlander Initiative Course.* Houghton, NY: Doris Nielsen, 1982.

Karl Rohnke, *Cow's Tails and Cobras: A Guide to Rope Courses, Initiative Games and Other Adventure Activities.* Hamilton, MA: Project Adventure, 1977.

Journal of Christian Camping

Christian Camping, International
Box 646
Wheaton, Illinois 60189

Backpacker

Backpacker, Inc.
P.O. Box 2784
Boulder, Colorado 80321

Summit

Summit
P.O. Box 1889
Big Bear Lake, California 92315

American Whitewater

American Whitewater Association
Box 1584
San Bruno, California 94066

Canoe Magazine

American Canoe Association
4260 E. Evans Ave.
Denver, Colorado 80222

16

Weekend Retreats

Retreat! The word is filled with excitement, adventure, relaxation, and fun. But when "retreat" is coupled with "coordinator," the very sound of it strikes panic into the hearts of grown men and women! Unfortunately, most retreat coordinators are cajoled into their positions with at least one of these clever tactics:

- It won't take much time—we've already picked the date.
- You're perfect for it, Herman. You've got a station wagon.
- You won't have to do much—you can delegate the work.
- We know you can do it. Here are the menus, schedule, and workers from last year. And here's the list of troublemakers that we said couldn't come back.
- You gotta do it. No one else will and it's just two weeks away.
- George, the Lord has led our committee to ask you to be retreat coordinator this year.

Retreat coordinators, no matter how they are drafted, recognize that weekend retreat planning is hard work. Individuals who accept the leadership re-

---

John Pearson is the Executive Director of Christian Camping International's U.S. Division.

sponsibilities must take the task seriously and should plan to spend ample time on the project. A poorly planned and executed retreat is far worse than no retreat at all.

Seven basic steps to weekend retreat planning are included here as resource material for the retreat committee. Youth leaders involved in the retreat process are encouraged to read and discuss the material together.

STEP 1: PURPOSE

A retreat should not be something that happens just because it has happened before. Ben Franklin said, "Living without a goal is like shooting without a target." A retreat must have a purpose. And that purpose should be carefully defined. The retreat committee should work on each of the following areas before the decision is made to have the retreat.

■ *Write down the objectives of the youth group.* A retreat is usually planned to help a group accomplish one or more of its objectives for the year. If one of the group's objectives is "to challenge youth to consider missionary vocations," then a weekend retreat with a missionary from Japan might accomplish that purpose.

While this first step may seem obvious, it should not be skipped. If a retreat does not fill a need in the objectives, the leadership should avoid the pitfalls of planning one "because we've always done it this time of year."

■ *Write down the specific objectives of the retreat.* "Well, we all know why we're here tonight," is too often the preamble to a retreat planning session. Instead, use a chalkboard or a large sheet of paper to write down the exact purpose of the retreat. Be sure the committee agrees and insist that there be youth group members present who have strong input into the entire planning process.

"To have fun" is not a good objective. "To provide fellowship, recreation, and guided activities so the youth group members will become better acquainted," is much better. The best way to evaluate whether or not an objective is specific enough is to ask, "When the retreat is over, how will we know if the objective has been accomplished?"

While some retreats have multiple purposes, many youth groups are using a weekend retreat to accomplish one specific objective. A 48-hour or more concentrated time together can often accomplish more than several months worth of weekly meetings. For example, retreats can be used for these special purposes:

- Evangelistic weekends with youth group members inviting non-Christian friends.
- A Leadership Development Retreat for serious-minded students who demonstrate a willingness to be involved in special training.
- A prayer weekend designed specifically to explore the subject of prayer.
- A sports weekend with "Olympic-style" events to fit all interests and abilities using a concurrent biblical theme.
- A special weekend with parents and teens highlighting communication, family conflicts, spiritual growth, and fellowship.
- A "How can I know God's will?" retreat with the senior pastor.
- A midterm "Study Weekend" with college students attending as tutors with strict study hall hours, great recreation, and a 2 Timothy 2:15 theme.

The list of ideas is endless. The key is to focus on accomplishing one objective. Be sure to involve youth group members in the planning; they'll have a bundle of creative ideas.

■ *Write down the major events and activities and compare these with the written objectives.* If the youth group's annual fall retreat features the surprise dunking of all the freshmen in the lake, the leaders may want to scratch the written objective that says, "One of the purposes of this retreat is to promote unity and cohesiveness among our youth."

It is essential that each activity and tradition be scrutinized to ascertain that the scheduled events harmonize with the objectives. Even the pastor's best skit may have to be scrapped for a future retreat more in line with his talent!

STEP 2: PROMOTION

"We're trusting the Lord for 125 students for this retreat," is a great goal. But when only 35 kids show up, everyone assumes the weekend was a big flop. If the goal had been 35 students, it would have been a great success.

Good promotion begins by setting a goal that can grow as excitement and enthusiasm mounts. Bad promotion can reduce attendance significantly. And overinflated goals will only cause disappointment for the individuals who attend. Rarely does a youth group have 100% of its members attend a retreat. Yet too often the promotion is slanted to suggest that if everyone doesn't attend, the leaders will be very disappointed. "We're doing an awful lot of work for you kids, so you had better come and appreciate it."

Toothpaste advertisers use a technique called "market segmentation." One toothpaste appeals to those who want fewer cavities. Another advertiser keys his message to the white teeth crowd. Sales departments have given up on reaching the entire population with their product, so each advertiser zeroes in on the specific group of people who are most likely to respond to a certain benefit of the product. Likewise, retreat promotion should be aimed at the most likely youth to attend the retreat. Don't use a shotgun when a pistol will do.

The wise retreat coordinator will recruit one person whose sole job is to promote the weekend retreat. The following suggestions will help that person avoid wasting precious time and energy.

- *Be specific when communicating the purpose.* If the retreat is a study weekend on the doctrine of God, the promotion should not mislead your young men into thinking it is all volleyball, swimming, and girls! By communicating the purpose of the event, youth will weed themselves out or in, depending on their interest. Tricking kids into attending an evangelistic weekend hardly squares with the ethics of the gospel. A brief paragraph in the church bulletin or the retreat flyer should spell out exactly why the retreat is planned.
- *Highlight the registration deadline and late fee.* If Christians had to mail in registration cards for heaven, many would never make it! Many leaders have found that a registration deadline and a $5 late fee for registrations received after the final day encourages promptness. A nonrefundable deposit should also be required.
- *Publish a detailed program with a time schedule.* Youth group members will get excited about a program they can talk about in advance. (It may also show

them it won't have the "same old stuff" as last year.) The schedule, again, will help communicate the purpose. Usually two responses will be common, "Hey, this retreat is just what I need," or "No way am I going to waste my thirty bucks on sittin' through a bunch of meetings." Negative responses in advance are helpful because the retreat committee may still make changes to salvage the weekend.

STEP 3: PERSONNEL

"Ah . . . sorry, George. I'm busy that weekend. Wish I could counsel at your youth retreat though." Recruiting personnel for weekend retreats is not easy. Who really enjoys sleepless nights, corn flakes in your sleeping bag, and having to act cool around high school kids all weekend?

Quality leadership for a weekend retreat is just as important as the program. You can't have one without the other. How do you recruit the right people? Where do you find them?

The local church usually has a good reservoir of volunteers if the youth leader looks hard enough. They include parents of youth group members, college students and young singles, pastoral staff and their spouses, and perhaps the traveling businessman who can't accept long-term church jobs but can clear his schedule for a weekend. When recruiting, remember these key points:

■ *Provide orientation, training, and motivation for all personnel.* Tell your volunteers they will be trained for their responsibilities. Too many people are recruited under the guise that "you really won't have to do much." If willing and capable leaders cannot be found, the retreat should be postponed until all the positions are filled.

The coordinator should recognize that greenhorns in the retreat ministry will need constant encouragement and motivation. Some reticent helpers will get last-minute cold feet and will offer 17 different excuses why they can't come. A thorough training and orientation session several weeks before the event will pay off in leader preparedness and confidence.

■ *Provide each leader with a written job description.* The retreat coordinator's most difficult task is listing all the jobs that need to be done. Written job descriptions will prevent misunderstanding and overlapping of responsibilities. Write down the obvious tasks.

For example, I once recruited a couple to be counselors at a weekend snow retreat. When the husband and wife arrived at the camp they were shocked to find out that they couldn't sleep together! No one had told the husband that a counselor was supposed to room with the campers! A written job description would have avoided the misunderstanding.

■ *Give leaders an overall view of the weekend.* Distribute a list of participants so volunteers will sense that many people are working hard. Depending on the kind of retreat you're running, your list could include:

Retreat Coordinator
Head Counselor
Men Counselors (one counselor per eight students)
Women Counselors (same ratio)
Head Cook (and necessary staff)
Transportation Coordinator
Promotion Coordinator
Registrar
Speakers
Musicians/Song Leader
Recreation/Special Events Leader
Retreat Emcee
Prayer Coordinator (back home warrior)
Nurse

Men or women counselors could also assume some of the responsibilities such as nurse or transportation coordinator.

■ *Ask each person to make a time commitment for the retreat.* The time required for volunteer work should never be underestimated. All personnel should be asked to give their time not only for the retreat, but also for before and after. Prior to the retreat the leadership will meet for planning and orientation. Each person will also need to set aside time for prayer and preparation.

Following the retreat, some time will be needed for evaluation, thank-you letters, finances, follow-up of decisions and new people, and reporting. Volunteers should be sure they have the time to give and that their continuing responsibilities, family life, and spiritual life will not suffer because of an added task.

(For special help on recruiting leaders, consult the resource list for the four-page article, "Recruit, Train, and Love Those Volunteers," published by Christian Camping International.)

STEP 4: PROGRAM

Lurking in the mind of any red-blooded youth pastor is a best-selling book on weekend-retreat program ideas. "If only those guys in Wheaton could see the fantastic stuff I do at Camp Awayfromitall, they'd beg me to write a book for them," beams the local youth pastor.

And it's almost true! Consequently, any discussion of weekend-retreat programs will be incomplete at best. Yet there are key concerns that are often overlooked. Several of these include:

■ *"Program" begins at the departure point.* The retreat has started when 15-year-old Sally shows up at the church two hours before the registration time. With four suitcases and her bulging sleeping bag, Sally may spend the first two hours of her retreat without another companion. Or the 90-minute bus ride from the church to the camp is rifled with shouts, screams, and threats to the kids from the hired bus driver. Meanwhile, the retreat coordinator is thinking the retreat's official beginning isn't until the 9 P.M. snack at camp! When the bus arrives at camp, most kids have already formed a mental picture of how good or how bad the retreat is going to be. The leaders need to program carefully for each event, scheduled or unscheduled.

■ *Inform the speaker and leader of the objectives for the retreat.* If a speaker is used, the coordinator should suggest the topic or thrust of the speaker's messages. Once again, the objective for the retreat should be the guiding factor in the selection of a speaker or other leaders. The temptation too often is to select a speaker who is popular, and then let him or her select the topics. However, if the committee has prayed and agreed that certain objectives for the retreat must be accomplished, then the speaker must understand the importance of helping to meet those objectives.

■ *Plan for the "Monday morning after."* The effectiveness of a retreat is not seen in what happens at the camp, but in what happens in the weeks and months after the weekend. And perhaps the greatest danger of retreats is that so many individuals make serious commitments to Christ on the weekend, and then are so emotionally and physically exhausted by Monday morning, that their first week as renewed Christians gets off on the wrong foot. The retreat schedule must allow for proper rest so that both campers and leaders do not burn themselves out. While many youth leaders cherish the Sunday evening service at their church as a great time for "camp reflections" from returning retreaters, maybe the young people should go straight home Sunday afternoons and catch up on their sleep.

▪ *Pace the program realistically*. Experienced retreat leaders learn quickly that the All-World Championship Team Pillow Fight should not be scheduled 15 minutes before a devotional talk around the campfire. "Pacing," or the proper positioning of activities, probably can't be learned from a book, but is extremely important. Youth leaders should find "old pro's" who have battle scars from poor pacing and learn from their errors. Some of the common mistakes in program pacing include:

- Running at full steam from Friday night until Saturday afternoon and then fizzling out only to see boredom and disinterest take over on Sunday.
- Saving all the "good stuff" until late Saturday night—and losing the group by Saturday breakfast.
- Scheduling a speaker late Friday night and right after Saturday breakfast—giving the impresssion that the whole weekend will be spent in meetings.
- Crowding meetings within five minutes of meal times, leaving no time for washing up or interaction.
- Sending kids off to bed too early at night.
- Scheduling each 30-minute time frame with activity, leaving no opportunity for one-on-one relationships and counseling.

Sample weekend schedules are included in many retreat sourcebooks. For other ideas look at past retreat files and consult the program staffs at nearby camps. The following sample schedule will help provide a framework for a group's own unique needs and agendas.

Purpose: Annual Fall Fellowship/Friendship Retreat

WEEKEND RETREAT SCHEDULE

FRIDAY

6:00 P.M. Leave Church
8:00 Arrive Camp—Registration, etc.
9:00 Get Acquainted Games, Mixers, Cartoons
9:45 Hot Dogs & Soft Drinks
10:15 Music, Singing, Weekend Plans, Introductions
10:35 15-Minute (maximum) Devotional Talk
10:50 Find Your Bunk
11:15 *Imperative* In-Hour
11:30 Counselor-led CabinTalk/Sleep

SATURDAY

8:00 A.M. Rising Bell
8:30 Breakfast
9:30 Unannounced Group Game (Polaroid camera scavenger hunt)
10:30 Music & Speaker
11:15 Small Group Interaction/Project (Act out a "still picture" illustrating the speaker's main point)
12:00 Free time
12:30 P.M. Lunch
1:30 Unorganized Games
3:00 First Annual Left-handed Olympics
4:15 Awards Ceremony
4:30 Free Time (sports, rest, talk, etc.)
5:45 Dinner
6:30 Optional Q & A Time with Speaker
7:00 Small Group Interaction/Project (Fill in a 12-month Youth Group Calendar that would rate a "Perfect 10")
7:30 Group Reports
7:45 Four-court Volleyball
8:30 Donuts and Apple Cider
9:00 Music and Speaker
10:00 Discipline of Silence (no one talking)
10:20 Feature Film
11:15 *Imperative* In-Hour
11:30 Counselor-led Cabin Talk/Sleep

SUNDAY

8:00 A.M. Rising Bell
8:30 Breakfast

9:30	Small Group Interaction/Project (Act out a one-minute modern-day version of a biblical story)
10:30	Music & Message by the Lake
11:30	Free Time
12:30 P.M.	Lunch
1:45	Depart Camp

■ *Utilize a variety of resources and idea books.* Retreat planners must always look for fresh ideas. Sometimes it is good to plan the traditional annual retreat without looking at last year's schedule. There are tremendous resources available for retreat planners today. Budget some funds from each retreat so new books and resources can be continually added to the retreat coordinator's file.

Two sources are especially good for youth. *Mini Camps,* authored by Richard Troup, is an 111-page volume that lists planning steps, schedules, training ideas, opening night tips, discipline procedures, menus, and Bible-study outlines. It was published in 1974 by Success with Youth Publications, 7348 Trade Street, San Diego, California 92121.

The second source is *Ideas,* compiled by Wayne Rice and Mike Yaconelli. Published quarterly, each volume of *Ideas* contains tried and tested suggestions of youth leaders from across the country. Chapters include crowdbreakers, games, creative communication, special events, camping, service projects, and publicity and promotion. It is published by Youth Specialties, 1224 Greenfield Drive, El Cajon, California 92021.

Christian Camping International, Box 646, Wheaton, Illinois 60189, provides resources, books, and a bimonthly magazine, *Journal of Christian Camping.*

STEP 5: PLACE

The selection of the retreat site is an important decision. Some groups enjoy using the same site year after year. Others select three or four camps and rotate each year for variety. Contracting for site, though, is much more complex than reserving the dates and submitting a deposit. The following suggestions will help the retreat coordinator consider the often overlooked details of choosing a location.

■ *Select a site on the basis of the retreat objectives.* A camp with lots of tempting recreational areas and equipment will only frustrate retreat-goers if the purpose of the weekend is to sit, listen, think, discuss, and think! Conversely, imagine what you would have if 150 kids have only one ping pong table and a checkerboard to share. Coordinators should always ask, "What type of place do we need to more effectively accomplish our objectives?" Other factors to consider include weather, accommodations for leaders and speakers, travel time, regulation of the camp, and the possibility of sharing the site with other groups.

■ *Visit the site before the retreat.* Camp directors are always delighted to meet with retreat coordinators and go over the use of facilities in advance. Careful planning at the site in advance will eliminate last-minute confusion and wasted time. A quick tour of the buildings noting room capacities will greatly help the leader. Items to be jotted down and noted for the committee's orientation could include travel directions, parking areas, off-limits areas, camp director's name, and emergency medical aid information.

■ *Read the camp rental agreement at the leader's orientation meetings.* Each camp has special details, rules, and traditions. If Camp Pine Tree requires guest groups to clear their own tables, the program leader will have to allow time for that. The recreational leader should know if the camp provides ping pong balls or sells them. Too many retreat coordinators fail to communicate the special details to the entire retreat committee. The result is disappointment, anger, and unhappy campers.

■ *Discuss the menu with the camp in advance.* When a camp provides food service for a retreat group, the group leader has the right to see and approve the menu in advance. Food plays a very important role in a retreat. If the weather is bad and the speaker is long-winded, top-notch food service can save the day! However, if campers paid $30 at the last camp for roast beef and ham dinners they will expect the same fare at the next retreat. If the camp's best meal is "Macaroni Surprise," leaders have two options: 1) pay more and request better food, 2) find another camp.

■ *Arrive at the site one hour before the campers.* Ask any camp director to describe the typical retreat opening: "Well, the first bus pulls up and 50 kids pile out and swarm all over the camp. Then I ask the bus driver where the leader is. He says he's the leader. Then he asks where he can set up for registration. Two hours later he has located all the kids and has given his discipline lecture twice and has threatened to send five kids home already." Early arrival for the leader, or his registrar, always provides a more relaxed and organized setting for the arrival of the campers. Many experienced leaders would label this practice as a prerequisite for effective retreats.

■ *Give the camp director a written evaluation of the site and the services.* Camp directors can best serve guest groups by knowing their likes and dislikes. If the site and personnel were substandard, the retreat coordinator has the responsibility of communicating this to the camp. Complimentary letters can also be sent and are always appreciated by the management.

Note: For a directory of camp sites available for rental, write to Christian Camping International.

STEP 6: BUDGET

The retreat budget need not be a complicated or painful problem. Basically, there are two major sections with key areas. For example, the following budget assumes that 100 youth will attend and their fees will cover almost all of the expenses including the leaders' meals and lodging.

EXPENSES	
Meals and Lodging	
100 students @ $30 each	$3,000
12 leaders @ $30 each	360
Promotion (printing and postage)	75
Program (films, props, awards, etc.)	125
Speaker & Music Honorariums & Expenses	500
Insurance (112 people @ $.50 each)	56
Transportation (church vans & gas reimbursement)	150
Staff Training (books, refreshments, etc.)	40
Miscellaneous	94
Total	$4,400
INCOME	
Retreat Fees	
90 Students @ $40 each	$3,600
10 Students on scholarship	—

Church Budget Subsidy	500
Donations for Scholarship Fund	400
Total	$4,500

Some churches ask their leaders to pay all or a portion of the fee. Other groups receive no subsidy. (If so, take the total expense of $4,400 and divide by 100 students to arrive at $44 per student fee.)

Other budget ideas to consider include:

■ *Give scholarships instead of reducing fees.* A popular concept in many summer camps today is to set the fees at a fairly high level so families who can afford camp will be paying what it actually costs. Then a scholarship assistance plan is made available for campers who need partial financial help. This plan avoids automatically subsidizing the fees of "the rich," and still provides a way for people of all income levels to enjoy camp. Therefore, it is recommended that youth groups do not subsidize the individual's cost from the group treasury, but rather provide for scholarships.

■ *Budget for a profit.* If the actual retreat costs are $44, some groups charge $46 as an added precaution against unexpected expenses. A small surplus will also be available to use as a deposit for next year's retreat. Some have assumed that it is almost illegal for a Christian group to make a profit on anything! Knowing that the retreat will be in the black will also allow the group leader to sleep nights!

■ *Determine policies on honorariums.* Every group wants to have a popular speaker at their retreat. (Who would want an unpopular speaker?) And groups that go for the top speakers in the city, the state, or the country need to honestly look at their honorarium policies. If a speaker is popular, he or she is busy. And if the speaker is busy, that person usually has become dependent on speaking engagements to provide for a portion of an annual income. Leaders should frankly discuss the financial arrangements with the speaker in advance. A written request to the speaker should include the following details:

- Amount of the honorarium,
- Amount for travel and expenses,
- Availability of space for spouse or family and if there is a charge for family members.

If a speaker has these details, he or she can then decide if the opportunity can realistically be accepted.

Many speakers find that after adding up costs of gas, preparations, babysitting, and clothes (besides time away from the family) they actually end up losing money by speaking. Group leaders should set the retreat fee high enough so a speaker's honorarium and expenses can always be met. The alternative, of course, is not to have a speaker from outside the group. (If more ammunition is needed to drive home this point, read *Let's Have a Banquet . . . or Will $1.36 Be Enough?* by Joyce Landorf, published by Zondervan. The chapter on "The Speaker" is both hilarious and sobering.)

■ *Consider policies on cancellations.* Monday morning the retreat coordinator calls Camp Swanee and reports, "We will have 100 people at our retreat next weekend." On Friday night only 67 campers show up and the group discovers they must pay the camp for the 100 reservations. How the leader handles a potential $990 deficit (33 no-shows at $30 each) should be determined early in the planning stages. Group leaders have suggested any and all of the following options:

- Require full payment in advance and no refunds for cancellations.
- Require nonrefundable deposits with a commitment to pay the full fee in the event of a last-minute cancellation.
- Refund fees for emergency cancellations only if the camp allows some deviation from the final reservation count.

Whatever the policy, leaders should be certain they understand the camp's contract and then set a policy with the campers accordingly.

STEP 7: POSTRETREAT EVALUATION AND FOLLOW-UP

"Whew, I'm glad that's over," is the typical benediction of most retreat coordinators. If the retreat was planned with specific objectives to be accomplished, the ministry of the retreat will continue for some time. Evaluations do not have to be time-consuming, lengthy, or critical. An effective review of a retreat can be helpful, encouraging, and even inspiring. The following suggestions will enable the retreat leader to guarantee that the retreat will continue to have an impact on people's lives long after the suitcases have been unpacked.

■ *Request feedback from campers and leaders.* As part of the retreat schedule, each person should be asked to participate in a brief evaluation period. This can be done on a detailed prepared sheet, or with an open-ended "list the good and bad points of this weekend." Other leaders prefer brief small-group discussions with a person from each group recording the comments. Even a show of hands for likes and dislikes on food, program, site, and other elements is better than no evaluation at all. Allowing the entire group to express its views gives each person a sense of responsibility and provides for excellent year-round communication. Some leaders watch for individuals who offer suggestions so that they can be recruited for retreat planning for the next event.

■ *Prepare a written report to be read and filed.* Evaluations are a waste of time unless they are reviewed and used. Mistakes are made every year by novice retreat coordinators only because "no one told me that 10% cancel out at the last minute." A brief outline of job descriptions, promotion, timetables, schedules, menus, site evaluations, and costs would provide tremendous assistance to the leader for the next retreat.

The retreat coordinator should meet with the committee no later than seven days after the retreat to gather ideas and recommendations for the report. Budgeting a modest amount to treat the committee to an early Sunday morning breakfast at a restaurant is an excellent way to show appreciation to each person and to get evaluations and feedback. Finally, the coordinator should write a report, distribute it to committe members, and place it in the group's records where it will be available for use by the next committee.

■ *Follow-up spiritual results immediately.* The impact of the retreat on individual lives should be noted in terms of the retreat objectives. While it is important that the evaluation indicate the spiritual results of the retreat, the most important postretreat activity is the follow-up.

A plan for personal follow-up of individuals should begin at the retreat and not wait until a committee meets to think about it. Individuals should receive literature and weekly phone calls or visits by a person who cares about their spiritual growth. Leaders should be assigned to follow-up prospects who are new to the group. All of this work, of course, is just as important as the retreat itself. And once again, it might be better to have no retreat than to fail to plan adequately for the important work of follow-up.

These seven steps of retreat planning will perform no magic for a retreat leader unless there is prayer and hard work. And a cooperative committee must believe in the importance of accomplishing the retreat objectives. An effective retreat can be a life-changing experience for every participant and with proper planning the results will more than reward the leader for the time invested.

ADDITIONAL READING

Virgil and Lynn Nelson, *Retreat Handbook, A Way to Meaning.* Valley Forge: Judson Press, 1976.

John Pearson, *Recruit, Train, and Love Those Volunteers.* Christian Camping International, Box 646, Wheaton, Illinois 60189 (reprints available).

______. *Seven Steps for Effective Retreats.* Christian Camping International, Box 646, Wheaton, Illinois 60189 (reprints available).

Wayne Rice and Mike Yaconelli, *Ideas.* El Cajon, California: Youth Specialties, (published quarterly).

Richard Troup, *Mini Camps.* San Diego, California: Success with Youth Publications, 1974.

Guide to Christian Camps and Conference Centers, Christian Camping International, Box 646, Wheaton, Illinois 60189.

17

Skiing Trips

The early morning sun shines brilliantly on the new-fallen snow. As the sun's rays glisten through the evergreens, their branches laden with new snow, you sense the quietness and beauty of the moment. Then you hear a faint sound from among the timber. As you watch, a lone skier appears from behind the trees and glides onto the slope. As he moves from side to side his movement seems almost effortless. When he is gone, all that remains are the tracks in the snow. It is a beautiful sight, one that you and I have watched on television or in movies many times. We have often longed to be that skier, to be able to share his enjoyment of this magnificent creation God has given us.

Every winter, if you travel, you can see cars heading for the mountains, equipped for skiing. Sometimes the skis are strapped onto the trunk, or even sticking out of the windows as people make their way to their winter funland. If you find yourself in an airport during the winter months, you may see travelers carrying ski boots, with skis slung over their shoulders, making their way to some resort to enjoy the beauty of downhill skiing. Each year, thousands of young people from ski clubs, the YMCA, church youth groups, high-school groups, Young Life and

Rusty Rogers is the Plains States Regional Field Director for Youth for Christ/USA, Topeka, Kansas.

Youth for Christ/Campus Life clubs travel great distances to seek the thrill of downhill skiing.

For the past twelve years I have been involved in ski trips for high-school age young people. These trips can be a lot of fun for the kids. I have had the opportunity to see these trips be the highlight of a young person's life. I have also been around when these trips were a real nightmare.

I was sitting in my office one fall afternoon when the phone rang, breaking my concentration. A youth pastor from a nearby community was calling for some help. Several high-school students in his youth group had heard about a ski club sponsoring a trip, and had decided that they would like to have their youth group do the same thing. Since he knew that I had been involved in several ski trips, he thought perhaps I could help him put a program together for his group. I was more than willing to help him, and as we talked, I recalled vivid scenes from the first ski trip I sponsored. I was much like the man who took a group of youngsters swimming and was asked if he knew how to swim. His reply was yes. When asked if he could save anyone, his reply was yes, myself. That's the way I was with skiing. I could ski a little bit for myself, but that was all. Oh, I could point someone toward the chair lift or the poma lift, or better yet, the first-aid station, but you didn't have to ask questions about all the fancy stuff skiers do on television. I had enough to do just getting my boots buckled and keeping my toes and fingers warm.

Having survived that first trip and many others since, I have discovered a fun-filled, positive ministry to young people in this beautiful mountain setting.

Most of the ski trips I take are to the Colorado Rockies, because I happen to live near them. Your trip could take you anywhere, as long as there is good snow and downhill skiing. No matter where you live, you can find slopes that will allow you to enjoy this fun winter sport.

If you are planning a ski trip, there are many things you should take into consideration. I hope that some of these ideas will be helpful to you in having a great time, and a fruitful ministry.

CHOOSING ACCOMMODATIONS

The selection of your hotel accommodations is very important because the physical plan will often dictate the kind of crowd control you will have and the kind of response you will receive from your group. When young people are happy with food and accommodations, they enjoy skiing much more. It is also much easier to communicate the message of Christ to them when they are content. If accommodations are uncomfortable or rooms are too large for staff supervision, your job will be much more difficult. If the meals are not what they ought to be, all the kids will do is complain. Having planned camps and conferences for young people for many years, I know that you cannot satisfy everyone, but giving close attention to meals can make a significant difference in the attitude of your group.

It would be ideal if you could have your accommodations close to the ski slopes where you can ski from your hotel to the lift lines. Often this is prohibitive because the hotels close to the slopes like to have liquor business. For this reason these hotels often frown on church groups or other Christian organizations. Often you can get a much better price and better accommodations a short distance from the slopes. Travel time to and from the slopes is not necessarily a problem. The staff and kids can use it to their advantage to catch a few winks, visit with a friend, or discuss where they are going to ski.

A hotel with an indoor pool, whirlpool, saunas, and game rooms is an excellent bonus for both young people and staff. These extra facilities provide alternative activities and relaxation. They're also good for the beginning skier who decides, after the first day or two, that he's not that interested in skiing. If these facilities are not available at your hotel, it's a good idea to check for other places locally where the kids can do something other than skiing if they choose.

Most hotels are willing to work with you. They can assure themselves of selling meals and accommodations and often will make a price break available to you for booking a group. It may become more difficult to find adequate accommodations for a larger group, but the local Chamber of Commerce should be able to assist you in this.

PHYSICAL EXERCISE BEFORE THE TRIP

I've watched many young people walk back to their rooms carefully after their first day of skiing, nursing hurts, and discovering muscles they didn't even know they had. One of the first things you can do in preparation for a ski trip is to encourage the young people to get ready physically for strenuous activity. It is important to do a lot of stretching exercises for ankles, calves, hamstrings, and quadraceps. Recommended exercises include:

- half squats—five at a time. Hold each one for ten seconds.
- side leg stretches—shifting body weight from one leg to the other. This strengthens the ligaments and tendons on both sides of the knee.
- strengthening calves—stand on a block of wood with heels hanging off. Move up and down on the balls of the feet.
- hurdler's stretch—A runner's exercise.
- jogging—increases endurance.

This can't be emphasized enough. Physical exercise prior to a ski trip is essential. It will allow each person to enjoy the entire trip, not just the first day. This will also help reduce the number of injuries in the group. The tired skier is often the one who is injured.

EQUIPMENT RENTAL

The first time I put on a pair of skis, I thought my feet would never be the same. The boots hurt, the ski bindings were very difficult to get into, and by the time I got the safety straps fastened I was worn out. Since then, I have learned the importance of selecting the right kind of ski equipment. This is one area where you should not cut corners in your planning. Although rental fees for ski equipment will vary with the length of time you'll use it and the area you choose for your trip, it does not cost much more to rent the finest available.

When your young people register for the trip, be sure to get accurate information from each person. You'll need to know each one's height, weight, shoe size, and degree of skiing ability. This information, provided in advance, will allow the rental shop to adjust the equipment properly for each person ahead of time. This will shorten the time you spend in the rental shop and allow for more time on the slopes. Encourage everyone to be honest about their weight; it has a great deal to do with the way the bindings are adjusted. If the weight figure is wrong, the bindings can come undone rather quickly as the skier turns corners.

When you arrange for equipment rental, check to be sure that the cost also includes breakage insurance. On our first ski trip, a young girl had taken her first lesson and felt she could conquer the hill. As she came down the first big run of the day, a tree loomed in front of her. She ran right into it. Fortunately, she was not hurt (I'll never know how she escaped it), but she snapped the tips of both skis. Our rental fee included insurance for breakage, so she just went back to the rental shop for another pair of skis.

Rental equipment is almost always available at the slopes, but it's often possible to get a slightly better price, and often better service, away from the slopes. At the slopes, skiers are in and out for adjustments and day-to-day rentals. A shop away from the slopes is more able to cater to a group. Often the shop at the slopes will be more than happy to help you with breakage or adjustments, even if you've rented equipment elsewhere.

The local Chamber of Commerce can suggest rental shops if you're not familiar with the area. They can probably tell you which shops will be able to handle a group of your size. Should you find that the shop you've chosen cannot handle your needs, the proprietor can often recommend a friend in the business who can.

The peak times of the year for skiing are the Christmas and Easter holidays. If your group is a large one, one hundred or more, or if your trip is scheduled for these peak times, it's a good idea to plan very early in the season to be assured enough equipment is available.

PLANNING THE PROGRAM

A three-day package seems to be the best for a ski trip. Two days of skiing is not quite long enough, and four or five days is too long, particularly for those who are beginners. They will often have to rest at least one of those days to recuperate from tired muscles and fatigue. If they spend one or two days resting, they're wasting their money and won't be too happy about it. On the other hand, if young people know that they have only three days, most of them will ski all three days.

The first day is just for getting the feel of their "ski legs." If a member of your group has never skied before, the first day should include a mandatory ski lesson. Anyone who has never skied before should not be allowed to go without lessons. "My friend will teach me," is not an acceptable substitute for professional instruction in the basics of skiing. Too many bad habits are passed on by well-meaning friends, making a beginner's skiing much more difficult. There is also a greater risk of injury, as friends are more likely to want to go (or be persuaded to go) to the top of the hill and show the new skier the way down from there. Taking time out for lessons on the first day will help the beginner enjoy skiing more the second and third days, and for years to come.

Unless you are willing to pay higher prices, your schedule will usually involve some travel time to and from the slopes. Most slopes open at 9:00, when there is excellent skiing on new powder. It's a little colder in the morning, but lift lines are shorter. You will want to have your group in line by the time the slopes open. To do this, be aware that novice skiers take from 15 to 30 minutes to get ready. This involves getting into their gear, getting their tow tickets, putting on lip ice, and wiggling their way into lift lines. You should probably allow 45 minutes plus travel time from your hotel. Breakfast served 45 minutes to an hour before departure time will help keep the group on schedule, although attendance at breakfast decreases as the trip progresses. Most slopes close lift lines at 4:00, and you'll be able to leave for your hotel by 4:30—the group will be really tired and ready to go. If you allow an hour or so before dinner, everyone will have time to relax, stretch out, take a warm shower, and rest tired muscles before the evening meal. An evening meeting that starts at 8:00 and ends by 9:30 will give staff and kids time to relax and get plenty of sleep.

To get your skiing day off to a good start, it's wise to send one or two of your staff to the slopes earlier than the kids to purchase tow tickets for the entire group. You should be able to get a group rate, depending on where and when you ski. You may even receive several free tickets for your staff, depending on the size of the group. By purchasing tickets early, your staff can meet the group on the bus or vans and distribute tickets as the kids get off and head for the slopes.

THE EVENING MEETING

It's a good idea to keep the evening meeting fun-filled and to the point. After the program one evening, a young man came up and asked if he could talk to me. Assuming that he had come for counseling, I was excited. We headed off to the corner with a couple of chairs. He began to quiz me as to why we did certain things in the evening meeting. I explained to him that we were trying to make everyone feel at ease; we wanted them to enjoy the program. He promptly said to me, "Hey, we all know that you want to talk to us about Christ. Why don't you get straight to the point and we will enjoy a shorter meeting." His frankness helped me realize that even though the young people had come primarily for skiing, they also knew we were going to share the message of Christ. They wanted us to get to the point. Kids enjoy a message and a program that does just that.

Good music is important too, music non-Christians enjoy. We all know that young people listen to a great deal of music, wherever they are. Be sure you have a group that can communicate well with them.

There are many short promotional ski films available at little or no charge through the ski area you choose. One of these can make an exciting preview for the first evening. The kids can get an idea of what can be done on skis, and the film gets them excited for the next day's activity. It's probably a good idea to preview these films, since they may promote some things you may not want to encourage.

During the day, have your staff watch for kids who have funny wipe-outs, and for the skier who appears to be the real "hot dog." Often the hotel will be more than glad to provide you with the hot dog for the "hot dog award." Sometimes the ski area will provide you with a broken pole to give to the person who had the most dramatic wipe-out during the day. You can also give an award to the person who had the most spectacular fall. (Often some beginner skier will fall out of the chair lift in the process of getting on.) You can present the awards during the evening meeting. Be creative with this, and build it up. The kids will look forward to it each evening.

The kids will usually be tired after a hard day of skiing. Encourage them to be in bed by 11:00. Some may complain about it, though rarely. Those who get overtired are the ones who end up with altitude sickness or broken bones.

If you are planning your ski trip primarily for Christian young people, you may want to change the nature of your evening meeting. You may want to do a little more group singing, or you may want your speaker to have a little heavier content from the beginning. You may also want to do without some of the frivolity. The size of your group will determine much of this. Regardless of what you are programing, it is important to decide before you go the kind of ministry you would like to have, and plan for it.

A MINISTRY OF SKIING

It is very important for you, in the initial stages of your planning, to determine just what kind of ministry you want to have with your youth group. Is it going to be an outreach ministry, or are you planning a discipleship ministry for the core of your group? If you decide that your ministry is to be an outreach to kids not presently involved, scheduling and programing are vitally important. Most kids will be attracted to the ski trip simply to go skiing. The rest of the program must be as exciting and appealing as skiing.

Your staff should be hand picked. Don't ask for volunteers. Many people may volunteer but they may not be right for this job. They need to understand that they are there to serve the young people and help them have the time of their lives. They are not there just to be leaders. It is important that your staff provide a positive model of Christianity for the young people. They need to see love and concern in you and your staff. If they see this and know that you are there to help them, your trip will be much more enjoyable as young people respond to your leadership. Train your staff ahead of time so they will know and understand their responsibilities for serving these young people and helping them have a great time skiing. The ministry results of many ski trips have been negated because the staff did not understand that they were there to minister through serving to the spiritual needs of young people.

Skiing is fun. It does not have to be a nightmare

for the sponsors. It can be a time of very positive ministry, a time when, planned right, can see many non-Christian young people come to know Christ in a personal way. If planned properly, a trip can help you disciple Christian kids so that they can be effective in reaching their friends with the message of Christ. Remember, there are many young people in your community who would like to ski. There are many young people in your community who may not be involved in your youth group. But they might go skiing with you.

18

Biking

During the mid-60s, while serving as the hero football coach at Taylor University, I began to sense that teen-age boys needed a serious adventure that would include maximum physical output along with excitement, stress, and touches of the romantic or poetic. In response to this we developed a three-week cycling program that eventually became known as Wandering Wheels. The first 1,000-mile tours were so rewarding that 3,000-mile coast-to-coast tours were introduced in 1966. Since that time, Wandering Wheels has offered one or two yearly coast-to-coast tours. The trips have long since become coeducational, include people of all ages, and have involved more than 1,000 young men and women.

The golden thread running through the Wheels' cycling program is the use of the adventure-related cycling activity to deepen religious interest on the part of the participants. Like it or not, an attitude on the part of teen-agers still prevails that it is "silly" to go to church, to pray, to read the Bible. By association, Wandering Wheels tries to identify the teachings of Jesus Christ with a full-blown "tough guy" experience. All the demands of a 1,000-mile bike ride

Bob Davenport is the founder and director of Wandering Wheels, a nationally known bicycle touring program based at Taylor University, Upland, Indiana.

mixed with prayer and Bible reading helped to make the idea of honoring God more appetizing to the teen-age riders.

BIKING AS A TOOL FOR EVANGELISM

A major problem in broadcasting any message is having an audience. Group cycling is an avenue that provides ready interest. The routes of travel are normally in populated areas. Few people can pass by without asking, "What is happening?" "Where are you going?" "Why?"

Group cycling not only provides ready interest, it provides a channel through which those in the group can share their faith. The news media is quick to pick up on a touring group, especially in smaller cities and towns. It usually does an excellent job of searching out the riders for their real cause or purpose. As a result of the media's questions the evangelical cause is helped with no expense for the large amount of exposure.

Printed data can be easily shared. This should be a tastefully designed tract or a specially printed brochure. There is wisdom in handing out printed material. It can serve as follow-up and allow for further communication.

DISCIPLESHIP AND LEADERSHIP DEVELOPMENT

A low leader-to-follower ratio is a major strength in developing discipleship and leadership. The ideal number of people per squad, including the leader, should be no more than six. The closer the one-on-one teaching ratio gets, the more learning takes place. Group cycling allows the squad leader to teach, but more importantly, to be observed. He is expected to do what he tells his followers to do. A twenty-four-hour-a-day living experience allows people to be seen as they really are. The physical demands of a ride bring out the best or worst in a person.

When observing Jesus, those being discipled not only listened, but watched. The disciples observed the teacher in action. It is often the chance circumstance that brings about some of the best teaching and a change of attitude.

One reason cycling is such a good tool for leadership and discipleship training is that it occurs on the highway, in the market place, and down the backroads where everyday things happen.

FACTORS TO CONSIDER IN GROUP CYCLING

■ *Leadership is important.* Superior cycling expertise is not necessary, but common sense and great respect for the physical welfare of the participants are critical assets for a leader to have.
■ *Junior-high age is a good minimum age for participants.* As a whole they are the easiest to get excited about a tour. Both boys and girls respond well. Older teens respond, but they seem more selective in the kind of activity they want. Adults, whether they be preprofessional, young marrieds, middle age, or older, all make prime candidates for a tour.
■ *The size of the group can vary.* However, there is safety in numbers! The ideal team size would be anything from a single squad of six to seven squads of six making a maximum of forty-two riders. This maximum number is built around the problems of feeding, housing, and maintaining equipment.
■ *Timing.* When to ride depends on the part of the country in which the group is located. November through March is an undesirable time span throughout most of the United States. Weekends, holidays, special school vacations, and summers provide the most logical time blocks.

GETTING STARTED

There are several ways to break the ice. Have a breakfast ride. Invite a number of people to assemble early on a Saturday morning and ride to a restaurant ten to twenty miles away. A distance ride is another way to get started, such as a half-century ride (fifty miles) or a whole-century ride in one day. Create a gimmick. Earning a patch for a jacket by riding so many miles is one many groups use. An "overnight," riding out one day and back the next morning, creates interest. Some groups ride to a summer camp. There are several established cycling tours across the nation that welcome any and all participants. Some of these tours attract as many as 5,000 riders. Taking a group to a major rally like this would be an excellent way to develop interest.

PERSONNEL

■ *Tour Leader.* There should be a tour leader. Someone has to take the lead, be the boss or head man. He will be the one to push, prod, and generally see to it that the trip goes and keeps going.
■ *Squad Leaders.* On even the simplest tours there is the need for at least one squad leader to every five or

six riders. The squad leader needs some basic experience in cycling. However, more important is the need for wisdom and common sense. For example, he should know when a road is unsafe; when weather makes travel unsafe; when the environment is unsafe; when courtesies need to be extended; what procedures to follow in case of an accident; how to be sensitive in the area of ministering, especially to weaker riders; how to create a good mix; and to be reasonable, fair, and a good model.

■ *Bike Mechanic.* The bike mechanic should be able to handle all normal bike adjustments. These would include: tire repairs, wheeling truing, derailleur adjustments, chain repairs, greasing and disassembling any of the major bearing areas. The mechanic should be responsible for all the needed tools and spare parts. His personality should be such that other riders will feel free to ask his help and not feel like a bother to him.

■ *Follow-up Driver.* This person is needed when the tour is large enough for a support vehicle. This is usually a person who enjoys the activity of cycling, but for various reasons cannot cycle. It is critical to have the right person for this job. He needs to have a caring, giving, and loving spirit.

■ *Cooks.* They are a breed apart—up early in the morning and to bed late at night. Most of their daylight hours will be spent searching out food and places to cook it. One good thing about cooking for a group of cyclists is that the cyclists will be hungry! The major complaint will result from the lack of quantity, not quality. Thick skin and a lot of "mama"-type sympathy is required.

PRETRIP PHYSICAL TRAINING

Most people grow up with a bicycle, although the ten-speed could be foreign to some novice cyclists. It is of prime importance that maximum time be allowed the riders so they can become comfortable with all aspects of the bike. They should especially know the bike's braking capacity, and this needs to be experienced under all conditions (i.e., heavy traffic, high-speed coasting, wet pavement, etc.). Along with stopping, riders should know how to use the gears and be aware of ways of experiencing maximum efficiency. These are of prime importance.

Beyond this there is the need to get in shape for the ride. Some people stay in shape year around, but most need to specifically prepare for a trip. A person cannot do too much riding prior to a tour. The better the condition, the more enjoyable the ride. The length of the ride and the terrain will dictate how much preparation is needed. If the ride is to be 1,000 miles over a period of three weeks, the riders know they will be pedaling about fifty miles per day. There should be several occasions before the trip begins when fifty-mile training trips are scheduled. This can be done during a solid morning ride on a weekend. As weather permits, shorter daily rides should accompany the longer fifty-mile periods.

On a percentage scale, the rider's seat suffers the greatest discomfort. A well-broken-in saddle helps to ease the pain, and a leather saddle seems to offer the best results for most touring.

The rider can also experience discomfort in his hands, but this can be eased by finding the proper measurement of gooseneck height to seat height. Cushioning the handle bar offers some relief as does the style in riding (i.e., regularly moving the hands around on the handle bar).

The rider's feet may also experience problems, so shoe fit is important. A shoe with a firm sole that allows for a solid platform over the pedal is a big help. The major foot complaint is that the toes go to sleep because of tight toe clips and poor shoe fit.

CHOOSING THE ROUTE

The single greatest item to be considered in successful touring is the route. The type of road available will greatly dictate the course the tour will take.

The most dangerous roads are the two-lane roads without a shoulder that carry a large amount of traffic, especially commercial traffic. These should be avoided at all costs. Some of these roads are heavily traveled only during peak hours, so make sure the tour is not conflicting with peak traffic hours.

Roads will graduate up to super safe as space for the cyclists increases on the highways (i.e., large, well-paved shoulders, lighter traffic flow). Many four-lane roads without shoulders are good cycling roads, especially if they are lightly traveled by cars and trucks.

Large cities present special problems. The people show less interest in the group as compared to the people from smaller towns. The possibility of accidents is higher (i.e., more concentration of cars, more crossroads, more stop signs). The unpredictable situations such as getting lost due to street signs changing, lost of direction, bike theft, and harassment, all make the large cities more difficult to negotiate.

Back roads and small towns offer a better chance for a successful tour. National and state parks provide some of the safest roads. The network of roads is sufficient to offer hundreds of miles of safe travel, and these roads are especially good for introducing novice riders to touring.

Maps are critical in touring. The American Automobile Association offers the best state maps. Most maps issued by the state are good and clear and show secondary roads well. County maps are the best for offering the latest information on secondary roads. The best overall map is the United States Geological Survey map issued out of Denver, Colorado, or Washington, D.C.

EQUIPMENT AND SUPPLIES

Bicycle

Wandering Wheel's experience in group cycling has brought about some basic conclusions about the choice of a group touring bike. There are several brands from which to choose. A good rule of thumb is to select a respectable bicycle dealer; one who has a good inventory of parts and bikes. It would help if he, himself, is reasonably versed in cycling.

Wandering Wheels has found its best success over the years to be with the Schwinn line of bikes. The major selling points are the no-nonsense, low-maintenance, strengths of the bikes. Wheels has found that the trade-off of low-maintenance bicycles to exotic lightweight bicycles favors the low-maintenance bicycles.

The Schwinn LeTour line is Wheels' recommendation for a bike. You can go up in quality from the LeTour, but you should use the LeTour as a model for reasonable success in group riding. There are similar bikes by other major manufacturers. The LeTour, however, will offer a measuring device for evaluating relative strengths in other brands.

Parts and Accessories

When putting extras on the bike, make them simple and maintenance free. Many accidents occur as a result of cheap and inefficient accessories.

The *rear rack* is the first extra to be considered. It

should mount so that it becomes an integral part of the bike. There should be no slipping of the rack on the frame.

The *bike bag* should be like the rack, simple and maintenance free. Check it out for its history of durability. There are many brands, but most of the better ones pattern themselves in material and hardware after the quality backpack equipment.

There should be one dependable *frame mount pump* with each riding squad. There should also be a quality deluxe foot pump with pressure gauge for the whole touring group.

The *cyclometer,* which is used for measuring miles pedaled, has not proven to be a reliable accessory. Sometimes, however, it is psychologically helpful to have someone in the group keeping track of the miles, so having one or two bikes with cyclometers can be helpful.

Water bottles are fairly consistent. The cage that holds the bottle should be the pressure type and not the snap-close type.

Kickstands are always up for discussion. Most experienced riders do not use them. However, the merit of a kickstand on a group ride makes sense.

Mirrors, like the kickstands, have advantages and disadvantages. I believe that a mirror is a critical accessory. The traditional handle-bar mount seems most consistent. In group cycling it is critical that the leader of each squad have a mirror.

Reflectors and lights are also pro and con items. Riding after dark is not recommended. The use of lights only encourages night riding. Lights as accessories for group cycling are unnecessary. Reflectors are required by law and it is wise to have them in case a squad is caught on the road after dark.

A *bicycle flag* and bright riding apparel are very important. The flag offers excellent early visibility to traffic, while an all-white shirt is the single most important item that can be worn to give traffic a full opportunity to see the cyclist at the earliest possible time. Anything that gives traffic the maximum advantage in seeing the cyclists early is important. Wandering Wheels also uses a tail patch. This is worn like an apron on the seat of the cyclists. It is bright orange and measures about a foot square and is attached to the rider by a belt.

Locks are important, especially if much city riding is to be done. Individual locks are good for squads. A long cable can be made to accommodate several bikes and eliminate the need for individual locks.

BICYCLE MAINTENANCE

Lubrication is the most common maintenance need. Silicone spray is the most simple type of lubrication, but it is expensive. A good lightweight oil put on carefully and then wiped off works about as well as the silicone spray. All metal-against-metal parts need regular attention. This is especially true of cables and other similar surfaces that are easy to overlook.

A regular check of spokes is important. Spokes in new wheels tend to seat after about 800 to 1,000 miles causing the spokes to loosen. It is critical that these be checked and the loose spokes tightened. Check regularly for broken spokes. The front wheel will have the fewest number of broken spokes while the back wheel on the cluster side will be where most of the broken spokes occur.

Tires need a regular check. Tires can wear in such a way that in one day's riding a serious condition can arise. Keeping maximum pressure in them is important.

A routine check of accessories, especially those that are held on by clamps, nuts, bolts, and screws, is critical.

The headset pits out early on some bikes and should be checked for incorrect turning.

Squeaking pedals are a sure sign of problems. Pedals that do not turn easily need to be cranked.

Three-piece cranks need attention if the bike is new or if the crank has been recently disassembled. The arms tend to seat and work loose. Any hint of sloppiness needs immediate attention. The same kind of attention needs to be given to the front sprockets.

Both front and rear derailleurs need to be kept clean. A toothbrush and toothpick, along with some oil spray, will free up the mechanism. Many of the more serious derailleur troubles occur when riders jam or overshift as a result of marginal working gears.

Simply keeping the bikes clean helps on overall maintenance. That would include everything from shining the chrome, polishing the paint, and keeping it as grease free as possible in dirt-collecting areas.

FOOD

The length of the ride and number of days on the road will help decide how much food preparation is needed. As a general rule the riders provide one meal per day at a fast-food restaurant and the tour organization provides the other two (breakfast and dinner by the tour and lunch by the riders). Keeping the price down is a major factor. A heartier, heavier breakfast is cheaper than a breakfast consisting of cold cereals, donuts, etc. Eggs, hot cereals, powdered milk, day-old breads, hot cakes, french toast, all go a long way. Lunch is simplest if sandwich spreads are used. They go on faster and are cheaper (i.e., egg salad, tuna salad, ham salad). All of the sandwich meals can be supplemented with chips, soup, cookies, and a simple drink. Dinner, as with the other meals, is cheaper when made in a big pot, such as stews and chili. Gravy-type mixes over bread help speed up food preparation and cut down on costs.

Using plastic or paper plates, and having the riders bring a spoon and drinking cup, helps streamline the cleanup operation and cuts down on the spread of sickness.

HOUSING

You should make sure the team is going to be dry when not riding. If tents are used they should be adequate to keep out the rain. Good success for housing can be offered through arranging ahead of time with churches, armories, YMCAs, civic buildings, and public and private schools. Information regarding bedding should be specific, especially if it is to be carried by the back-up vehicle.

FOLLOW-UP VEHICLES OR SUPPORT EQUIPMENT

There are several reasons for motorized help. It provides assistance for injured or ailing riders. Food, cooking equipment, tents, and bicycle parts can be carried in the support vehicle. This helps speed up operations. Vehicles can be used to search out "homes" or camping sites. Often there is a need to purchase unusual items while on the road (i.e., bicycle parts, special medicine, food, etc.).

CLOTHING AND PERSONAL EQUIPMENT LIST

Standard items for a Wandering Wheels three-week trip are:

Provided by organization:

1 jacket
1 pair riding shorts
2 riding shirts

Provided by individual:

1 dress pant (the type that would double as a warm riding bottom and dress pant)—sweat bottoms are recommended
1 dress shirt (could be top of sweat suit)
1 long sleeve shirt (preferably turtleneck) to coordinate with dress pant and shirt
1 pair shoes—good quality—something that can double as riding and dress shoe (may be thongs or sandals)
1 hooded sweatshirt (for warmth)
1 good upper raingear
1 bathing suit
5 pair socks or footies (wool socks are excellent)
6 pair underwear (suggest nylon for fast drying)
1 towel, washcloth, soap
1 Dopp kit (streamlined, such as a small plastic kit or simple zip lock bag)
1 sleeping bag (down filled or polyfiber filled only)
eating utensils (one cup that holds hot and cold drinks, one spoon)
Bible
camera (optional)
warm gloves (optional)
sunglasses (optional)
flashlight (optional)

INSURANCE AND DOCTOR'S CLEARANCE

Common sense will tell the story as to whether or not a rider is fit to ride a bike a particular distance. Usually, parents know a kid's physical history well enough to throw up any red flags. However, it is good to require a physical if the ride is going to be more than 500 miles.

Most families carry a standard health-insurance policy. Beyond the standard family health policy it is good to have a group accident policy to cover any marginal cases. Reasonable coverage would be a $5,000-First Dollar Accident and Sickness policy. Hand in hand with the accident policy the tour should have adequate liability coverage.

SAFETY TECHNIQUES

Many items have already been covered on ways to increase the safety of the cyclists. Some of these have been safe roads, flags, clothing, leadership, night riding, etc. Other items that need to be covered are helmets, city traffic, and road conditions.

The bicycle helmet is becoming more and more accepted, and there are many brands from which to choose. Enforcing the wearing of a helmet is worth the effort if one rider is kept from being seriously injured.

City riding has its special problems. Grates that cover drainage holes are a major hazard, especially if the grill work runs parallel to the street. They are even more dangerous if located in areas where riders are traveling fast as a result of coasting. Car doors opening on the traffic side pose a problem. Stop lights must be obeyed as though the riders were driving a car.

Road conditions present the most serious problems. Gravel is always dangerous and the rider should slow down when riding in it. The front brake, if applied when riding in gravel, increases the danger even more. Riders riding off the edge of the road onto the shoulder are likely to spill when coming back onto the road. This is due to the ridge created by the highway surface and the shoulder. Railroad tracks present the same kind of problems. Riders should try to cross them by riding perpendicular to the tracks if possible. Wet roads are dangerous because of the poor braking ability and the visibility on the part of the traffic to see the cyclists is poor. As a general rule, never start cycling in the rain. If the riders get caught in the rain, then personal judgments need to be made. Chuck holes, debris in the road, and unusual bridge surfaces, all create the need for alertness to road conditions.

RIDING TECHNIQUES

It is important that the individual riders be allowed to find their own comfort level. The ten-speed bike with the traditional drop handle bar will allow the rider to assume the best position for touring. His body will be at a forty-five degree angle. This allows the body weight to be spread more evenly over the bike. This position allows for better use of muscles and better control in steering the bike. It allows the cyclist to be more relaxed and wind resistance is lowered. The dropped bar also allows for a greater number of hand positions.

Proper gearing is the name of the game for long-distance touring. Riding in the correct gear will allow for more distance with less energy being used. When a person walks briskly he will take 120 to 130 steps a minute. When this is compared to pedaling, he will pedal 60 to 65 revolutions per minute. A constant pedal rhythm is more important than trying to maintain a certain speed. When going uphill, shifting to a lower gear slows the rider down but does not mean less revolutions per minute and usually the same amount of energy is used. Heavy winds and climbing long mountain roads will require more work. When riding with a tail wind or going downhill, the opposite will be true, allowing the rider to use a higher gear.

A reasonable pattern of riding with groups is to regroup at least three times a day. That means that all the individual squads come together at about 9:00 or 10:00 A.M., at 12 noon, and 3:00 or 4:00 P.M. Psychologically this helps the slower riders and creates a good situation for more fellowship.

The normal pattern for cycling with a squad of six is to have the squad ride single file about three yards apart. Double file can occur when traffic is almost zero and road conditions permit. The squad leader should maintain a rear position as much as possible. This will allow him to call out traffic and make better judgment calls. It is good to shift the individual squad members around from the windbreaking lead spot so no one person is in this position all the time. The squad should sound like a softball infield—chattering all the time—calling out holes, items on the road, approaching traffic, etc. They really need to communicate with each other.

COURTESY

A group as large as forty can be frightening to a small country-store owner. It is important, therefore, to impress on the team the effectiveness of being polite. Some of the most profound witness comes from the conduct of the group. Keeping the noise down, staying out of the way, allowing other customers to do their business, all are a part of group courtesy.

When stopping at a gas station, for instance, it is important to park the bikes away from the area that will compete for customer service. Clean up after the group. If the restrooms are used by the forty-person team, someone needs to make sure they are in better shape when the team leaves than when the team came into the station. This could even mean getting a mop and cleanser and performing janitorial duties.

The use of common riding attire, indicating some degree of organization, seems to put establishment owners at ease.

The impact of group cycling has been felt in the Christian community. It was Wandering Wheels that took the lead and rejuvenated long-distance touring nationally.

Long-distance group cycling experiences creates memories which, when combined with future teaching, will make for good Christian growth. Wandering Wheels calls it "evangelism in escrow." Or, one could say that the teaching, learning, and changing of attitudes that take place during a bike trip will be drawn on for years to come.

ADDITIONAL READING

Ray Adams, *Serious Cycling for the Beginner.* Mountain View, California: Bike World.

Building Bicycle Wheels. Mountain View, California: World Publications, Inc.

Tony Christopher, "Cycling," *Illustrated Digest.* New York: Stadia Sports Publishing, Inc.

Tom Cuthbertson, *Anybody's Bike Book.* Mountain View, California: World-Sports Library, Inc.

Fred Delong, *Delong's Guide to Bicycles and Bicycling—The Art and Science.* Radnor, Pennsylvania: Chilton Book Company.

Handbook of Cycl-Ology. Minnetonka, Minnesota: Cycle Goods Corporation.

Stephen Henkel, *Bikes.* Mountain View, California: World-Sports Library, Inc.

Keith Kingaby, *Inside Bicycling.* Chicago: Henry Regnery Co.

Irene Kleeberg, *Bicycle Repair.* Mountain View, California: World-Sports Library, Inc.

Joe Kossack, *Building Frames.* Mountain View, California: World-Sports Library, Inc.

Ross Olney, *Simple Bicycle Repair and Maintenance.* Mountain View, California: World-Sports Library, Inc.

Eugene A. Sloane, *The New and Complete Book of Bicycling.* New York: Simon and Schuster.

Lloyd Summer, *The Long Ride.* Harrisburg, Pennsylvania: Stackpole Books.

MAGAZINES

Bicycle Camping and Touring
Tobey Publishing Company
Box 428
New Canaan, Connecticut 06840

Bicycling Magazine
Bicycling Magazine, Inc.
33 East Minor Street
Emmaus, Pennsylvania 18049

Bike World Magazine
World Publications, Inc.
Box 366
Mountain View, California 94042

Travel by Bike
(By the editors of *Bike World*)
World Publications, Inc.
Box 366
Mountain View, California 94042

19

Summer Camping

CAMPING WITH A PURPOSE

After a long, cold winter and the new life of springtime, there is a mass urban exodus to the beautiful outdoor setting of mountains and lakes. Young people especially enjoy the exhilarating changes from their schedule to a camp setting.

Dr. Ted Ward, noted educator from Michigan State University, has said, "Christian camping offers the greatest environment for Christian education in America today."[1] A "teachable moment" is nowhere more evident than in a camping setting, and the Scriptures abound with stories of Jesus teaching His disciples and followers in the outdoor setting.

In camp surroundings, young people begin for the first time to make choices apart from their parents. Dr. Basil Jackson, a Christian psychiatrist from Marquette University, has underscored the important role Christian camping can have in the life of an adolescent. He calls the period of adolescence more accurately, "a period of separation." This is a period of time when the most complex changes occur physically, spiritually, psychologically, and socially.

The young person begins to develop a sense of autonomy and starts on the road of decision-making as a unique individual.

Edward Oulund is an international representative of Christian Camping International with over 40 years experience in all levels of camping.

The greatest contribution Christian camping can make to young people is to lead them to a life of joy, peace, and satisfaction as they begin to make daily choices with Christ as their partner. They learn that it isn't necessary to "walk alone," especially when parents aren't there, but that they can, like Enoch, "walk with God" through life.

Other purposes and goals for a camping experience could include the following:

- Teaching truths from Scriptures, especially those related to God's creation and the outdoors.
- Helping young people understand the details and complexity of God's creation and loving Him more for it.
- Teaching campers about a personal walk and relationship to Jesus Christ.
- Building strong relationships between campers and staff, and campers to their own peer group.
- Teaching scriptural truths that can be translated into daily actions.
- Teaching new skills of physical growth and achievement.

Each group should develop its own list of purposes for camping and continuously review them during the year. Purposes can be measurable in "quantity" as well as "quality."

Cathy Nicholl, veteran camp director of the Canadian Inter-Varsity camps, has said, "It is possible to have quality in large quantities and it is also possible to have very poor quality in some very small quantity. It is also possible to substitute quantity as a measure of success when we fail in quality. We are apt to substitute the use of quantity of camper days for the quality of results because of its immediate satisfaction. In our culture this has become greatly important and unfortunately has found its way into Christian activity."[2]

TYPES OF SUMMER CAMPING

Our modern culture has added many varieties to camping in the past fifty years. Our churches have borrowed many of these programs and have assimilated them into new creative camping approaches. There has been a growing trend away from the larger family conference approach, toward more youth-oriented action types of programs and wilderness experiences.

Camping programs may be either centralized or decentralized. "In its purest form the centralized camping approach focuses mainly on large group activity. Minimal initiatives are required from cabin unit leaders. It seeks to fulfill the camping purpose mainly through preaching and teaching in all-camp meetings. The remaining parts of the camp programs, while not discounted as to physical values, are not seen as primarily involved in fulfilling the spiritual purpose of the camp. In contrast, the decentralized camping approach focuses on the cabin unit led by a capable counselor. The program is designed to provide maximum involvement in small-group activity. In its purest form, the campers would rarely assemble for some meals, award-giving, or orientation."[3]

There are strengths and weaknesses in both types of programs and those responsible for camp planning must carefully weigh the best approach for their group. There is still room in many camps for the youth-oriented teacher-preacher who is able to motivate campers through his presentation of biblical truths. Often the same person can multiply his effectiveness by teaching counselors how to teach campers in smaller groups.

The ultimate in decentralized camping is trip, trail, wilderness, or stress camping. Skills are learned in the wilderness that often have a life-saving effect and change attitudes toward a Christian living experience with real depth.

Wheaton College and other Christian colleges have offered courses in stress camping for several years to incoming college freshmen. The courses offer such stress experiences as mountain climbing, rappelling, long-trip canoeing over rough, white rivers or open waters, and then living on edible natural foods of the land.

Some years ago I interviewed Dr. Hudson Armerding, who was at the time President of Wheaton College, for his appraisal of their new stress program for college freshmen. He confirmed the growing evidence of students having many "teachable moments" and "stretching" through their wilderness experiences to become campus leaders. He said he felt that students, though they might still find areas of campus problems and disagreements, were now looking for new options and solutions to these problems.

CHOOSING THE CAMP SITE

You should choose your camp site carefully. Since camping makes the maximum use of the natural out-of-doors, it is important to provide facilities that will bring the camper and leaders into a close relationship with God's great creation. Too often, especially in a conference setting, the pointed tower of a chapel becomes the focus of the conference site. This may tend to instill the idea that God can be worshiped only in buildings, whereas the camping experience ought to emphasize the fact that God can be worshiped anywhere in His creation.

The amount of land available at the camp site should be considered. Most camping organizations recommend at least one acre per camper in order to provide adequate natural interests, privacy, and isolation. Some camps have effectively achieved this goal by locating their site adjacent to a state or federal park or land. Truman Robertson, director of Fort Wilderness youth camp in Wisconsin, has said he has a site of 50,500 acres—500 belonging to the camp and 50,000 that is the American Legion State Forest. His staff uses the state property for horsemanship and hiking in the summer and for the winter sports of skiing, snowshoeing, and snowmobiling.

The accessibility of the camp site is also important and should be measured in terms of time. Interstate highways, air lanes, and even waterways can bring distant areas close. You must decide how much time and expense you want to commit to travel to the site. Both the distance from the camp and the mode of transportation will help determine how far you should travel.

The question of owning or renting the facilities of another organization is a vital consideration. Often there are camps that have adequate facilities and are looking for a limited source of income in order to keep staff employed year round, for regular maintenance and security. There are a limited amount of facilities available on public lands, but it may be worth investigating. Some of these lands may be available on a long-term lease for development. Of course, renting a site often will limit an organization to using the site in less desirable weeks of the year. It would be wise to check out the rules and regulations of the camp you are renting. You may find that these rules will inhibit the type of program you were planning to conduct and create a negative environment.

To assist you in choosing a camp site, Christian Camping International, an association of major Christian camps around the world, has an outstanding program of certification for Christian camps. Look for those camps that are "marked by excellence" in their facilities, staff, program, food services, and long-range planning. More information regarding the camp certification program called *Foundations for Excellence,* as well as a U.S. and worldwide directory of camps, may be secured by contacting Christian Camping International, Box 646, Wheaton, Illinois 60189.

PREPARING A SUMMER CAMP

Some of the larger West Coast conferences, where both adult and youth camps are held in the same location, have had successful thematic camping programs. Camp Forest Home in California has an Indian Village for 4th- through 6th-grade campers. The drum sounds through the canyon pines—where, under the supervision of trained "Indian Chiefs," campers (braves) enjoy hiking, Bible study, swimming, crafts, council fires, Indian games, and just plain fun. Camp Rancho, another location, is for 7th- and 8th-graders. Horses, old western activities and skits provide a setting where Jesus Christ becomes relevant. High schoolers are challenged to an "Olympic Village"; a take-off on a modern version of a competitive athletic program. The emphasis is on dialogue and communication between campers and listening Christian counselors.

In every camp there should be a good balance of time spent in learning new skills, as well as studying the Word of God. Even such programs as horsemanship or ceramics can be taught creatively using the Bible as a textbook.

Campers also need to learn the appreciation, understanding, and wise use of natural resources for the greatest good for future generations. Campers can learn by doing. Cleaning up trails, roadways, riverbanks and lakeshores, planting cover brush for eroded areas, planting trees on hillsides; all help campers learn principles of conservation.

No Christian camp should overlook the many opportunities and places for Christian growth. The campfire meeting with well-planned programs can easily be the most meaningful and lasting experience for the campers' spiritual growth. Music can greatly enhance the programs with skits and devotional talks. Superior campfires and programs don't just happen the last minute; they come from careful, detailed planning.

Hiking along familiar and new trails can be enhanced by new objectives and goals, such as learning orienteering (use of a compass). A list of special types of hikes might include:

- A nature-study hike—looking for signs of wildlife, butterflies, birds, trees, etc.
- A historical hike, discovering the remnant of an Indian mound or battle.
- A rain hike.
- Overnight hike, learning cooking and tenting skills.
- A cemetery hike, discovering unusual, interesting dates found on the tombstones.
- Hill or mountain hike.
- Night or moonlight hike, listening to the night sounds of animals and birds.
- Conservation hike, cleaning up trails, roadways, and riverbanks.

For the safety of campers and to keep insurance rates from skyrocketing, "contact games" such as Capture the Flag need to be carefully monitored in order to eliminate broken bones. Games such as baseball would be better to have than new games that can be played outdoors in a natural setting.

FINANCING AND PROMOTING THE CAMP

Setting fees for a summer camp must be realistic. In the long run, it is better stewardship to do the job right than to put together a camp that is substandard in its leadership, food, and program. Many groups raise scholarship funds from their supporters to assist campers who cannot afford part or even a part of the total camp fee. Fees often are reduced for larger families for two or more members of the family. Each year the fees need to be reviewed and should project an adequate increase as the cost of living rises. There is a real danger in overlooking increases for two or more years and then adding a whopping 25-35% camp fee increase.

There is another advantage in collecting registration fees as early as possible. A sizable nonrefundable fee will help assure that campers will come, and they are often a source of additional income. I was told by a director of a large camp on the West Coast that they registered people to return the following year while still at camp. The registration fee was then banked, earning more than $10,000 in interest during the year. You have to be big to accomplish that, but it's worth thinking about.

Promotion, particularly early mailings, is essential. Organizational and private camps are usually much more alert to the need for early promotion. As Scout Masters, we were trained to have all Scout camp registrations sent into headquarters on a date at least five months prior to the camp date. In the average Scout camp it would be almost impossible to register for summer camp after February 15 of any year.

Honesty and ethics are an important part of camp promotion. Too often beautiful four-color brochures exaggerate the facilities and programs. If water skiing or any such specialty is promoted, there should be adequate equipment and personnel to carry out the program that is indicated.

SELECTING YOUR LEADERSHIP TEAM

The number-one problem on which camp directors agree unanimously, in both independent and organizational camps, is the difficulty of recruiting adequate leadership for the camping ministry. Both need and solution are illustrated in 1 Chronicles 12. The setting of the story was at a crucial point in the life of David, anointed to become king. He was having one victory after another. Every tribe now, as in a presidential nominating convention, was getting on his bandwagon. Each tribe contributed from 3,000 to 120,000 warriors to assist David, except for the tribe of Issachar, of which we read: "Men of Issachar, who understood the times and knew what Israel should do—200 chiefs, with all their relatives under their command" (1 Chron. 12:32).

Dr. L. Ted Johnson, youth secretary for the General Conference of Baptist Churches, has said of leadership: "A leader is a person who moves progressively forward in a prescribed path toward a pre-determined goal that he may lead others to similar personal achievement. He is in effect a bridge builder. He constructs a span across which others can safely and profitably move toward desired goals. . . . A leader is a responsible person, able to communicate his ideas, plans, and desires to others. He has vision without being visionary. He is decisive without being soft. He is adaptable to changing situations and circumstances without being guilty of wavering in every persuasive wind that blows."[4]

But looking for leaders doesn't necessarily mean you have to look for upfront, platform personality types. Cathy Nicholl, veteran camp director, says it succinctly: "One of the things I have learned over the years is that I would go completely and absolutely 'hairy' if I ran a camp that was all personality leaders. Very often a quality camp is undergirded by the quiet, steady, faithful folk you can always depend on. The foundation of quality camping is quality relationships. The Lord used the word 'servant' throughout His ministry. A quality leader is a servant. He says this about Himself: 'Even the Son came not to be served but to serve.'"[5]

These leaders can be found in Christian or secular schools and colleges, but the first place to look is among your own group. Campers who have grown up through the camp program can often be singled out to become the finest leaders. School teachers and nurses whose summer vacations may be longer, can often be encouraged to give leadership that is required.

During the early teens there is a need for more careful leadership counselor selection and training. During high school and college camps or retreats, it is even more important to have older, mature, experienced leadership who can be trained to motivate campers by their examples of Christian life. Harvey Chrouser, dean of camp directors from Wheaton College's Honeyrock Camp has often said that the most important objective and reason for the existence of their camp is the development of staff and counselors for Christian leadership in the years ahead.

In training counselors here are a few positive and negative characteristics to emphasize:

A good counselor:

- Has a good sense of humor and can smile even in the face of criticism.
- Leads by example and is a good listener.
- Recognizes "fun" to be a chief reason why campers come to camp.
- Gives praise publicly and can usually see some good to commend even in a weak camper. Praise is given in public.
- Uses discipline sparingly, and even when aggravated does not show his temper.
- Tries to treat all campers alike, even the rich kid, or campers from the more affluent families.

Conversely, a good counselor:

- Does not act as a master sergeant or judge.
- Is not a slave to the campers, nor does he enter into a free-for-all wrestling match.
- Is not a detective—snooping through belongings of the campers.
- Does not easily give up on a camper who is a prankster. Often creative leaders come from the group of kids who "test the limits."
- Avoids disciplining a camper in front of his peers. He never uses physical punishment.
- Avoids problems of campers who have a "crush" on him/her. These campers are steered into more productive involvement in the camping program.

Over the years I've been privileged to see God work in the lives of countless young men and women as they encountered Him in the setting of a summer camp. I'm confident that as you use the vehicle of a summer camping program as part of your ministry, you'll experience rich rewards.

FOOTNOTES

[1]Dr. Ted Ward, Christian Camping International Convention, October 1979, French Lick, Indiana.

[2]Cathy Nicholl, "Quality Versus Quantity," Christian Camping International, Wheaton, Illinois, 1978 (a monograph).

[3]Werner Graendorf and Lloyd Mattson, *An Introduction to Christian Camping* (Chicago: Moody Press, 1979), pp. 50–51.

[4]L. Ted Johnson and Lee M. Kingsley, *Blueprint for Quality* (Chicago: Harvest Press, 1969), p. 42.

[5]Nicholl, "Quality Versus Quantity."

20

Short-term Missions Projects

Five thousand miles from home, in the dense jungle of Brazil, a missionary was clearing a much-needed airfield of stumps, five hundred of them. That's not unusual work for a missionary, but this one was a thirteen-year-old girl who had never before been outside her small midwest town. She wasn't alone, however. She was part of a team of thirty young people who were summer missionaries. They were learning what it meant to put their faith into action.

WHAT SHORT-TERM MISSIONARY OPPORTUNITIES EXIST FOR HIGH SCHOOL STUDENTS?

Many mission organizations list short-term opportunities for individuals who have basic skills to contribute. These skills may include teaching, secretarial work, construction or medical work, to name a few. The assignments may be for periods ranging from two weeks to two years. The longer assignments are generally for those who have completed a minimum of high school.

Most opportunities that exist for high-school students, however, center not so much on individual talent, but in the activity of an organized group of ten to fifty students. These young people may not be skilled workers, but they combine their efforts to assist an existing mission.

Bob Bland is the Executive Director of Teen Missions International, Merritt Island, Florida.

The types of projects that can be accomplished depends on the skills and training of the students and their leaders. Untrained teams generally do simple projects of repair, painting, cleaning, landscaping, and odd jobs.

Teams with additional training may take on more complex jobs such as construction of schools, homes, churches, orphanages, and youth camps. In some cases the work teams may have opportunity for a direct ministry and in other circumstances they may not, but not all short-term groups are work teams. There are:

- *Singing Groups* who share in churches, camps, and open-air meetings.
- *Literature distribution teams* who blanket communities with gospel literature.
- *Vacation Bible-school teams* who put on a one- or two-week Bible school in places that otherwise would not have one.
- *Puppet groups* who operate children's camps or share at open-air meetings, fairs, and festivals.
- *Bicycle teams* who travel mostly in North America and Europe conducting open-air evangelistic meetings.
- *Sports teams* who use their athletic skills to open opportunities for personal and group evangelism.
- *Boat teams* who use large ships operated by Operation Mobilization or canal boats operated by Teen Mission, Youth for Christ, and other organizations for a ministry to those at ports of call or along the waterways.
- *Parks teams* who travel to national parks in the United States and Canada. Although permission to hold religious services in National Parks by outsiders is generally not granted, often the campers can share one-on-one or hold their own campfire meetings, inviting others to attend.

In recent years the opportunities for serious high-school students who want to have a ministry during the summer months have increased significantly. Local churches, denominations, mission and parachurch organizations are offering a large variety of short-term service opportunities.

ARE SHORT-TERM MISSIONS WORTH THE SUBSTANTIAL TIME AND FINANCIAL COMMITMENT?

The end result of short-term missions opportunities can be seen both in the completed project and in the lives of the students participating.

One group of students traveled two days and nights by river launch to a remote part of the jungle where they built a floating hangar to provide a place to service a mission float plane. Prior to this, the nearest place of service was four air-hours away, round trip. Words are inadequate to express the gratitude seen in the eyes of a family whose home has been rebuilt by a group of students following a devastating hurricane, or a group of believers who now for the first time have a place to worship together because a group of students has built a church for them. Work teams of high-school students have made significant and tangible contributions to the world in recent years. Those involved in sending students on such missions agree, however, that the most significant contribution made is not in the building of buildings, but in the building of lives. Hardly ever does a young person return from such an assignment with the same set of values he or she started with.

One young man recently said, "Christ becomes real when you sit with a friend and a broken-down jeep somewhere between Barraquilla and Santa Marta under the stars, waiting for help. You begin to realize God's total control of every circumstance. As I look back, I can see how that jeep was used to put us in touch with people who hadn't heard the gospel, simply because the jeep broke down at the right time and the right place. This summer taught me the need of absolute, unreserved surrender to the will of God."

A young lady wrote, following her experience, "My heart was broken in a million pieces this summer over extreme poverty, sick bodies and souls perishing without hope of ever sharing eternity with the Lord."

SHOULD I PLAN THE ENTIRE PROJECT MYSELF, OR SHOULD I WORK THROUGH AN EXISTING AGENCY?

Once you as a youth leader make the commitment to provide a short-term missions experience for your group, you need to decide if you will create the entire experience yourself or work with an agency already engaged in these activities.

There are several advantages to putting your own group and program together. Some of these advantages include being the leader of your own group, setting your own time of the year, length of stay, and the project itself. You may set the size of the group and the age parameters of the participants. Generally, the cost may be less because you're not paying for organizational overhead. You can establish your own training program and preparation can become a part of your year-long program.

On the other hand, you may not be as familiar with the proper travel procedures including visas, legal problems, customs of the country, and the project itself. You take on the additional responsibilities of deciding who qualifies to be part of the team. You can become involved with parents who may think you are treating their child unfairly, particularly if some form of disciplinary action is needed. Above all, you and the church take on a tremendous legal liability for a group of high-school students in a foreign land.

In addition to the many denominations that provide short-term mission experiences for churches within their own group, there are several missionary and parachurch organizations providing these experiences as well. Following is a partial listing of these organizations:

Child Evangelism Fellowship
P.O. Box 348
Warrenton, Missouri 63383

Gospel Missionary Union
10000 N. Oak
Kansas City, Missouri 64155

The Evangelical Alliance Mission (TEAM)
P.O. Box 969
Wheaton, Illinois 60187

Greater Europe Mission
P.O. Box 668
Wheaton, Illinois 60189

Regions Beyond Missionary Union
8102 Elberon Avenue
Philadelphia, Pennsylvania 19111

South America Mission, Inc.
5217 S. Military Trail
Lake Worth, Florida 33460

Teen Missions International
P.O. Box 1056 TMT
Merritt Island, Florida 32952

Unevangelized Fields Mission
P.O. Box 306
Bala-Cynwyd, Pennsylvania 19004

Worldteam
P.O. Box 343038
Coral Gables, Florida 33134

The Worldwide Evangelization Crusade
P.O. Box A, 709 Pennsylvania
Ft. Washington, Pennsylvania 19034

Youth for Christ (Project Serve)
P.O. Box 419
Wheaton, Illinois 60189

IN CONCLUSION

I am confident that the experience we are talking about may be one of the most life-forming periods of your young people's lives. You may decide to create the entire experience yourself or you may decide to work with an existing agency. In some situations you may be able to work with your own group as a self-contained unit within an existing agency.

Whichever direction you choose, the following guidelines may be helpful in making your experience as worthwhile as possible:

- Don't take a group without proper training and preparation.
- Be mindful of safety. Many good things can happen; so can many bad things. A young person could lose his or her life.
- Know your purpose.
- Be willing to sacrifice. It is not a vacation.
- Check and recheck on set-up. Overseas organizations think tomorrow, and you have only a few weeks there.
- Guard the actions and dress of young people closely. Remember that missionaries have to live there after you leave. A bad incident by the group could close the door to a witness for a long period of time.
- Find out the culture of the national church. In most cases, missions have been there long enough so that a national church exists. Their standards are usually more strict than

we're used to as it relates to manners and dress code. Do not be the "ugly American."

Let me encourage you to talk with some of the agencies involved in this type of mission outreach, to seek out other youth directors who have had experience with their own youth group's mission involvement, and to seek the mind of the Lord for His direction regarding your students. I know He will honor you for it.

IV SHARPENING THE TOOLS OF YOUTH WORK

21

Practical Suggestions for Keeping Current on the Youth Culture

Walking into a living room full of teen-agers can be intimidating, even for an experienced youth worker.

"What can I talk about with this crowd?" "Will they reject me just because I'm a few years older?" "How do I get through to these young people?" All these questions storm into the youth worker's mind as he anticipates spending the next hour or week or year with a new crop of teens.

If it's any comfort, most youth workers never get over the sense that they are in a different world when they are surrounded by teen-agers.

"Even after four years of working in the same high school," one youth worker from upstate New York said, "I never felt totally at ease contacting kids at school. I don't think you ever feel comfortable—a twenty-eight-year old—eating lunch with high schoolers in the school cafeteria."

Nor, perhaps, should an adult forget the fact that he *is* an alien in this teen-age world. A youth worker should not simply be an overgrown teen-ager. Too many youth workers make that mistake. Unfortunately, by becoming nothing more than "one of the guys" or "one of the girls," you run the danger of losing the respect of the young people, to say nothing of your credibility with their parents.

Marshall Shelley, a former youth worker and adjunct instructor in Christian Education at Denver Seminary, is assistant editor of LEADERSHIP journal.

Effective youth workers walk that delicate balance of being an adult in a teen-ager's world. They participate fully, but without becoming teen-agers themselves. As much as Christians are commanded to be "in the world but not of the world," so must youth workers live among teen-agers with that same tension.

That caution being made, however, the youth worker must be intimately acquainted with the youth world if he or she is going to minister effectively in that culture.

How do you do that? How can you keep current in the ever-changing youth culture? Vocabulary, interests, and fads are constantly shifting. While the deeper needs of young people tend to remain the same, the expression of those needs will vary. One year the group may be sports-oriented, and anyone wishing to be accepted by them must be able to talk sports. The next year the sign of acceptance may be keeping track of a certain musician.

"My junior highers are into noises this year," said a youth director from a church in Illinois. "As long as you can do a respectable car crash or dive bomber or drum-solo imitation, you're immediately in."

The expressions may vary, but the need for love and acceptance remains. How do youth workers learn to communicate meaningfully in the youth culture with expressions and ideas their young people can understand?

One of the keys is what Jay Kesler once called "creative hanging around."

This means that you find ways that fit your personality to meet teen-agers on neutral ground, not just in church or in the youth group where the situation is "controlled." Maybe this will mean inviting one or two guys from the group over to help you work on your car. One brave junior-high Sunday school teacher invited his class to his home to make tacos. He said, "Here's the meat, the lettuce, the cheese, and the shells. You guys are in charge." And the group had to do the cooking and preparation. It provided a great opportunity to let some of the guys, who perhaps weren't the smartest in class but who could cook, a chance to perform what they could do well. It also gave the teacher a chance to get to know his class in a way that never would have happened during the regular class time.

School events are another way to meet students on neutral ground. Plays, concerts, athletic contests, all give you time to spend with youth and give you a natural topic of conversation. Ask questions—probing questions if the situation is appropriate, about their likes, dislikes, and reactions to happenings around school. It will give you a glimpse into the minds of your young people.

School newspapers are an indispensable source of information. If you work with high-school students, write their school or schools and request a subscription to their school paper. Many schools have a mailing list of subscribers. If they don't, most faculty newspaper advisers wouldn't mind mailing you a copy if you pay the postage. The insight into the inner ticking of the school is well worth the minimal investment. You may even get ideas from the papers that you can use to base a lesson or group meeting on.

Become acquainted with some of the magazines that your young people are reading. If they are junior highers, pick up a copy of *Mad* magazine (if you're like some youth workers, you've been a subscriber ever since *you* were in junior high), or *Pizzaz,* or *Bananas.* If you work with high schoolers, start reading *Seventeen.* More than being merely entertaining, each of these publications will have thoughtful features that will help you understand some of the issues young people are currently struggling with. Two magazines that do an excellent job of integrating the Christian faith with the problems of high school are *Campus Life* and *Group.* Both are well-written and professionally designed so that the personality of these magazines is warm, up-beat, and informal, but with the right touch of helpful advice. Both magazines also can be used in group settings. *Group* has a discussion section built into each issue, and *Campus Life* has a separate leader's guide available with ideas for group use.

The music that young people listen to can also help you stay in touch with them. "Some of the best opportunities I had to share with my kids what it means to be a Christian," said one former youth leader in Denver, Colorado, "was when I was driving the van during our summer trips. We'd listen to the radio and critique the songs, both the music and the words. I also learned a lot about the kids' attitudes and some of their deeper thoughts."

Don't feel obligated to try to enjoy Top-40 music just because your junior highers do. You may want to listen occasionally when you're with them, or perhaps to keep up your working vocabulary on the current musicians. But if rock music isn't part of your personality, don't force it. Teen-agers enjoy people whose tastes are different, as long as they can joke about them.

Because I tend more toward country western music, on our last church-group retreat I demanded equal time on the radio—for every song we listened to on "their" station, I got to listen to one on "mine." It turned out to be a great time of talking about what we liked about music and why. After that two-hour ride, all of us in the car felt we knew one another a lot better.

Experience, listening, and time spent with young people probably are the best teachers. But they aren't the only ones. Besides those forms of "creative hanging around," other sources are available to help you keep current in the youth culture.

Some youth workers feel that because they spend long hours with their group they know what the kids' needs are. That's true to a point, but experience alone doesn't always give you a broad enough perspective of what's happening in the lives of the kids.

Let me give an illustration. My father, a church history professor, once accompanied a group of tourists to the historical sites of Germany. One of the stops was the famous Wartburg Castle, where Martin Luther was held "prisoner" for his own safety by his friend Frederick, the ruler of Saxony. While there, Luther translated the Bible into German. He also was deeply troubled there, and the devil became so real to him in a vision that Luther hurled an inkwell at him.

When my father stood in that room where Luther had struggled with the direction of the Reformation and saw the stained wall, a reminder of Luther's battle with the devil, he was deeply moved. The other tourists weren't. To them it was but one of a long string of historical sites.

What was the difference in the two reactions? My dad and the others in the group had had the same experience—they had seen the same bare room with a desk, bench, and stained wall. But it meant more to my dad. Why? Because he knew what to look for. As a result, even though everyone saw the same objects, my dad saw more than the objects themselves. Because he had studied and read, he had the background that enabled him to get more out of the experience.

The same is true for youth workers. They can observe attitudes and behavior in the teens in their youth group, but unless they know the significance of the attitudes and behavior, the full importance may be lost.

Thus, study of the age characteristics and developmental stages of adolescents is important. It helps youth workers know how to react when one of the kids starts feeling self-conscious about his height, or lack thereof. Or about his or her body. Or when tensions develop between young people and their parents.

Three excellent books have been written from a Christian perspective dealing with the young person's passage through the teen-age years. *Junior High Ministry* by Wayne Rice (Zondervan) is perhaps the best of the Christian age-characteristics books. It includes not only descriptions of problem areas, but also offers programing ideas for youth workers to use with junior highers. Marlene LeFever's *Toward Freedom* (Cook) is only 64 pages, but it is a helpful summary of the physical, emotional, mental, moral, and social development that adolescents go through. And John Westerhoff deals with the spiritual stages that adolescents work through in his book *Will Our Children Have Faith?* (Seabury).

From a secular point of view, but still very helpful to youth workers, is Dr. Haim Ginott's widely read *Between Parent and Teenager* (Avon). Though some of his illustrations are a bit dated (the book was copyrighted in 1969), it still remains the standard book in the secular field on parent-teen relationships. And the principles of communication and understanding that Ginott discusses are just as true for Christians as for anyone else.

And finally, a book that deals with a problem almost every youth worker has is Tim Hansel's *When I Relax I Feel Guilty* (Cook). A former staff member with Young Life, Hansel certainly knows the youth ministry and the real danger of burn-out. Though not dealing with age characteristics, this book may prove even more valuable to youth workers by helping them remember to bring the most important ingredients to their youth group—themselves.

Books aren't the only source of helpful background for dealing with young people. Two newsletters also do a good job of keeping youth workers in tune.

Success With Youth Report (Grafton Publications) is filled with succinct information on current trends among youth, the latest findings of nationwide polls, events that will affect youth, and other youth-related news.

Youthletter (Evangelical Ministries, Inc.), though often borrowing heavily from *Success With Youth Report,* does include a one-page editorial from a Christian perspective plus a two-page annotated bibliography that provides a constant source of new materials.

It's also helpful for youth workers to meet one another to discuss their ministries; to find out what's working and what isn't, and to encourage one another.

Many cities throughout the United States and Canada have Sunday school conventions that offer excellent workshops and resources for youth workers. Youth Specialties, Inc. annually sponsors the National Youth Worker's Convention in different locations and, usually in the spring, conducts a series of Youth Worker's Resource Seminars in most of the major metropolitan areas of the United States. These gatherings are a helpful way to meet other people involved in youth ministry and to discover trends in the youth culture.

Perhaps the most important way of staying fresh in the youth culture and of making sure you are effectively addressing the youth culture is by staying personally fresh. No matter how efficient the medium, unless solid content is coming through, the whole process is in vain.

How can a person keep himself from going stale? From where comes our freshness?

In youth ministry, with so much activity demanded, it's easy to overlook the need for spiritual nourishment. This can take a number of forms. Certainly involvement with God's people in a church is vital, and so is daily communication with God.

Bible study is important, but most of us have to admit that it's hard to work into the daily routine. For me, Bible study is like jogging; almost impossible for me to do alone. The motivation simply isn't there. But if I have a group of friends who are expecting me to show up, either for exercise or Bible study, then it will get done. I'm thankful for the people in my life who hold me to these disciplines.

Seek out people who can provide a spark for your spiritual life, people who ask questions, hard questions, and then doggedly search for honest, satisfying answers. If this kind of personal spiritual life can be developed, it will become apparent in your youth ministry.

People who have learned to think freshly and honestly before God will speak freshly and honestly with their young people. Don't settle for leading youth groups directly from printed curriculum products. These can be helpful idea starters, but run them through your own life first, and try to come up with one concept or application that's new for *you*. By making sure that at least one item is fresh to you, you'll accomplish two things: first, you'll keep yourself growing spiritually, and second, your times with the group will have more life. Chances are, if the material you present to your group isn't fresh for you, it won't be fresh for them.

Help develop your ability to think freshly by reading some of the thoughtful Christian periodicals, such as *Eternity*, LEADERSHIP, *Reformed Journal*, *Christianity Today*, or the newsletter *Context*, edited by Martin Marty. These publications do an effective job of relating spiritual truth to the realities of the world. And if you can learn to do that, you'll be a long way toward effectively addressing youth issues.

SUGGESTIONS

Besides these important spiritual keys to staying fresh personally, a few simple practical steps can also help.

1. Begin to list prayer requests in a notebook, especially those involving your youth group. Every month or so, review each of those items. You'll be encouraged as you see God working in ways great and small.

2. Once in awhile take an inventory of the experiences you're glad you've had—

- An icy root beer on a hot day.
- A snowball fight.
- Thunder.
- Handel's *Messiah*.
- Christmas.

3. Start a humor file. If you see something that makes you laugh—not that's merely amusing—but that makes you chuckle out loud, jot it down or clip it out and put it in the humor file. It may be a fractured proverb such as: A bird in the hand is messier than two in the bush. Or it may be a true story, such as the youth leader who was telling the story about Lot being told to take his wife and flee from the city. One of his ninth-graders said, "I know what happened to his wife; what happened to his flea?" Humor files are fun to thumb through when you're feeling down, and they're also a valuable resource for working with young people. Humor is just as effective in the youth culture as it is in the adult world.

4. Start a youth-group scrapbook for yourself. Keep track of what you've done with the group with photos, clippings, ticket stubs, things you've written together in the group, and event calendars. These serve as a reminder of the people you've worked with and the progress you've seen in their lives. One church youth director said, "Every time the group comes over to my house someone says, 'Let's get out the scrapbook!' They enjoy it as much as I do."

These are just a few ideas. I hope they spark more ideas in your own mind. All of these suggestions are ways of building contacts with the youth culture and ministering effectively in it.

But remember, the best youth worker isn't necessarily the one who does the most right things. It's usually the one who cares about the young people in the group and loves them enough to find his own ways of expressing that love.

22

Speaking to High-school Students

A cynic once said the three hardest things in the world are: to climb a mountain leaning toward you, to kiss a young lady leaning away from you, and to keep youth interested for twenty minutes with a speech. He was almost right. Only the third item is questionable. Once you begin to master the art of sharing a message it becomes both enjoyable and rewarding. God can and does use the spoken word. I challenge you to seriously consider your role as a spokesman for God.

At the outset we need to be reminded that a good Christian message boils down to three basic ingredients. If these are evident, everything else is superfluous, regardless of what the speech teachers and homileticians say.

First, it must be *biblical.* Our only claim to a hearing is that we have a word from God. All kinds of voices are clamoring for a hearing, but only God is absolutely trustworthy. We are privileged to share an infallible Word with youth. Unless we build our messages on the Scriptures and what they teach, we can get lost in subjectivity and personal opinion. Don't be afraid to be biblical. There is an incredible hunger for God today. As one of my teachers put it, "Drive the text!"

Dan Baumann is pastor of the College Avenue Baptist Church, San Diego, California.

Second, it must be *present tense.* Some of our messages get lost in the past. We never bring our hearers into the here-and-now. As a result, we give the impression that the Bible is for our ancestors, not for us. It is no surprise to discover that young people don't get too excited about the Jebusites and Moabites! A useful message will always build a bridge between the past (exegesis of the text) and the present (the theological truth that is *always* pertinent). In other words, a worthy message occurs at the intersection of what God said (in the Bible) and what God is saying (to us right now).

Third, it must be *interesting.* It is a sin to be boring. The gospel is never dull; only teachers, preachers, and speakers at youth groups are. We therefore need to be fresh, full of enthusiasm, and present material that wins a hearing. Incidentally, a well-chosen illustration will often lift the interest level of your hearers. A novel approach to an old subject will also stimulate a bored group.

Let us now proceed with a step-by-step process of message preparation and delivery.

STEP 1—AUDIENCE ANALYSIS

Who will be in attendance? What are their needs?

Unless you are the guest speaker for a "new" group you will have numerous clues to their needs. And even if you are brought in from the outside you should secure some need assessment from the people who invited you.

Assuming that you have had some ongoing relationship with the group you are to address, take note of the following: What overall weaknesses are apparent in the group? Are they clannish and do they need teaching on "Body Life"? Do they lack guidelines for making Christian decisions? Are they immature in their understanding of the Bible and do they need instruction in Bible study? Do they have freedom to share their faith or do they need instruction in personal evangelism? Are many of the kids unsaved and do they need to be introduced to Christ?

In other words, "What do they need?" This information is gleaned from informal conversations, counseling of youth, sensitive observation, and direct questions addressed to articulate leaders among the youth themselves. Unless you have a handle on their particular needs, you will be shooting in the dark when you speak.

STEP 2—PURPOSE OF THE MESSAGE

Following a need assessment comes the moment when you select a goal for your message. For example, if there are a number of unsaved kids you may need to share a clear, simple salvation message. The goal then is to see them come to faith. Or, if your youth have become enamored by "situation ethics" they may need a good dose of Christian ethics. The goal then would be to see your youth develop personal convictions based on the Bible. Additional worthy goals for individual messages might include: to teach a basic approach to Bible study, to encourage personal conviction regarding the use of alcohol and drugs, or to encourage kids to find strength by sharing their troubles with each other.

If our message is like Abraham "who went out not knowing where he was going," we are in trouble. Choose your destination before you begin your trip.

STEP 3—STRUCTURE OF THE MESSAGE

If the group is highly motivated and friendly toward your message you can be *deductive* in approach. That is, you state your thesis and then develop your message in logical fashion.

For example:

Thesis—"Bible Study is Rewarding"
Development—1. It helps me understand God
2. It helps me understand others
3. It helps me understand myself

If, however, your listeners are either unfriendly toward your subject or are suspicious of you, it is imperative that you choose to be *inductive*. That is, begin where they are. You should find points of contact with them and build a relationship. You take them to *your* destination, but you take *their* route.

On one occasion I was invited to share at a religious emphasis week on a secular state university campus. I spoke for thirty minutes on crises in my life (a serious football accident that had me hospitalized for six weeks, my five-month-old daughter Lynette's bout with spinal meningitis, and the death of another shortly after her birth). As I recounted each experience I mentioned how much one of my friends meant to me. Never once did I refer to the Bible, Christianity, or God in that message. I concluded that talk by saying, "Oh, incidentally, that friend's name is Jesus." A one-hour question-and-answer period followed. In the succeeding hours a number of students gave their life to Christ. I'm convinced that if I had begun with biblical categories I would have prematurely turned some off. As it was, I first earned a hearing.

A helpful structure is called the "Motivated Sequence." I recommend this approach over all others. It has some wise psychology behind it. And it is very adaptable to youth settings.

Alan H. Monroe, the originator of this method, outlines five steps:

- Attention
- Need
- Satisfaction
- Visualization
- Action

You begin by a short attention-getting device. It may be a striking quote, a humorous incident, an event in the world of sports, or anything that makes them sit up and take notice.

Next, you create a feeling of need for action of some sort. This should leave the listener with a sense of unrest, dissatisfaction, or hunger.

Then, you show how that need can be satisfied in Christ. This step may be the longest of all. Here, typically, is where you teach the Scriptures.

It is now time to help them see themselves participating in the change you suggest. They should "see" how it would be like to be forgiven, to be a Christian, to be spiritual, etc.

And finally, you call them to decide. Now is the moment to do something. Spell it out carefully—assume nothing.

STEP 4—SOURCES FOR THE MESSAGE

The world is full of material for the Christian speaker. When you are alert to the resources you will never be at a loss for content.

Consider the following:

1. The Bible—I am surprised to discover how little of the Scriptures Christian people know. If you set about to be a careful student of the Word you will be congratulated for your creativity and originality. People do not know their Bible! Most of our youth, even those with strong church backgrounds, have a very elementary view of what the Scriptures teach. Use the Bible not only as a quarry for illustrations, but teach its truth.

2. A personal biblical library—We are living in a day when Christian bookstores are jammed with resource material—much of it very good. Every speaker should have at least: a complete concordance, a Bible atlas, a biblical encyclopedia, a Bible dictionary, two or three sets of evangelical commentaries, and individual volumes on evangelism, the church, counseling, devotional classics, and contemporary social issues.

3. News magazines and newspapers—Learn to be a gleaner of articles from the news. Each day there are new items of interest, sometimes in world events, sometimes in sports, occasionally in the comics. Be a gleaner and a jotter. Clip anything that might be of use.

4. Observation—Record events around you. Put them on slips of paper and save them for future use. A bumper sticker, a radio interview, a popular song, a quarrel between two kids; these and many more can add to the "nowness" of your message.

Illustrations need to be an important part of your messages. For the most part, avoid the "canned" illustrations that are found in illustration books. All too often these are old, unbelievable, and worn out from overuse.

Be your own anthologist. An illustration that is yours will always be fresh. Develop an eye for illustrations. The world is full of them, if we have the eyes to see them.

When selecting illustrations be certain they are *typical* so that the truths they teach can apply directly to the listeners who hear them. Abstract illustrations are a useless novelty. A good illustration helps the listener place himself in the situation. He can see himself in the position that you describe. This means that illustrations out of old history books or old devotional books need to be carefully used, if used at all.

Most of the time we should concentrate on contemporary illustrations, and these should help your listeners see how other youths handled a situation.

One word of warning about personal illustrations. Let me strongly suggest that you avoid constant reference to yourself. An occasional personal illustration is in order, but not if it always records your successes. We need to see your struggles, your failures, and your inadequacies. This gives us hope. When you admit failure we can immediately identify with that. We can then learn to positively cope together.

STEP 5—INTRODUCTIONS AND CONCLUSIONS

Introductions and conclusions are doors to get us into or out of your message. Make them clear, short, and pertinent.

Introductions should create interest, garner a hearing, and establish the direction you want us to move. Don't yield to the temptation to tell introductory stories that really don't introduce. Get us into your subject as quickly as possible. Your first few sentences are crucial—grab us, start us moving immediately into a predetermined direction.

Conclusions should generally call us to a decision. A few wrap-up sentences should answer the listener's question—"What should I do now?" Don't add new material at the end. Summarize quickly and call us to do something! Be specific and succinct.

STEP 6—DELIVERY

Use as few notes as possible. The important issue is communication. If you need a few notes, don't feel guilty. Notes are a tool. If you can speak with minimal notes, so much the better, but freedom is important.

Some of the best preachers in American history used complete manuscripts. Although I don't recommend the use of a complete manuscript, I hate to see content severely sacrificed just so someone can say he speaks without notes.

Be yourself—your best self—when you speak. Allow gestures to flow out of your material. They should be natural.

Vary your volume. Too often we are tempted to confuse volume with unction. Often a point can be more forcefully made when it is almost whispered. The key is variety. Most youth, incidentally, are not thrilled with the loud bombastic speaker. They prefer an animated conversational style.

STEP 7—HOLY SPIRIT

God does not expect you to do it all. He has given His Holy Spirit to instruct you, to fill you with power, to enable you to speak His truth, and to be the agent of change in the life of people.

Your task is to be a yielded instrument in His hands. When you are prepared, have a genuine love for kids, and speak with enthusiasm borne out of conviction—God will use you.

He can be trusted!

23

The Creative Use of Music

Music, the universal language, is perhaps the most powerful communication and therapeutic tool that God has designed into every human being. Almost everyone can sing. It's built into us. In fact, this very moment, as you are reading this page, your vocal chords are vibrating to the sounds around you. They even vibrate to sounds that are happening in your dreams as you sleep. I am telling you this because most people have no excuse for not singing.

Oh, you may say, "But you've never heard me!" The problem is generally not the inability to use the vocal chords, since most people can talk and this is the same voice used for singing. It's the inability to let go and just sing. The voice is an involuntary muscle like the heart, but when people try too hard to sing (by imitating or trying to sound pretty), they turn the voice into a voluntary muscle and frustrate the natural process of singing.

Why am I saying all this? Because music leaders must understand how difficult it is for some people to sing (I would say for about 80% of the U.S. population), and that it is absolutely one of the most personal, scary, and powerful things to do. These leaders often seem to intimidate people into not singing.

Yohann Andersen is President of Songs and Creations and is actively involved in the Young Life ministry.

A child will sing when left to be a child. Crying is a form of singing. In other cultures, singing in unison is a definite part of their heritage, and kids grow up participating in unison singing. They know the tune and grow confident in singing it. It happens automatically.

In dominantly technological and specialized societies like the United States, "being musical" is equated with reading notes or having a sophisticated degree of brain/ear/vocal chord coordination without natural unison singing preparation and encouragement from parents and teachers.

Instead, kids grow up watching performers. They are told to be quiet, or told they don't have a singing voice, and are even put into nonsinging sections of school classrooms. People grow up thinking that only a select few can really sing. Even in our worship services, the pervading dynamic is to leave it to the experts (i.e., the organ or piano takes over playing the tune). This is the worst thing we could possibly do for group singing, or any kind of singing. Listen for a moment to your favorite recording of a vocalist, or simply turn on the radio. Listen to the background instruments. They are not playing the tune. They are backing up the singer or singers with rhythm and flavor and a moving chord structure that follows the basic shape of the song. All the singer has to do is fill the vacuum created. This is why guitar accompaniment is very good, since the tune usually is not being played. One can accomplish this on a piano or organ too, by just playing the chord structure with rhythm.

Another example of the "leaving it to the experts" syndrome in most churches is the hymnbook. It's usually geared to those who read musical notes. About 85% of the population do not read music, and an even higher percentage cannot, when they are asked to sight-read a new song on the spot, let alone sing in four-part harmony. This is absolutely intimidating to a great number of people who are already feeling insecure about singing, and it doesn't help the matter when the leader has started singing before some have even found the page.

The high degree of importance placed on performance of certain skilled musicians is another problem. Kids grow up thinking performance is only for a few, or if they don't like the screeching soprano in the choir, they (usually the guys) would certainly not want to be associated with anything like singing. Or it's that guys and gals just don't feel adequate compared to the current musical hero that everyone is swooning over and they are so scared that they do not want to reveal their own imagined inadequacy.

Of course, everyone can sing in the shower. Why? All the dynamics are there. It's safe. Good acoustics are present, i.e., sound bounces off hard surfaces and the person can hear the true voice, there is background noise (running water), etc. The big item here is that the shower space is *safe*. The same dynamics can be transferred to any meeting room space. This is a problem in many building structures. The room is dead because there is no acoustical aliveness, so the singing sounds dead.

The way to get singing (or for that matter, any form of communication) going is to create an environment that is safe and nonintimidating; an atmosphere where the message corresponds to the communication process. Seating, lighting, temperature, attitudes, and acoustics are all important. In fact, everything you do at a meeting is the message. Leaders forget this point and sometimes go directly to a method or technique, bypassing their own attitudes and the attitudes of the group, not being aware of their own discounting mannerisms and negative body language, therefore turning that good technique into a gimmick and harming the original purpose of the message.

Form needs to always follow function. This is basic to good design in the arts and needs to be followed in the communicative arts. But when methods, programs, seating, architecture (forms), are not equally plugged into the message, then content, process, attitudes, mannerisms (function), whatever one is doing (music, speaking, worship, discussion, play, etc.), becomes less than best and, in most cases, becomes a loser. Singing often is bad because of this point. The song leader sometimes doesn't even know the song or says apologetically, "Let's all sort of pick up your hymnbooks and let's kinda sing." And all that will come back is "kinda, sort of" singing. Look at your body language before the group. This might even help you know what your feelings are about being there. What are your attitudes? Do you want to be there? Are you scared? Are you on an ego trip as a "hot shot" singer, guitar player, or power-hungry youth leader? These are questions you must ask or else your meeting will be weak and you'll end up intimidating people.

"Scratching them where they itch," meeting their needs, and doing what's appropriate to the situation (like singing songs where lyrics and music meet the needs of the mood in your situation), can be practiced only when you are aware of your own needs. Then the attitudes of the group can be plainly seen. When a person is not aware of himself, that person is out of control and might be saying and doing something out of touch with the scene happening at the moment. Some communicators claim that approximately 92% of what a person remembers and retains over the years is nonverbal. By this I mean that the way we communicate through body language and tone is often remembered more than what we communicate verbally. Most people seem to concentrate on the other 8%, which is words. Whenever I am leading music, I see myself not as a performer, but as a catalyst for others to be the performers, and then I join with them as a group coming together as almost one personality. I relax, they relax. I enjoy and sing, they enjoy and sing. If I'm pushing or my ego is "out there" or I'm not feeling the lyrics, group singing does not happen. You don't make people sing. You create the atmosphere and allow them as "little children" (whatever age they are) to sing. It's that child-like ego state where communication takes place and singing takes off. That means you as the leader need to be in that child-like ego state yourself. The best communicators, song leaders have that unpredictable, surprise quality of childlike spontaneity.

When you understand this philosophy of relational (incarnational) "medium equals message" type of communication, then some of the following song leading techniques and creative use of lyrics will make sense and won't be used as gimmicks.

First, some song leading hints. (Remember, these hints are to be integrated into your own personality to the point where you are comfortable with them. Then they will be authentic and people will follow, as they will have permission to be comfortable and authentic too.)

BE REAL YOURSELF

As we have already discussed, the first item is for you to be real. Some leaders try to razzle-dazzle and pull a power trip, but this does not wear well in the long run and can really intimidate kids. This does not mean a leader is not to be assertive. In fact, if the leader is not clear and definite and he passes on a lot of insecurity about singing, then the group he or she is trying to lead will be insecure about singing. The instrumentation should always provide rhythm (i.e., percussion: spoons, kitchen utensils, key chains, blocks of wood, shoes banging, tambourines, etc.). In fact, if you don't have anyone to play guitar, piano, organ, etc., or if they won't just play chords and rhythm, then just go with doing rhythm.

CHOOSE SONGS YOU KNOW

Choose songs ahead of time that you know, are confident with, and that fit the setting and mood of the group. I always plan more songs to sing than I will actually use in order to have a list of songs available to pull from that I know and that I'm comfortable with. When choosing, be sure to have a variety of moods in the songs so you can be flexible enough on the spot to meet people where they are. You always start where people are and then move toward where you want them to go, learn, and experience. That's leadership. This does not mean you are a dictator, because you are constantly monitoring your own feelings and those of the group so as to be sensitive to their needs.

CHOOSE SONGS THAT EXPRESS THE GROUP'S FEELING

Music works magic with groups to help them express what they are feeling. It provides a buffer zone between where they are coming from and in being totally involved in the meeting. I cannot emphasize enough the powerful tool that participation music is when used to bring a group together, to help individuals feel that their particular needs and feelings are being acknowledged, to help them feel they are participating. It helps them feel they have something to say and that their voice is actually heard, instead of just watching a performance. Participation music is a way to teach content in a most enjoyable and effective way. Foreign languages are now being taught through music. Values are better transmitted through music than through any other method.

This tremendous tool, of course, can be misused. Negative values are seen in much of today's music. Just because a song is labeled religious doesn't mean it is exempt from shallow, clichéd, theological thinking. In fact, song after song starts sounding alike, and the words seem to fit the same pattern. Creative lyrics that help someone see life, faith, and theological understanding in picturesque language are refreshing. This is the type to look for when you are planning songs to sing. They have a classic feel to them. Even the music has a major tune shape to it. It's easily sung. Much music goes up and down for no particular reason, with no real identifiable shape to it.

CHOOSE SONGS THAT ARE APPROPRIATE

PICK A VARIETY OF SONGS

In Scripture (Eph. 5:19, Col. 3:16), Paul tells the early Christians to sing using ". . . psalms, hymns and spiritual songs." It seems that Paul is exhorting the early believer to sing a variety of music. He could have just said, "Sing religious music." Have you read the Book of Psalms lately? That body of material in the Old Testament from Ecclesiastes to the minor prophets includes real-life lyrics, common-sense wisdom, protest, romance, relationships, praise, prayer, feelings of depression or elation, anger, sadness, gladness, conversion, change, etc. Therefore song lyrics of all types about life, love, and feelings can all be sanctified by a believer and used to help express what's going on inside. Thus a modern-day psalm could be written by a person just blurting out his or her feelings. To me, some of the classic "psalm" songwriters are people like John Denver, Bob Dylan, Gordon Lightfoot, Mac Davis, Joe South, Paul Stookey, Peter Yarrow, John Fischer, Ralph Carmichael, Marcus Uzilevsky, Mike Mirabella, Mark Spolstra, Pam Mark Hall, and many others. These writers have the freedom to get out of the way and write down effectively what is happening in life, faith, and society at that particular moment. They happen to write in a classic style that many people can relate to. The more spiritual writers who are classic don't seem to preach, but simply state what's going on. John Denver's song "Follow Me" is a prime example of this type. You can sing it as if God is speaking to you. It covers sharing, praying alone, and listening to God speak to us. We sang this at our worship service on Easter morning in response to

Jesus' dialogue with Peter asking him to "Follow Me." Open up the lyrics of Denver's song "Sweet Surrender" and see the beautiful Christian meanings of a surrender come through. Gordon Lightfoot's "Rich Man Spiritual" can be seen as a person trying to buy or work his way into the kingdom. He can't, and in the last verse he accepts the gift of God's grace and lets the "smiling angel" come to take him home. The songs "Catch the Wind," "Sounds of Silence," etc., were all written in response to Old Testament passages.

The song "Get Together" was written as a hymn. The song "Games People Play" is a beautiful confession hymn. "Puff the Magic Dragon" is about growing up and also about getting rid of attachments. A song like "Weave Me the Sunshine" is a beautiful dialogue between God and us, emphasizing the fact that God fills my cup and gives me sunshine out of the falling rain. "Come and Sing a Simple Song of Freedom" can be sung as if God and all of heaven is singing these words to us. The list could go on and on, but what is important is that in becoming a spiritual person, all of life becomes sacred and breaking open lyrics will happen all the time when listening to radio, records, or television. A person should always be thinking of lyrics and putting them into the context of his or her own faith. Of course, there are some bad lyrics that are just plain disgusting and don't fit wholesome values at all. These are to be avoided. The best way to get kids off trash is to provide exciting, deep, meaningful alternatives. The Psalms also include spontaneous praise directed to our Lord, just blurting out uncensored, beautiful feelings or statements about what is.

The next category is hymns. These constitute more premeditated, careful thinking, expressive lyrics, with meaty content. Usually they are of a nature that states an objective truth about something and that something is usually about God or our condition as human beings. Prime examples would be the lyrics to Martin Luther's "A Mighty Fortress Is Our God," or "In Christ There Is No East or West," and "The God of Abraham Praise." Modern songs that have this feel are Ray Repp's "I Am the Resurrection," Jim Strathdee's "I Am the Light of the World," or my own song "Abundantly." These are stating in

God's words or human words, objective truth.

These first two categories can be sung by anyone, believer and unbeliever alike (just like reading the Bible), and the authenticity still stands. But when we come to the next category, "spiritual songs," we have to be discrete about the personal quality of the lyrics so as not to force people to sing a lie. This next category has that dimension. These songs are more personal expressions of how a person's faith is being activated in life, sometimes a story song, sometimes a personal witness. They are more intimate. Sometimes these songs are avoided by certain intellectual groups who treat faith more as an academic discipline and are apt to defend the faith and God at the expense of intimacy. Some of these songs anthropomorphise God (i.e., "He Holds My Hand") or make it intimate (i.e., "In the Garden" or "My God and I"). This intimacy is good at times, but if that is all we get, then we miss the other categories and have no balance. In fact, one of the best ways to get people out of their "heads" and experience faith is through the use of music. It activates the "child," thus letting the warmth of faith come through. Sometimes, as is the case of songs such as "Pass It On," "He's Everything to Me," "They'll Know We Are Christians By Our Love," and "Jesus My Lord," the song states a truth but is sung as truth by the singer(s) as their own. They own that truth. Its truth becomes intimate. So be careful who the audience is when you sing these types of songs. If you're in evangelistic work, be sensitive to the fact that you have people before you who have never made any real choice for God. Sing songs that assume they believe that way. A song might have a catchy tune, but would be inappropriate, lyric-wise, for whoever is singing the song. I usually tell kids in a Campus Life or Young Life camp or club meeting, when one of these songs comes up, to be careful and perhaps sing only parts of the song. They appreciate the fact that I'm recognizing their intelligence and am not trying to get them into some kind of emotional "jag" where they are coerced into saying something they don't believe.

These "spiritual songs" that Paul, in my opinion, is speaking about are very subjective songs about one's own personal belief. They tend to border on "psalm-like" lyrics sometimes, but seem to have a customized, home-made quality to them. And they are like hymns, but tend to personalize content more, i.e., "Fairest Lord Jesus," "Be Thou My Vision," "Who Do You Say I Am?," and "My Jesus Rose on Easter Morning."

In summary, in singing there needs to be variety. A steady diet of just one type of song or hymn is unhealthy. An emphasis on Psalms leaves out the content and personal faith feelings of the other two. Likewise, an emphasis on hymns might tend to keep kids just in their heads, to the detriment of social concern, praise, and a recognition of a personal relationship to the Savior, or a defending of God to the exclusion of intimacy. An emphasis on spiritual songs can lead to a kind of pop-spiritual feeling, always depending on other people's faith story. Don't get me wrong. There are many good, solid lyrics in this category, but a growing movement to write personal songs with clichéd, formula-like commercials for God tacked on the last verse can lead to a dearth of good, solid content songs about God, where people catch the truth rather than have a finger pointed at them, and which can lead to a dearth of beautiful-feeling psalm songs of life or caustic psalm songs protesting social injustice.

In most of this discussion, I'm separating the music from the lyrics. As you may know, most of our "psalms, hymns, and spiritual songs" music comes from the "folk" culture of the people. In Germany, during Martin Luther's time, it was appropriate to use the tune of a common German folk drinking song. Or in England, John and Charles Wesley took tunes from the folk songs sung among the people, whether in the "pub" or in the village square. If you were a missionary going to a foreign culture, you would want to sing musical tunes that that culture would understand. Of course, we are now getting a world-wide type of universal music that is understood by most cultures. It seems to be a folk-rock-country type that has a dominant shaped tune. Oftentimes it has a Latin or Eastern bent to it. The group Abba has the most worldwide, universal musical appeal. Musically, the Beatles had a very efficient universal sound in their more mellow songs like "Let It Be," and "Hey, Jude." John Denver and Kenny Rogers reflect a universal, current, singable tune.

Look for music that doesn't border on the extremes. It's hard to sing hard rock or jazz, whereas blues, country, or folk songs can be remembered because they are classics and stick to one shape in the melody line. This kind of song can be sung immediately, even before kids know it. When rhythm and a strong voice are present, people will sing, especially if there are no notes and the tune is not on the instruments. Choose songs, then, that have a strong melody line and not something that just goes up and down for no apparent reason. *Choose songs where the words fit the music.* So often the music is inappropriate to the feeling in the lyrics, i.e., a real feeling song set to a "flighty type" plastic formula sound, or a joyful lyric set to a "downer," heavy, depressing musical shape. Remember, everyone is a musician. You don't have to read notes to be one. Feel the song. Use your God-given, intuitive nature to know when things all fit together. Consider your youth group as a choir. Call what we now call "choir," "special music from the choir." If this is the attitude, people will sing much better.

SLANT THE SONG RIGHT

When starting a song, remember to wait for the kids to find the page. Look around for those who don't have books. Make sure lighting and seating arrangements are relational. When starting, find that first chord, and the pitch level you will start on, play it, sing it, hold it until the group is with you on it. If you're leading while playing an instrument (which is a great talent to have), this can be an automatic flow, often starting on the first syllable of the first word and holding it. If you're not playing an instrument, then you must be in absolute control and dialogue with the accompaniment. Also, make sure that the instrument players are singing too, as they tend to get faster if they are not singing. Nonsinging instrumentalists tend to look more like "performers," and this makes the group the "watchers." Make sure you, the musicians, and all others, use the hymnbook or songbook (even if you've memorized the song), as it tends to free up people to realize they can use it too and they don't have to have the song memorized. This is comforting for new people, as they probably don't feel "in" in the first place.

So, hold that first note pitch and when, in a playful way, everyone is on it, start the song slowly. This helps people to get on board, or else they will *get* bored, by not getting involved with the song. Starting slower gives you somewhere to go. Most songs are started much too fast, and it's hard to keep the same intensity all the way through. Also, the song usually gets burned out this way, as it gets boring. Or to do something different with the song, some leaders will (under the guise of creativity) do inappropriate things to the music without any regard for the lyrics. Venting off steam on a deep, meaningful song would be one example. I've seen groups do Ray Repp's "I Am the Resurrection" in such a manner as to really defile the song. Sung much too fast and with little phrases like "Blah! Blah! Blah! Blah!" after "I Am the Resurrection," or yelling out "1, 2, 3, 4" between verses and chorus. There are other examples of how some slaughter songs, but I'll sum it up by saying: Let the music shape and rhythm be appropriate to the lyric meaning. Sometimes within a song, some verses can be sung fast because that's appropriate to those lyrics, and sometimes the verses demand slowing up and being more reflective. Don't just crank out a song. Feel it! Move with it! Paint a feeling, experiencing picture with it. Music is one of the best ways for people to feel the message.

What you are aiming for is intensity. Many think that for a song to be celebrative it must be sung fast or loud or rowdy. This couldn't be further from the truth. If it's appropriate to the lyrics and music, fine. Otherwise, singing a song softly, in a whisper or slow and blues-like might be more intense. The word enthusiasm in Greek means: enthoes or in-God, and that's what appropriate mood singing is all about. Wait to start clapping if that's what's appropriate to do. I always say, "Play your hands." (It's a less intimidating word phrase.) Play hands when the feeling is there, don't force it. When you force it, I call that "Plastic Soul." Playing hands is great fun and I even have folks play each other's hands. This gets the kids sitting closer and gets them in touch with each other, promoting the one-unit, group feeling. Remember, music is not only the group builder, crowd breaker, but in itself, with it's dynamics, is the message verbally and nonverbally, all wrapped up into one item.

O.K.! The song is started. Now, as the group and you start feeling the song together, you can move into more of the faster rhythm. But always remain in control of the rhythm. It's the secret for creating mood and having the group experience together the song in the most enjoyable fashion. Sometimes stop in the middle of a song and point out some meanings. This lets everyone know you are in control and they will be more comfortable when they know that. They see you have experienced the song and really know about it, and they can then experience the song in new dimensions. When it's appropriate to clap (play hands), do so. But don't push it if the feeling is not there. Clapping too much can be irritating and intimidating.

CONTROL THE MOOD

PLAN THE ENDING

Ending the song takes some forethought. Slow down in the last phrase so there is some warning that the song picture is in the process of completing and then really end it. Don't let it just disintegrate. I sometimes like to end songs not at the last period, but I like to sing the first phrase or sentence over again, or stop at a certain word that I want to emphasize to fit the mood or theme of that moment or the mood of what's coming next. Speakers can be set up to launch into their talk if they would pay attention to what just went on ahead of them. Then there is a flow.

If you ask for a request, have the courage to say no if the song is inappropriate or if you don't know it. Tell the person you'll learn it or sing it another time. A lot of kids will hear some songs done a certain way at a camp experience, on a recording, or at a concert, and be higher than a kite to keep doing the song "that way," when it may not be appropriate to the new setting and the people who are there, or it would be too hard for the group to sing that way. This not only burns out that song, but it intimidates those who were not at that particular experience. It takes strong leadership, not technical music ability, to be in control of this.

For a long time I didn't consider myself a musician, and didn't play a "uke" until I was 26 years old and in seminary. But I did have some strong leadership training and apprenticeships in Young Life and Campus Life organizations, so I'm telling you these things from a nontechnical standpoint. I had to work at it. I still do. But I'm learning my own sound and what I can do to free it up, being the "child" as a leader, so others can be in their "child" and participate. I see music as part of the message and spend as much time with it as I do the talk.

Actually, music takes up almost as much time as the talk, perhaps even more. Get the two together, or else they could cancel each other out.

I say this to encourage you to be a leader of music. You have it in you. God gave it to you. It's one of those universal gifts, so just open yourself to it as a child. Whatever age you are, start! It's never too late.

Remember, you are communicators, which involves being an atmosphere-setter and not a music-technician. You are not the performer, you are the artist, the catalyst, the one who blends music with the atmosphere, the one who paints the picture. In fact, it's better to be a little awkward, raw, and real than to be too polished.

Be open, take risks, be ready to be the "fool." (If you can't be a "fool" sometimes, then you *are* a fool.) But know when to turn off being a fool or else you'll be foolish. Monitor your own feelings and be aware of what you're doing and place yourself in the group's shoes and ask: Would I like whatever the leader is doing to be done to me?

The creative use of music is up to you, the leader. "How-To" techniques are fine, but they must be incorporated into your personality, or the techniques become gimmicks. Start with you singing. See, feel, hear how much fun it is for you personally, then with that aliveness, everyone will want to sing with you.

Music is the universal language that everyone knows!

CHECK LIST FOR GROUP INVOLVEMENT SINGING

1. Look at yourself and your motives.
2. What kind is the group? (outreach, worship, neutral, fun)
3. What songs fit the group? What songs fit you? Attitudes?
4. Why sing? Is it appropriate?
5. Where do you want the group to go?
6. Prepare song list. (Overprepare number of songs so you can go with the mood, even though you won't have enough time to sing them all.)

7. Do you know the songs? Do others understand the lyrics?
8. How are you going to teach the song? (Start with yourself and core group. The others will come along automatically.)
9. Is there good communication between song leader and instrumentalists? Maybe they're the same, and that's great.
10. Do you know what subject material is going to be discussed? If any is (depends on group . . . i.e., beach party, worship), plan mood of song around that.
11. Do you have enough songbooks?
12. Can everyone see to read?
13. Can people hear the first note? Start slower and ease into rhythm.
14. Are you intimidating the group with your mannerisms?
15. Are you in control? Does the group lead you, or do you lead the group?
16. Can you start and stop a song as well as end it? Even in the middle?
17. Do you use your voice properly? Projecting to be heard?
18. Is your instrumentalist a "hot dog" performance type or really into serving as back-up catalyst? This applies to you if you do both. (Never *play* tune, *sing* it!)
19. Are you enthusiastic without being obnoxious? Be appropriate.
20. Do you portray variety?
21. Are you performing or leading? (Or both?)
22. Are most people involved as a unit? Where they are *one,* don't push them.
23. Did you lead them somewhere? Was it the place and space you wanted them to be? Did the group have a chance to perform? Were they the "star"?
24. Were the songs compatible with the message?
25. Did *you* enjoy leading and experiencing with others what went on? Were you one of the crowd? (That's important for relational ministries.)

24

Principles of Informal Counseling

SHOULD I TRY TO HELP?

We are all called upon to help. By virtue of our position as youth leaders we will be sought out by parents, teen-agers, friends, and acquaintances to provide guidance, comfort, advice, and a listening ear. How helpful will we be? Will we be effective counselors? The following are some guidelines that, when practiced, will increase our ability to be helpful to hurting people.

Whether you are a professional youth minister or a volunteer, you are called to be a part of the body of Christ and to serve the church according to your God-given gifts. All Christians are called to be servants and helpers. Jesus taught His disciples that service and servanthood are fundamental to being part of the kingdom of God. (See Matt. 25.)

My hope is that you will find counseling to be one way of using yourself more effectively in Christian ministry. In this chapter you will be exposed to some ways of thinking, responding, and behaving that will enrich and expand your current approaches to being God's ambassador to young people who are lost, confused, and hurting.

Counseling will be a useful tool in your repertoire of ministering approaches. No doubt you have already

---

Dave Carlson is Director of Arlington Counseling Associates and Visiting Professor of Counseling at Trinity Evangelical Divinity School.

been consulted to assist people who are having difficulty coping with life situations. Whether or not you believe you are qualified to help, your choices are only two: Will I be an effective or ineffective helper?

Relating to others in helpful ways is a complicated and serious matter. You will want to be careful that you do not underestimate the need for prayerful, thoughtful, intelligent, knowledgeable activity on your part as helper. It is not uncommon in ministry to be confronted with people and situations that make us feel inadequate, insecure, and unprepared. Therefore, it is imperative that we as ministers of the gospel continue to learn and grow in our ability to help. Since many of the people we talk with will probably need more help than we as amateurs are prepared to give, it is important to ask for help for ourselves and to learn to direct others to resources that can better help them. As a rule of thumb, offer only the assistance you are capable of and then encourage people to seek more professional help when that seems needed.

TO COUNSEL OR TO CONVERT?

A primary emphasis in Christian work is proclaiming the "good news" of Jesus Christ. Some Christians fear that evangelism will lose out if church workers accept a style of helping that is not directly preaching or witnessing. When preaching or teaching methods are not sufficient to bring a person to Christ or help him solve problems, counseling strategies are very useful. Counseling is compatible with converting activities when a person's needs are used to determine what styles of help are correct.

Since most of us have more training in witnessing and preaching than in counseling, our tendency is to teach, preach, and give answers more than to listen, ask questions, and paraphrase what we hear others are telling us. In many ways it is easier to proclaim what we know than listen to what people are asking for and need. The emphasis in counseling is on preparing a person and helping him process information and feelings rather than on giving him an answer and final end product. Counseling is not the answer any more than witnessing is the answer. It is merely one way, a uniquely different way, of helping people get to the answers they need and utilizing the answers in their daily life. Therefore, a person does not have to choose between converting or counseling because the choices are ones of methodology, not message.

WHAT IS COUNSELING?

1. Counseling is helping a person get his own information in his own language and using it in his own way. Many people confuse *giving* counsel with *offering* counseling. Generally, it is easier to tell someone the answer than to help him discover ways to get to the answer. A key difference between counseling and giving counsel is the skill of *thinking with,* more than *thinking for,* another person. Counseling then utilizes the active participation of the person seeking help. Unlike a physician, the counselor asks the person what his problem and need is rather than tells him the diagnosis and prescription. For the novice, learning to ask more than tell is a difficult skill to develop. But effective counseling is built on the attitude and belief that people have value and divine potential. Therefore, the counselor utilizes the skills and abilities of the person seeking help. Rather than *doing for* the hurting person, the counselor *does with* the person as an affirmation of his worth and dignity.

2. Counseling is respecting and understanding the person regardless of the problems they are facing. The counselor does not assume he knows what the person is up against without first exploring the nature of the difficulties and what gets in the way of resolution. Effective counselors first respond to what people need, not to what a counselor thinks they need. When we listen actively and attentively we respond understandingly, warmly, and objectively. This means that our responses are more questions than comments. A common error is to assume we know what another means, needs, and experiences without first getting verification from him.

Humility then characterizes the counselor's attitude. He does not consider himself more intelligent or better than the hurting person. Rather, he sees himself as privileged to be invited into the person's life, acknowledging that no temptations are uncommon to human beings. (See 1 Cor. 10:13.)

3. Counseling is understanding human nature and the reasons for human behavior. Behavior makes sense only to those who are willing to learn the complexities of human motivation. The counselor must

start with the assumption that all behavior makes sense, or he is lost before he begins to try to help. "All behavior has purpose" is a key belief of effective counselors. This means that a person's behavior and feelings make sense even when it appears as nonsense. Together the counselor and counselee explore the purpose and meaning of the problematic actions, attitudes, and affections that are up to this point hidden from obvious view. To explore the sense of behavior that is illegal, immoral, fattening, sinful, or hurting, one must set aside any tendency to criticize, condemn, or condone.

4. Counseling is a relationship in which a person seeks help from another. In counseling, help is possible only when the relationship between counselor and counselee is warm, genuine, honest, truthful, and accepting. Relationship is the communication bridge between people. Without a relationship, helping is not possible. This is due largely to two factors; first, it is risky letting someone into our life. "If I tell you who I am and you don't like who I am, I am all I have."[1] Secondly, help is possible only when we risk letting others make themselves known to us.

The best counselors possess at least three personal characteristics: accurate empathy, nonpossessive warmth, and genuineness. In fact, professional counselors have learned that these three characteristics are more important than counseling techniques.[2] No doubt many of us are surprised to learn that who we are as a helper is more important than what we do or say.

Effective counselors are empathetic. Empathy is the ability to feel with a person, to imagine what it is like to live inside his or her body, mind, and soul without getting yourself lost; plus the ability to communicate this understanding to the person being helped. Counselors understand and experience people more than "psych them out." Our job is to empathize, not analyze. Empathy is different from sympathy and pity. Empathy is feeling *with* while sympathy is feeling *like* and pity is feeling *for* another. When we remember our own humanness it becomes easier to feel with and know what another is experiencing. As humans we are all basically alike. Jesus understands this because He became a man in order to relate to us. His empathetic example and experience through His incarnational priestly ministry is summarized in Hebrews 4:14–16.

Effective counselors are nonpossessively warm. Many of our relationships have "strings" attached. A counseling relationship allows the hurting person to be himself, struggling, failing, confused, and uncommitted without demanding he change in order to be helped or loved. Counselors respect people as human beings, as made in God's image, as brothers and sisters in Christ (1 John 4:11). The counselee is perceived as a person of worth and dignity who has needs and potential. He is recognized as trying to solve his own problems even when his attempts are ineffective, inappropriate, illegal, or sinful. To respond warmly and positively to another is possible when we believe that people can be loved without condoning or judging their behavior or feelings. Jesus related to sinful people without condemnation (John 3:17; 8:10, 11). Let us follow His example of loving without condemning. Another belief that helps us accept people as they are is our understanding that people desire to grow and mature but resist and fear change. Also, relating warmly to people is possible when we believe behavior makes sense even when it makes no sense at first hearing. And lastly, we can relate to people warmly when we remember that Christ loves us and them even when we are God's enemies (Rom. 5:8).

Effective counselors are genuine. A genuine person is as "in tune" with his "real" self as he is with his "ideal" self. He does not need to hide from the person he really is. He can accept his strengths and weaknesses, his accomplishments and failures, his victories and temptations, and his finished and unfinished problem solving. A genuine person gives up the temptation to wear a mask. This means he is in touch with his humanness and can allow other people to know him for who he is. As the counselor creates an atmosphere of openness he provides an opportunity for the hurting person to be open, honest, real, and more genuine.

Who we are as people then determines the quality of the counseling relationship. The most important ingredient in helping others is the relationship we build with them. How does one build relationships? Jesus taught us, "Here I am! I stand at the door and knock. If anyone hears my voice and opens the door, I will come in and eat with him, and he with me" (Rev. 3:20). To whom will people open the door of their lives? To persons who are empathic, warm, and genuine. People will trust us when we are trustworthy and keep confidences.

5. Counseling is maintaining confidentiality. When a person shares secrets with a counselor he needs to retain the person's secrets. It is the promise of privacy that encourages people to open their lives to us. People seeking help need to know they are in control of the information they share. Counseling is recognizing that people seek help only in a sanctuary of confidentiality. It is our responsibility to bury the person's confessions to us like Christ does, in the deepest sea. If and when these secrets are to be revealed is the prerogative of the confessee, not the counselor. Therefore, another's hurts, mistakes, and sins are not coffee-hour topics or stories with which to entertain.

6. Counseling is listening thoughtfully. We cannot be empathic, warm, or genuine without listening. The most common error counselors make is to talk to the person before they listen to him. Job, the well-known sufferer, asked his friends, "How long will you torment me and crush me with words?" (Job 19:2). When they still did not remain silent and listen, Job pleaded, "Listen carefully to my words; let this be the consolation you give me" (Job 21:2). Do you want to help? Then listen before talking. As the wise man said, "He who answers before listening—that is his folly and his shame" (Prov. 18:13). Let us remember to "listen with the ears of God that we may speak the words of God."[3]

What are some of the major blocks to listening? These include a closed mind, prejudgments, preoccupation with our own needs, and anger at the person for his behavior or attitude. Helpers have learned that it is crucial to listen for the other person's point of view more than decide from their own perspective. Also, it is helpful to remember that what people say and what they mean may be different. Words usually have several layers of meaning. Therefore, listeners tune into the feelings, needs, hopes, fears, and expectations of what people are saying behind their words. As someone has said, "Love hears the hurt." To put it another way, the problem presented at first may be only part of a much larger concern the person is unable to expose to himself or to another. As helpers, we need to develop the capacity to hear what people are not putting into words, to hear what they may never be able to say. To do this we must learn to listen with their ears, see with their eyes, and feel with their heart.

7. For the amateur counselor, counseling is responding nonjudgmentally. Much of what we hear will be shocking and repulsive. We will be tempted to respond critically and judgmentally. Experienced counselors have found it possible to respond warmly and nonjudgmentally when they remember that hurting people seek out help because they too are bothered by their actions or feelings. People seek help when they are convicted about their own behavior. They need the opportunity for confession, not condemnation.

8. Counseling is teaching a person to satisfy his or her needs in personally, socially, and spiritually acceptable ways; considering alternative courses of action. New ways of thinking and creating new values are often part of the counseling process. In counseling, teaching is seldom as direct as in a classroom. It is more often accomplished through the counselor facilitating learning by noting options to the counselees' plans, pointing out consequences of carrying out the plans, and noting benefits and liabilities of various courses of action. These kinds of responses by the counselor utilize the counselees' own decision-making capabilities and encourage maturity more than dependency.

9. Counseling is serving as a *facilitator and catalyst of change.* We do not change anyone, but we help people to change. Counseling is a process of assisting people to solve their own problems. We may know the answers, even give the answers, but this is quite different from helping people learn how to solve their own problems utilizing their own resources. We can even make choices for people, but that does little to help them learn how to make better choices for themselves. Counseling then is working with people more than working for people, listening more than talking, asking more than assuming, understanding more than advising, and exploring more than explaining. One of

the goals of counseling is to assist people to become their own problem solvers. Whatever we do or say is initiated for the purpose of building, supporting, nourishing, instructing, or converting. In biblical terms the counseling goals are similar to the goals for the body of Christ as expressed in Ephesians 4:12–17. However, the primary goals of counseling are first to be a mediator for the hurting person—to himself, others, and God. And secondly, to help the person develop his own mediatorial skills. As Christians we believe in the priesthood of believers. When counseling, this means we assist the person in removing the blocks that hinder him from being his own priest.

Anyone can give advice, answers, or solutions. But counseling is most effective when we are willing to take the time and energy to let the hurting person tell us what his problem is, how he has tried to solve it, what hurdles got in the way of his problem-solving attempts, and what help he would like from us. As counselors we support, encourage, guide, explore, and clarify, but ultimately the person must make his own choices and changes. He may or may not choose to utilize our help or God's help. But the choice is always his.

TWO STYLES OF HELPING

Counseling differs from giving counsel. We need to be clear about which activity we are engaged in and which activity is most helpful to the person seeking help. In studying Jesus' style of relating, I have discovered two basic approaches to helping people: prophetic and priestly.[4]

Prophetic relating is giving counsel. This style assumes that the helper knows what people need and knows what is helpful. The prophetic relater is convinced he is called by God to tell people what is wrong and how they can right it. This approach is characterized by such responses as convicting, preaching, proclaiming truth, giving advice, lecturing, and in general disturbing the comfortable.

A second style Jesus used for relating is *priestly*. It assumes the helper needs to ask for what is needed and how he can be of help to the troubled person. The priestly relater is convinced that he is called by God to listen to what is wrong because the person is convicted of wrong. A priestly relater is a confessor who affirms the truth when he hears it, interviews to discover the problem, and comforts the disturbed.

While helping often utilizes both prophetic and priestly styles of relating, the priestly approach is considered by me to be counseling. The task for you is to learn when the prophetic or priestly approach is needed and helpful. Both approaches are legitimate, but not necessarily useful when used only to the exclusion of the other style. It is my experience that most Christian workers are better at prophetic relating than priestly relating because they have received more training in witnessing than listening. My encouragement to you is to develop a repertoire of ministering approaches. No one way to help is right for each person in need. There are many effective ways to help. The right way to help is determined by what a hurting person needs at that moment.

Some authors have tried to put helping into a pat formula. Unfortunately, helping is not that simple. It is crucial that we be flexible, creative, and discriminating in our efforts to help. Generally speaking, by the time someone seeks you out he or she has read books, listened to sermons, attended seminars and meetings, but is still having difficulty solving the problems. Therefore, I recommend beginning with the priestly approach because it encourages us as helpers to begin where the hurting person is rather than where we as helpers are.

CONCLUSION

Counseling can take place anywhere. As a youth worker, you may do more listening, reflecting, empathizing, and exploring with another outside your office than anywhere else. The telephone, coffee shop, car, or hall is often the setting for youth counseling. Informal counseling is really no different than formal counseling in terms of the kind and quality of conversation and help that takes place between a counselor and a counselee.

In this chapter I have tried to encourage you as a youth worker to offer help to the limits of your training and experience. When confronted by a person's problems that demand more than you can competently handle, don't hesitate to get supervision and help for yourself or to refer the person you are helping to a professional counselor whom you know, have confidence in, and who shares or sympathizes with your Christian beliefs and values.

Also, you are encouraged to develop personal-professional characteristics of effective helping. These include empathy (feeling with, not feeling sorry for or like another), warmth (accepting, respectful, loving), genuine (honest, open, real, sinner saved by grace, nondefensive), listening (attentive, thoughtful, quiet hearing of a person's needs, feelings, unspoken concerns), and responsive to what people need (humble willingness to explore more than explain, struggle with more than do for).

Lastly, you are encouraged to model your approach to helping after Jesus' style of relating; an approach to people characterized by variety and sensitivity to individual needs.

FOOTNOTES

[1]John Powell. *Why Am I Afraid to Tell You Who I Am?* (Chicago: Argus, 1967).

[2]R. R. Carkhuff. *Helping and Human Relations: A Primer for Lay and the Professional People, Volume I, Selection and Training* (New York: Holt, Rinehart and Winston, 1969).

[3]Dietrich Bonhoeffer. *Life Together* (New York: Harper and Row, 1954).

[4]David Carlson. "Jesus' Style of Relating: The Search for a Biblical View of Counseling," *Journal of Psychology and Theology,* Summer 1976. Also a revised edition of this paper in Gary Collins, *Helping People Grow* (Santa Ana: Vision House, 1980).

ADDITIONAL READING

Gary Collins. *How to Be a People Helper,* Santa Ana: Vision House, 1976.

Gerald Egan. *The Skilled Helper.* Monterey: Brooks/Cole, 1975.

———. *Exercises in the Skilled Helper.* Monterey: Brooks/Cole, 1975.

Grinder Bandler, Satir. *Changing with Families,* Palo Alto: Science and Behavior Books, 1976.

Norman Wright. *Training Christians to Counsel.* Denver: Christian Marriage Enrichment, 1977.

25

The Creative Use of Media

If you've been involved in youth work for any time at all, you've no doubt had the experience of standing in front of a group and spotting a newcomer, who quite obviously has never been in a church or Christian group before. Perhaps you had been in this position yourself as a teen-ager, or conversely, you may have been raised in the church and never experienced the awkwardness of those moments.

As a youth leader, I find myself focusing on those individuals, wondering what they are hearing, feeling, and experiencing. I am questioning how the matrix of their learning mechanisms is translating both what I am saying and how I am saying it, for these young people have come to learn through sophisticated forms of communication from their earliest years.

When they were children, Sesame Street and the Electric Company were a regular part of their daily routine. Now, if they happen to live in the right part of the country, they can make use of the many advantages of television with its various forms of viewer feedback.

The small electronic games they play with are the result of major breakthroughs in microchip de-

---

Gary Dausey is the Executive Vice President of Youth for Christ/USA, Wheaton, Illinois.

sign. Without such breakthroughs, it would take a computer hundreds of times their size to produce the same results.

The school they attend has a sophisticated learning center that may incorporate devices for self-paced learning and small personal computers with individualized instructional software to guide the students toward their educational goals. The learning carrel in which they study is equipped with a device capable of random-accessing any one of hundreds of video tapes that are integral parts of their instructional program.

Then, one of these young people, who has been exposed to all of these technological advances, attends a Sunday school class for the first time. There he meets his class teacher, who is armed only with a quarterly and a recent paraphrase of the Bible.

Years ago, the late Marshall McLuhan tried to convince us that the medium was the message. If there was a sliver of accuracy in this thesis, the message that this young person must be getting is clear: "Whatever these people in church are trying to communicate to me can't be all that important because their means of communication is so antiquated."

While it is true that the most sophisticated means of communication without a message is worthless, it is also true that those of us who feel we have an extremely important message ought to find the most effective means of communicating it. In this chapter I would like to focus on selected audio-visual tools of communication that I believe can make our ministry with high school students more effective. This is not an attempt at an exhaustive study of all audio-visual resources, but rather a look at specific media most suited to this age group and which are generally available to most churches.

Media, in any form, helps the communicator and the learner focus their attention on a common base of information. Without such a focus, the communicator may be meaning one thing and the learner, working with a different information grid, can be perceiving something altogether different.

The communicator must always begin with the question "What do I want my group to understand, retain, or experience?" Once that question is properly addressed, he may then ask a second question: "What forms of audio-visual resources can best assist me with my goal?"

As you apply these questions, consider these audio-visual tools as valuable resources for your ministry.

16MM FILM

Historically, when one thought of 16mm film in the church, he thought of a full-length feature film. While it is true that some of the recent films produced by Christian film makers are well suited for the high-school age group, other problems exist. Many of them are too long to fit into a typical youth program, and cost is often prohibitive. (If your budget is large or if you can combine an activity with another church, cost may not be a factor.)

Whatever film you use, you must be very careful to preview the film for content and quality. Choosing a film is not unlike choosing the topic of a message. Don't approach it by asking what films are available. Start with the questions, "What do we want to accomplish in this meeting?" and "What is available that will help us achieve our goal?" If the quality is poor, it will detract seriously from the message, even if the content is suited to your needs. The Christian film maker has the sizable task of trying to compete with secular productions that cost millions of dollars to make, while his budget is only a very small fraction of that . . . yet the audience expects the same quality they see elsewhere.

Although the full-length Christian feature film does have a place in youth work, other 16mm film formats are used more frequently. Often a portion of a secular film lends itself well for use in a youth meeting, while the use of the entire film may be inappropriate. Using part of a film can be a great way to start a discussion or enhance a singular point. Many public libraries make such films available to not-for-profit groups for little more than the cost of inspection and servicing the film.

In youth work, the short film is the most frequently used form of 16mm film. It ranges from three to fifteen minutes in length and usually conveys one point. These short films are generally brief dramatic vignettes or animated productions. Because of their brevity, they are to the point and the rental fees are minimal, making them more practical to use than longer films. Some distributors have package plans that allow unlimited use of their films for a fixed annual fee. If you plan to use 16 mm films frequently, this is an attractive offer.

SUPER 8 FILM

Although not as widely used in youth work as 16mm, Super 8 film can provide some additional life in your meetings.

Many photography and discount stores have a wide variety of Super 8 titles available. These commercially provided films include everything from major sporting events to animated cartoons. Generally, both silent and sound versions are available in a variety of lengths. The major advantage of these films is their price. They can usually be purchased for what it would cost to rent a 16mm film.

With a little creative thought and your own script, those films can be used to make announcements more interesting or to add some life to your crowd-breakers. What better way could you promote a summer camping program than to write your own script and use the film "The Three Stooges in 'Bear Facts'" or promote competition with another group by showing some appropriate footage from a World War I documentary?

If you're looking for a way to get your group involved in their own creative expression, give one of your core groups or modules a camera and a supply of film and assign them a specific theme to portray in film for some future meeting. If you can round up enough cameras from friends in the church, you might have several groups producing films to be shown at your own film festival. Appropriate prizes might be offered for the team producing the best film.

VIDEO TAPE

Perhaps in no other area is the advance in technology more apparent than in the development of video-tape equipment. Not many years ago, the only video-tape recorder available was approximately 6′ x 6′ x 2′ in size, required special air conditioning and a full-time engineer, consumed costly 2″ tape and was very expensive to purchase and operate.

Because of the development of solid state and integrated circuitry and new video formats, videotape equipment has become available to the consumer market. Hundreds of thousands of units, which can now be measured in inches instead of feet, can be found in homes throughout the nation. This opens great new areas of potential for the creative youth worker. Video tape is flexible and adaptable for meetings—you can start and stop it, freeze frame, rewind and review sections with relative ease.

Commercially produced tapes on a wide variety of topics are available for rental or purchase through university libraries, stores selling video equipment, some public libraries, film distributors, industrial corporations, parachurch organizations, and church denominational headquarters. When appropriate, these tapes can be used in their entirety or, as with 16mm film, selected portions can be used as discussion starters.

In addition to the commercially available tapes, it is possible with almost all home units, to record programs as they are broadcast. If there is a program airing on television that would be useful in a future youth-group meeting, tape it and keep it on file for later use. One word of caution about your use of broadcast programs you've taped. There have been long-standing legal struggles over copyright laws as they relate to taping broadcast material. Many programs that appear in the public broadcasting channels are excellent sources of usable material. Each month the Public Broadcasting Service issues a "don't copy" list of the programs they air that are not cleared for taping. Use caution with any programs you do tape for future use. The PBS "don't copy" list appears in *Educational and Industrial Television* magazine, a publication of C. S. Tepfer Publishing Co., Inc., Danbury, CT.

In addition to commercially available tapes and any you may make of broadcast materials, most video-tape recorders also have provision for the use of a video camera. The typical camera designed for use with home recorders is generally in the $1000 or less category. Don't be disappointed if your results don't compare favorably with the standards of commercial television. Their cameras can cost fifty times that amount.

With the combination of camera and recorder you can pretape interviews to be used in your class or youth-group meeting, tape dramatic or musical presentations by your group for critiquing, tape a typical youth-group meeting as a training tool for new sponsors or, again, give the camera to a group of students, along with a creative assignment, to produce material to be used in a later meeting. It's a useful tool that will add variety and interest to your youth group programing.

A brief technical note may be helpful. There are three popular formats of video cassettes currently being used in North America. None of the three are interchangeable with the others.

¾″ Video Cassette

The ¾″ video cassette is the most widely accepted industrial and educational standard. This is also the format used by most television stations for their minicam reports. This equipment is usually not found in homes but is available in high school and university learning centers and audio-visual rental agencies. Nearly all ¾″ machines are interchangeable.

½″ VHS Video Cassette

The ½″ VHS cassette has some acceptance in educational and industrial markets, but is used most widely for home entertainment. Many commercial tapes are available in this format. Most ½″ VHS cassettes can be used on any VHS machine, but some will not interchange. The key to be aware of is the maximum playing length of the recorded tape. This is an indication of both the length of tape and the speed at which it was recorded. There are several tape-speed combinations in these machines and your playback machine must be capable of playing back at the speed at which the tape was recorded.

½″ Beta Video Cassette

The ½″ Beta cassette is very similar to the ½″ VHS, but is neither electronically nor physically interchangeable with it. Although some inroads have been made into other markets, these machines are used primarily as home entertainment units. Commercially recorded tapes are available, but these machines have the same problem with varying tape speeds as the VHS machines have, and care must be taken to ensure that the tape and machine are compatible.

OVERHEAD PROJECTION

The overhead projector has been in existence for more than four decades, but it has moved into the church as an acceptable teaching tool only in recent years.

Originally designed for use in the armed services, this helpful teaching device has been slow to be accepted in the church for a number of reasons, including the lack of commercially prepared visuals, a normal resistance to anything new, and the lack of understanding of the preparation of custom-made visuals.

In the youth program, this projector is best suited to teaching sessions, either in a Bible-study setting or in "talk-to" situations where difficult concepts can be visualized better than they can be verbalized. It is also being used in many youth groups for the projecting of words of songs in group singing situations.

As a teaching device, the overhead projector has many advantages over other means of visual communication. It allows the instructor to stay in the front of the room so that eye contact may be maintained. Because of its location, the instructor can manipulate the materials himself, setting his own pace for the revealing of information. The large brilliant image is unique among projected visuals in that it is designed to be viewed in a lighted room, again providing better eye contact with the group.

The overhead projector's major advantage over the chalkboard is the unbroken flow of communication between the teacher and the group. When you write on a chalkboard, your back is to the audience. The overhead projector offers a wide variety of creative uses, and does not force the teacher to lose essential eye contact with the group.

Overhead projection provides a variety of options for the creative teacher. The following types of transparencies are most frequently used:

Write-on Transparency

The simplest form of overhead transparency is the "write-on" visual. In this situation, the communicator begins with a blank sheet of acetate on the projector stage and, with a felt-tip pen or grease pencil, writes on the acetate as he talks. This use of the projector is similar to using a chalkboard.

Static Transparency

The static transparency is a single acetate sheet bearing the preprepared information for projection. It has no overlays or moveable parts. Normally, this type of transparency is shown in its entirety at its first projec-

Figure 10

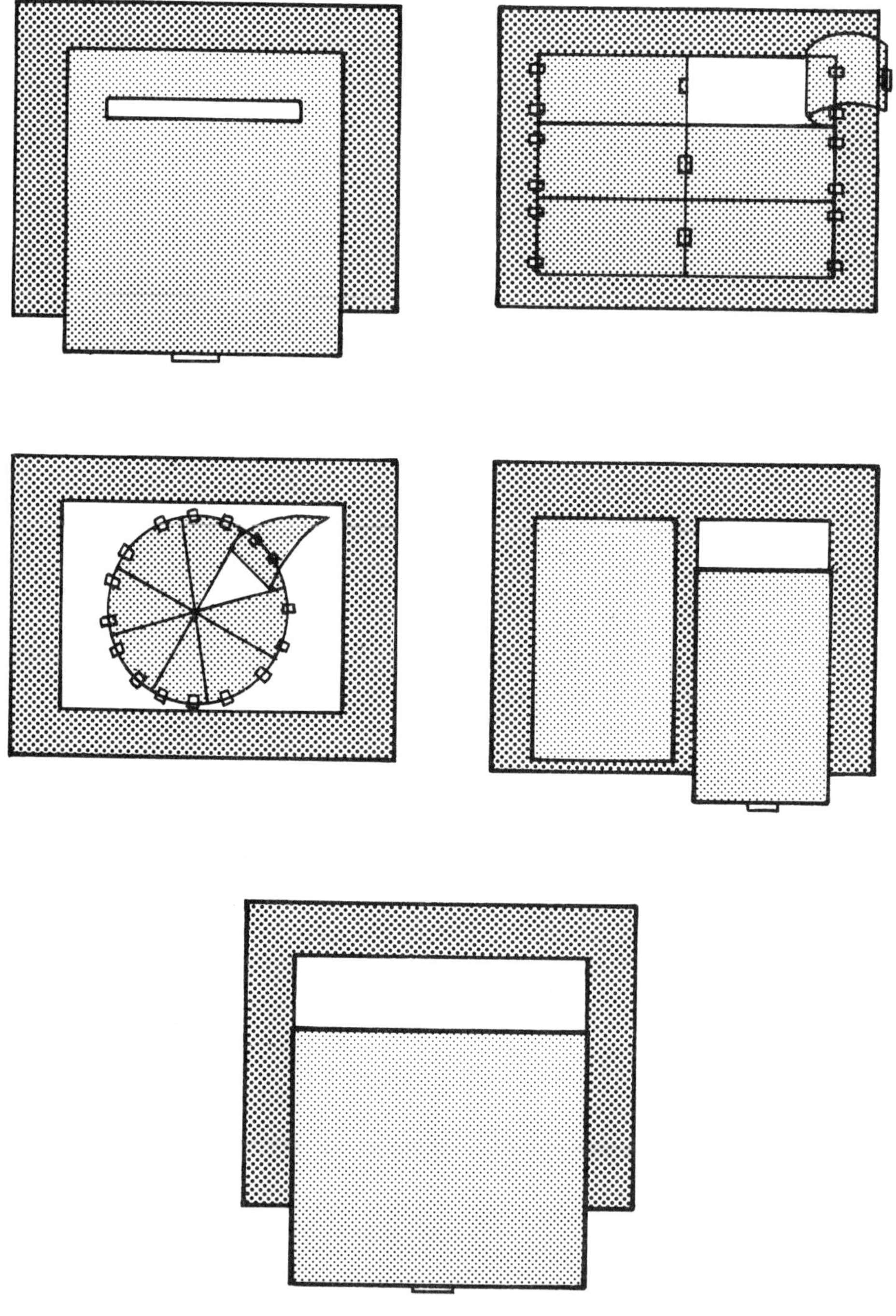

tion. Static transparencies are most useful in communicating single thoughts and general material. A good example of this would be a visual depicting the location of buildings and trails at a camp orientation session.

Progressive Disclosure

It is often desirable to reveal only a part of the transparency at a time so that the class will not get ahead of you, and so that you may develop your outline at your own rate, without disclosing the entire visual. This controlled disclosure of the visual allows you to isolate one thought from another for clarity and to present it singularly and without visual distraction. Progressive disclosure may be accomplished by several means. The simplest of these is to block out the unwanted portions of the visual with a sheet of paper. The paper may be moved to disclose the desired part of the visual. Figure 10 illustrates several other masking techniques possible to achieve the same effect on more complex transparencies.

Figure 11

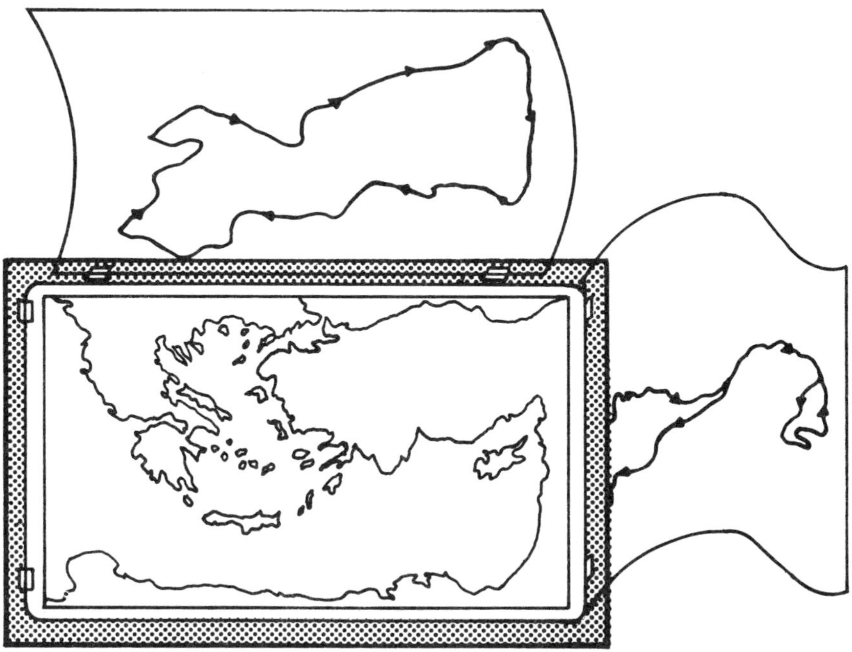

Overlay

Another important technique in overhead projection utilizes one or more overlays. Overlays are transparencies that can be placed over other transparencies to show the breakdown or development of the material being taught. A visual using the overlay technique usually consists of a basic transparency mounted in a frame and one or more overlays connected to the frame by metallic or vinyl hinges. Although the number of overlays for each basic visual is almost unlimited mechanically, optically it is not advisable to add more than four at a time. The addition of more considerably cuts down on the luminosity of the projected image. Figure 11 (see page 315) shows an example of how this technique can be used to isolate Paul's three missionary journeys, using a map on the basic visual and the three routes on three separate overlays.

Roll Chart

A technique that is especially useful for linear charts and other continuous subject matter is the roll chart. This chart may be produced on an acetate roll. Its length is limited only by the capacity of the projector. Many projectors have provisions for the mounting of a roll attachment. Some projectors allow only for rolls that move horizontally, while others also allow for vertical movement of the information. Generally the roll is placed on spindles on the attachment and the chart may be moved back and forth by means of a crank or wheel.

Technimation

Perhaps one of the most advanced techniques used in overhead projection is Technimation. It was developed by the American Optical Company and is designed to produce horizontal, vertical, circular, diagonal, or flashing movement on the projected image. This device is used to draw the viewer's eye to predetermined parts of the visual. You may use it to underline statements or locate places on a map.

As you may know, when one piece of polarized material is placed on another so that their polarized grains are at right angles, all light is effectively cut off. Changing the angle at which they cross allows the light to pass through again. In overhead projection, the effect is achieved by placing adhesive-backed polarized material on the specific part of the visual you want to emphasize. Then a circular piece of polarized material is mounted under the projector's head. When this wheel is turned either by hand or motor, the effect of linear motion or flashing is achieved.

SOURCES OF TRANSPARENCIES

Commercially Produced Visuals

Although these were almost impossible to find a few years ago, now a variety of sources exist for commercially produced overhead transparencies designed for the evangelical church. At present, the primary sources for these materials are the Christian publishing houses, particularly those that specialize in Christian education curricula. Most of their visuals relate directly to their curricula and textbooks. There are a few companies that manufacture visuals on general Christian themes. Some of these are listed at the end of this chapter. These are adaptable to many teaching situations.

Custom-made Visuals

Although commerically available overhead transparencies are attractive and desirable, you'll often find that none exist for your particular need. That should not deter you from using the overhead projector to enhance your presentation. You probably have at your disposal one or more of several means of producing your own transparencies.

- *Write-on Method.* As discussed earlier, this is one of the simplest methods you can use to produce your own visuals. Felt-tip marking pens designed for use on acetate are available in a modest range of colors. With these pens and clear acetate, the creation of your own visuals is limited only by your ability to print or draw.
- *Rub-on Lettering.* Art-supply stores offer a wide variety of lettering and designs that are sold under a number of trade names and are suitable for direct transfer onto clear acetate. One note of caution: Most dry-transfer artwork has a wax base and care must be used to rub down the letter only. The wax base surrounding the letter is more opaque than transparent and will project as black smears.
- *Lift Process.* This is a simple process that makes it possible to actually "lift" an image from a printed page onto a transparency. It is most suited to the use of color photos from certain types of printed material and will work only with materials that have been printed on clay-coated paper. This is the type of paper used by most of the better magazines. There are com-

mercial acetate products available through audio-visual dealers designed for this purpose. There are alternate means producing "lifted" transparencies using products found around the house, but their results are not generally too successful.

■ *Photocopying Method.* If you have access to a photocopying machine and have some opaque artwork that you would like to project, you have all you need to make an attractive overhead transparency. All xerographic and dry-heat photocopy machines that use single sheets (rather than rolls of paper) are capable of producing transparencies. Check with your photocopy or audio-visual dealer for information on the proper types of transparency films available for your machine.

■ *Overhead Transparency Makers.* In addition to these methods there are machines specifically designed to produce overhead transparencies. Most use either the dry-heat method or a diazo process. The diazo process is used in producing blueprints and, when used to make overhead transparencies, it produces visuals of very high quality in a variety of vivid colors. Your audio-visual dealer can give you full details on these machines.

MULTI-IMAGE SLIDE PRESENTATION

The use of multi-image slide presentations is growing rapidly in youth work. It is presently seen in its most sophisticated form in parachurch and "Son City" type youth ministries. The multiple use and potentially larger audiences that these ministries have make the expenditure for a more advanced presentation more cost effective.

Perhaps a word of definition is in order. The words "multimedia" and "multi-image" are often interchanged. If you read a number of authoritative sources on this topic, you will see that there is no universally accepted definition of either term. Multimedia generally refers to the use of any two or more forms of media for a presentation, the most common being the slide-tape presentation.

Multi-image most often refers to a multi-projector slide presentation, although motion picture film may also be included. It generally involves more than two projectors and can use as many as 60, occasionally even more. Its special effects are created in the way the material is projected, rather than being created in the film laboratory, as is true with motion pictures. Because there are several images on the screen at one time, multi-image forces the viewer to select and choose between the pieces of information he is seeing.

In Christian youth work, multi-image presentations are used to illustrate songs, communicate a spiritual message, advertise an event, start a discussion, or report on a ministry. When the presentation is done well, this tool can command and hold the attention of young people in a way that few other approaches can duplicate.

One of the most frequently asked questions about producing a multi-image presentation is "Where do I begin?" Begin at the same place you would with any form of media, by asking the question, "What do I want people to understand, retain, or experience?" In planning a multi-image presentation, your answer to this will not only affect the content of your presentation, but the format as well.

The inexperienced person often feels that the more slides on the screen or the more projectors used, the better the presentation. In many cases, the opposite is true. If you are trying to create a visual experience with some form of emotional response, a fast-paced, many-image presentation will be more effective. However, if your goal is to explain a difficult concept or to encourage retention of material, you'll want a slower-paced presentation, probably with fewer visual images to select from, and you will generally include more graphics (as opposed to photos). These are both generalizations. If you are interested in more exacting detail on media format and audience response by age group, let me recommend the theory and research section of *The Art of Multi-Image,* edited by Roger Gordon and published by the Association for Multi-Image. This is one of the best resource books available on the topic of multi-image.

After you've determined the response you're seeking and have established a preliminary format, move on to the script stage. Go no further until you have a script that you feel communicates your message well; one that you feel you can support visually. If you are not a writer, find someone in the church who is. Tell him or her what it is that you want to say, and let your writer put it into words.

Be aware that not all people who are capable of writing for the printed page can write equally well for the spoken word. You'll need someone who is more interested in how smoothly a sentence flows when spoken than how it would look on the printed page.

The next step is to "storyboard" your presentation. Basically, this will be your blueprint for how the presentation should look. Use 3 x 5 cards to represent each of your screens for any given point in the script. It is at this stage that you decide which visual vehicle best communicates your message. It may be a photo, a design, or simply words. You may decide that there is no practical way to visualize certain parts of the script. In most cases you'll find it is better to rewrite the script than to have a weak verbal/visual combination.

Your sources for slides may include your own collection of originals, reproductions from magazines, or commercial slide sources. Volumes have been written on this subject alone, and I'll not attempt to duplicate that information here. One of the best recent publications on this subject is *Images, Images, Images,* published by Eastman Kodak, Rochester, New York.

After your storyboard is complete and you feel confident that you can visually support the script, proceed to the recording of your audio track. Most medium and larger churches have recording equipment and personnel knowledgeable in its operation. It is highly likely that they will be capable of producing a near professional quality sound track for your presentation. You may want to record in stereo, particularly if there is much music. Whether stereo or mono, you will want to record in a format that allows a spare track for program pulses.

The final stage in your production is the synchronization of your visuals to the audio track. When only one projector is involved, this is simple. It can be done manually or with the use of a "beep" on the unused track of the tape. The tone is generally standardized at 1,000 Hz for .45 seconds. Earlier models of synchronizers used pauses of fixed lengths, holes punched in the audio tape, and the use of metal foil on the tape. This prerecorded tone feeds into a synchronizer that may be free-standing or integrated into a recorder. Whenever this tone is received, it closes contacts, which advance the projector to which it is connected.

Two projectors may be connected to a single synchronizer through the addition of a dissolve unit. When a dissolve unit is used, two projectors are focused on one screen. A single pulse to the dissolve control turns the lamp in one projector on and the lamp in the other projector off at a predetermined rate. The unit will also advance the projector whose lamp was shut off to the next slide position.

Two-projector dissolve effects don't have to be costly. While on an assignment in Africa, I was viewing a two-projector presentation a missionary youth worker had put together. The presentation was well done and the dissolve effect added a level of quality to it. When I turned around I realized he had achieved the dissolve effect by setting two projectors side by side, and with his hand moved a V-shaped piece of cardboard back and forth in front of the lenses. This was, without question, the cheapest dissolve unit I've seen, but the effect was good.

Once we move out of the range of two projectors, simple synchronizers, and dissolve units, we move into the more sophisticated area of multi-image programmers. Depending on what is required of them, these units may cost between a few hundred and a few thousand dollars. Again, remember that the most expensive equipment may not be the best for meeting your needs. There is no sense in paying for features that are not needed for the normal scope of your productions. Also, you don't always have to think about purchasing equipment. Within most churches there are people with tremendous resources for accessing this type of equipment. Check with educators or men and women who work in corporate offices that run sophisticated training programs. In addition to these resources, this type of equipment may be rented from audio-visual dealers in larger cities.

The reason programmers become both more complicated and more expensive is that we require so much more of them. Think, for instance, of the possible combinations of "lamp on" commands in a four-projector production. There are 15 different combinations possible:

"Lamp on" in projector (1) or (2) or (3) or (4) or (1 & 2) or (1 & 3) or (1 & 4) or (2 & 3) or (2 & 4) or (3 & 4) or (1, 2 & 3) or (1, 3 & 4) or (1, 2 & 4) or (2, 3 & 4) or (1, 2, 3 & 4).

These commands simply turn the lamp on. More complicated commands can include "lamp off," "forward," "hold," "back up," "flash," "cut," "dissolve" (variable rates), "home" (all slides back to 1 or 0), and "hunt and find" (random-accessing a particular slide).

The latest generation of equipment is capable of locating the proper slide to be shown at any given point in the audio. If a projector jams, blows a lamp, or someone trips over a cord, it will bypass the slides it missed and go right to the next slide to be called for in the presentation.

The equipment used in multi-image presentation is developing and changing rapidly. For that reason, no specific equipment is described here . . . the information would be out of date before this book is printed. The resource section of this book includes a list of the major manufacturers of multi-image equipment. Your request to any of these companies for brochures describing their latest equipment and a list of dealers in your area will surely be welcomed.

Many manufacturers provide training schools and seminars in the use of multi-image equipment. The person seeking to develop a high level of competence in this area can gain much by attending various workshops and multi-image festivals sponsored by the Association for Multi-Image. Information regarding their activities may be addressed to them at 947 Old York Road, Abington, PA 19001.

IN CONCLUSION

Media can add a new level of creativity and professionalism to your youth program. If you already have an interest in this area, you are probably now using many of these approaches. If you don't feel particularly competent or even interested in this area, find someone in your church who is, and put him or her to work! (That is sometimes preferable, as it doesn't take up your valuable ministry time doing things that someone else could do as well or better than you.) Continue to develop your strengths in ministry, but be sure to provide for the enhancement of your program, and your ministry, through the creative use of media.

SOURCES FOR PREPARED OVERHEAD TRANSPARENCIES

David C. Cook Publishing
850 N. Grove Ave.
Elgin, Illinois 60120

Milliken Publishing Co.
1100 Research Blvd.
St. Louis, Missouri 63132

Scripture Press
1825 College Ave.
Wheaton, Illinois 60187

Bible Believer's Evangelistic Association
Rt. 3, Box 92
Sherman, Texas 75090

GT Luscombe Co., Inc.
P.O. Box 622
Frankfort, Illinois 60423

Bill Hovey & Associates
5730 Duluth St.
Minneapolis, Minnesota 55422

Faith Venture Visuals, Inc.
P.O. Box 685
Lititz, Pennsylvania 17543

Moody Press
820 N. LaSalle
Chicago, Illinois 60616

Cokesbury Press
201 8th Ave., South
Nashville, Tennessee 37202

Baptist Sunday School Board
(Southern Baptist)
127 9th Ave., North
Nashville, Tennessee 37203

ADDITIONAL READING ON MULTI-IMAGE PROJECTION

The Art of Multi-Image. Roger L. Gordon, Ed. Association for Multi-Image, Abington, PA 1978.

Images, Images, Images. Eastman Kodak Company, Rochester, New York, 1979.

Jerome P. O'Neil Jr., "101 Ways to Make Copy and Title Slides . . . Some of Them Good," *Audiovisual Notes from Kodak* T-91-9-1, T-91-9-2 and T-91-9-3. Eastman Kodak Company, Rochester, New York.

V RESOURCES FOR THE YOUTH LEADER

A Topical Listing of Resources

The following is a partial listing of major resources available to the youth leader. In most cases, no attempt has been made to include the many fine materials available through denominational publishing houses, nor have we sought to include the work of many excellent individual or smaller ministries.

CHRISTIAN CAMPS AND RETREAT CENTERS

For a complete listing of Christian camps write to:

Journal of Christian Camping
Christian Camping International
P.O. Box 646
Wheaton, Illinois 60189

For additional resources, see further reading suggestions at the end of chapter 15.

CLIP ART

Nido R. Qubein & Associates
P.O. Box 5367
High Point, North Carolina 27262

CROWD BREAKERS

Group Books
P.O. Box 481
Loveland, Colorado 80539

Success with Youth
P.O. Box 27028
Tempe, Arizona 85282

Youth Specialties
1224 Greenfield Drive
El Cajon, California 92021

CURRICULUM, BIBLE STUDIES, AND PROGRAMING IDEAS

Awana Youth Association
3201 Tollview Drive
Rolling Meadows, Illinois 60008

Here's Life Publishers
Subsidiary of Campus Crusade for Christ
P.O. Box 1576
San Bernardino, California 92402

CAMPUS LIFE Magazine
Leader's Guide
465 E. Gundersen Dr.
Carol Stream, IL 60187

Christian Service Brigade
P.O. Box 150
Wheaton, Illinois 60189

David C. Cook Publishing
850 N. Grove Avenue
Elgin, Illinois 60120

Creative Youth Ministries
500 Common Street
Shreveport, Louisiana 71101

Moody Press – Sonlife Ministries
820 N. LaSalle Drive
Chicago, Illinois 60610

Pioneer Ministries
P.O. Box 788
27 W. 130 St. Charles Road
Wheaton, Illinois 60187

Nido R. Qubein & Associates
P.O. Box 5367
High Point, North Carolina 27262

Reach Out Ministries
120 N. Avondale Rd.
Avondale Estates, Georgia 30002

Salt Mine Resources
4561 Calle de Tosca
San Jose, California 95118

Scripture Press Publications
1825 College Avenue
Wheaton, Illinois 60187

Serendipity House
P.O. Box 1012
Littleton, Colorado 80160

Shepherd Productions
c/o Roger Press
915 Dragon St.
Dallas, TX 75207

Standard Publishing
8121 Hamilton Avenue
Cincinnati, Ohio 45231

Success with Youth
P.O. Box 27028
Tempe, Arizona 85282

Word, Inc.
P.O. Box 1790
Waco, Texas 76796

Young Life
P.O. Box 520
Colorado Springs, Colorado 80901

Youth for Christ/USA
(Campus Life/Youth Guidance)
P.O. Box 419
Wheaton, Illinois 60189

Youth Specialties
1224 Greenfield Drive
El Cajon, California 92021

Zondervan Publishing
1415 Lake Drive, S.E.
Grand Rapids, Michigan 49506

FILM SOURCES

Most of the sources listed below are producers. Write to them for catalogs and the name of their distributor nearest you.

Ken Anderson Films
P.O. Box 618
Winona Lake, Indiana 46590

Augsburg Publishing House, Audio Visual Department
426 South Fifth Street, Box 1209
Minneapolis, Minnesota 55440

Cathedral Films
P.O. Box 4029
Westlake Village, California 91359

Family Films
14622 Lanark Street
Panorama City, California 91402

Gospel Films
P.O. Box 455
Muskegon, Michigan 49443

Mark IV Pictures
P.O. Box 3810
Des Moines, Iowa 50322

Mass Media
2116 N. Charles
Baltimore, Maryland 21218

Moody Institute of Science
12000 E. Washington Blvd.
Whittier, California 90606

Outreach Films
P.O. Box 4029
Westlake Village, California 91359

Pyramid Films
P.O. Box 1048
Santa Monica, California 90406

Quadrus
610 E. State Street
Rockford, Illinois 61104

R O A
914 N. 4th St.
Milwaukee, Wisconsin 53202

World Wide Pictures
1201 Hennepin Avenue
Minneapolis, Minnesota 55403

MEDIA SHOWS FOR HIGH-SCHOOL STUDENTS

Camfel Productions
136 West Olive Ave.
Monrovia, CA 91016

Heavy Light Productions
Route 3
Howe, Indiana 46746

Paragon Productions
Campus Crusade for Christ
Arrowhead Springs, California 92414

TransLight Media Associates
1N045 Morse Street
Wheaton, Illinois 60187

Twentyonehundred Productions
InterVarsity Christian Fellowship
233 Langdon St.
Madison, Wisconsin 53703

PERIODICALS AND NEWSLETTERS FOR THE YOUTH LEADER

Adventures with Youth
P.O. Box 5367
High Point, North Carolina 27262

CAMPUS LIFE Leader's Guide
465 E. Gundersen Dr.
Carol Stream, IL 60187

Essence Publications
168 Woodbridge Avenue
Highland Park, New Jersey 08904

Group Magazine
P.O. Box 481
Loveland, Colorado 80539

Resource Directory for Youth Workers
1224 Greenfield Drive
El Cajon, California 92021

Serve Magazine
P.O. Box 27028
Tempe, Arizona 85282

Sources and Resources
1224 Greenfield Drive
El Cajon, California 92021

Success with Youth Report
667 Madison Avenue
New York, New York 10021

The Wittenburg Door
1224 Greenfield Drive
El Cajon, California 92021

Youth Leader Resource Deck
845 Chicago Avenue, Suite 224
Evanston, Illinois 60202

Youthletter
1716 Spruce Street
Philadelphia, Pennsylvania 19103

SHORT-TERM MISSION OPPORTUNITIES

Group Magazine Work Camps
P.O. Box 481
Loveland, Colorado 80539

See the listings in chapter 20.

SONG BOOKS AND HYMNBOOKS

Hope Publishing Co.
380 S. Main Place
Carol Stream, Illinois 60187

InterVarsity Press
P.O. Box F
Downers Grove, Illinois 60515

Manna Music
2111 Kenmere
Burbank, California 91504

Songs and Creations
P.O. Box 7
San Anselmo, California 94960

Zondervan/Singspiration
1415 Lake Drive, S.E.
Grand Rapids, Michigan 49506

YOUTH WORKERS' TRAINING CONFERENCES

Campus Crusade for Christ
High School Department
9948 Hibert St.
Suite 200
San Diego, California 92131

Group Magazine
P.O. Box 481
Loveland, Colorado 80539

International Center for Learning
2300 Knoll Drive
Ventura, California 93006

Moody Bible Institute—Sonlife Ministries
820 N. LaSalle Drive
Chicago, Illinois 60610

Reach Out Ministries
3117 Majestic Circle
Avondale Estates, Georgia 30002

Shepherd Productions
Box 25
Columbia, Tennessee 38401

Serendipity Training Seminars
P.O. Box 1012
Littleton, Colorado 80160

Youth for Christ/USA
P.O. Box 419
Wheaton, Illinois 60189

Youth Specialties
1224 Greenfield Drive
El Cajon, California 92021